the
five
smooth
stones

the
five
smooth
stones

Essential Principles for Biblical Ministry

Robertson McQuilkin

PUBLISHING GROUP

Nashville, Tennessee

© 2007 by Robertson McQuilkin
All rights reserved
Printed in the United States of America

ISBN: 978-0-8054-4518-3

Published by B & H Publishing Group,
Nashville, Tennessee

Dewey Decimal Classification: 259
Subject Heading: MINISTRY

07 08 09 10 11   15 14 13 12 11 10 9 8 7 6 5 4 3 2 1

To Deb,

God's gift of a gifted "wing-man"

for my final flight.

TABLE OF CONTENTS

Table of Contents

WHY I WROTE THIS BOOK

Follow the Lord's rules for doing his work.
(2 TIM. 2:5 TLB)

As I began my first ministry assignment, I was bemused by the constant rising and falling of new methodologies. What was must-do at any given time did well to make it into a historical footnote decades later. I longed to know what would endure. Which of our activities will survive the light of eternity? Does it make any difference to God how we go about doing his work? I've been revisiting this question constantly over the past half century.

I figured the Bible might shed some light on my questions, but then I discovered a problem. At the end of seven years of formal theological education, I began to wonder: why were the solid academic disciplines sealed off from the practical ministry departments? Sealed on both sides of the divide, I noted. Theologians rarely examined the implications of their theology for practical ministry. And practitioners, though interested in theology for the content of their message, seemed oblivious to any implications theology might have for how they did ministry. Actually, each seemed to express less than complimentary views of the other!

I began to ponder: if theology were wed to ministry, what sort of healthy offspring might we have? That was in 1950 and thus began a lifetime quest for how best to integrate theology and ministry by applying key Bible doctrines to ministry.

I began this quest backward. Rather than starting with a search of Scripture for some theological bases for ministry, I decided to look at methodology—the way ministry had been done—and see if clues emerged as to what theology might have done to aid or hinder success, however defined. I began with New Testament church history. In a graduate course, designed to explore my quest, I assigned students different portions of Scripture to report back on what was discovered about how the apostles went about ministry. This was not only the typical ploy of getting students to do the professor's research, but I thought we would gain in objectivity by having many minds interacting on the issues that surfaced. As the profile emerged, we concluded the Plymouth Brethren had it right—they were most similar to the early model, other models of church and ministry emerging as the church developed and expanded. This research into apostolic practice naturally led to the next stage of research, church history.

As we looked at the broad scope of church history, we discovered that those who adhered most closely to the way the apostles did ministry did not show significantly greater prosperity. In fact, we discovered in church history no correlation between strict adherence to apostolic practice and blessing in ministry viewed in any measurable terms. This discovery led to a quantum leap forward in my hermeneutics of applying Scripture: historical passages (as the book of Acts) have no normative authority unless Scripture—either in that passage or elsewhere—makes the reported event or response normative.[1] So I was forced to begin where I should have begun—with Scripture's direct teaching. I discovered five major doctrines that seemed to have great significance in how I would do ministry.

Those five major doctrinal categories were: Bibliology, Christology, Pneumatology, Ecclesiology, and Soteriology. In each of these categories certain elements that seem to have primary implications for ministry were chosen: Bible authority, Christ's lordship, those activities of the Spirit aimed at church/ministry, and those elements of God's redemptive plan that require the participation of Christians and/or the church. Among the major doctrines, why did I leave out eschatology, for example (one of the few major doctrines omitted) and why not include other elements of any theological cluster that was chosen? For example, in Christology, why not focus, as most theological systems do, on Christ's nature and work? Because doctrines brought into play are those which have strong implications for ministry issues. So I began to pick up my "Five Smooth Stones" to prepare for battle against the spiritual Goliaths of the day.

But first, one further historical research piqued my curiosity. How would those doctrines be evidenced in contemporary churches noted for great revival blessing? So I sent questionnaires to the leaders of the explosive church movements of that day in East Africa/Rwanda, Ethiopia, Colombia, and Korea. When the questionnaires finally arrived I was already into a church-planting ministry in Japan, striving to implement the implications of "my" five basic doctrines. Imagine my consternation, in evaluating the returns, to discover none of "my" doctrines! In fact, I found few similarities among these groups other than spiritual dynamism and explosive growth. One, charismatic, three not; one episcopal in government, one presbyterial, two congregational (sort of). Not only organizationally diverse, but different

---

1. For justification of this position, see McQuilkin, *Understanding and Applying the Bible* (Chicago: Moody, 1992), 233, 301–304.

leadership styles and every other methodology I was looking at as well. It was a dark day for me. Was this the culmination of eight years of research? As I examined the profiles of these churches, however, at last a bright light burst on the horizon of my future ministry: every one of those church movements showed adherence, in their diverse ways, to every one of the basic doctrines!

I was elated. And also I was emboldened to use these conclusions as the outline of the commencement address for the first graduating class of a newly formed Japanese theological seminary. I planned to speak on "The Five Smooth Stones" because I felt those graduating seniors needed all the encouragement they could get as they headed out to face the spiritual Goliaths of one of the world's peoples most resistant to the Good News. The school was wholly indigenous, so why did they invite a neophyte foreigner to speak on this auspicious occasion? I suspected they may have heard rumors about what had happened in our city in the new churches started during those five years. Whatever their motive, when I stood before the group I was not prepared to find, on the front row, not only the founders of the institution but also church leaders from across Japan. What should I do? It was too late to change, so with great trepidation I spoke on "The Five Smooth Stones." How did it go down? I had to wait five years to see.

Pastor Akira Hatori, premier evangelical leader in Japan and chairman of the seminary board, gathered a small group of us to meet over lunch atop a downtown Tokyo building. There Hatori asked if I recalled the commencement address. Of course I did—it was my life. Then he said, "For five years I've crisscrossed the world, seeking to determine if your thesis is true. I've discovered that it is, and I want you and Professor Ariga to research the church in Japan and prove it!" We protested that a true research doesn't begin with a predetermined outcome, but we took the assignment to do the research. Hundreds of churches and pastors and thousands of believers later, a massive amount of data had been accumulated. The results were startling—those who seemed to be most under the control of those five doctrines were the churches that prospered. Those that did not prosper were missing out on one or more of the basic biblical principles!

The acid test was yet to come. Donald McGavran, father of the mission-oriented Church Growth Movement and doubtless the most influential person in missions for the second half of the twentieth century, was in Japan to research and speak. I was his interpreter for the private conversations we had set up with leaders of all denominations. They opened up to this distinguished foreign guest, so for a few months, at least, I knew more about the church in Japan than anyone else! We spent a lot of time together, so I had occasion to share with Dr. McGavran the Five Smooth Stones. He was skeptical. To a thoroughgoing missions pragmatist, those principles were too "spiritual." But he was courteous when I invited him to check the data.

Professor Ariga presented large charts displaying the results of the study of the church nationwide, and McGavran sat back on the sofa, courteously listening. About halfway through the presentation, he leaned forward to examine the charts, then he moved to the edge of his seat with great enthusiasm. A data-based man, the data seemed to mesmerize him. He agreed the principles were worthy of consideration though I didn't catch him, in the years following, ever preaching about the Five Smooth Stones!

So, though the evidence was strong that the principles were effective in the church setting, what of nonchurch or parachurch ministry? I was soon to test that. After twelve years of church-starting ministry in Japan, I was called to lead Columbia International University (Columbia Bible College at the time) and for the next twenty-two years tested those five principles in an institutional setting. They proved worthy. A quarter century later I reviewed an old personal journal entry written about a decade after my tenure began. In it I explained to myself why I no longer taught certain courses, courses focused on each of the basic biblical principles. In fact, with one exception, I concluded that within that decade those principles had so come to permeate the institution, perhaps none of those courses were any longer needed!

During those same years, however, something infinitely more significant was taking place. On the other side of the world, an explosive growth that dwarfs anything in the two thousand years of church history—China! When my wife and I were young we planned on going to China where one-fifth of the world's population lived. At the time, there were fewer than a million evangelical believers in that vast nation. And by the end of the century? Perhaps a hundred million! How did it happen? In the July 1980 *Chinese World Pulse*, the dean of China watchers, David Adeney, made a startling statement. He told why the Three-Self, government-approved church in China had made no advances during those years of communist rule. Then he defined what the Chinese church must be and do if the stagnated churches were to live again. He spelled out what kind of church it must become. It did in fact become just what he spelled out in advance, and the rest is history! What essentials did he enumerate at the beginning of this incredible burst of life?

- For the church to survive and thrive it must live under the authority of Scripture, not the surrounding culture. Christ's own worldview must be theirs, he said.
- The church must experience "the reality of true fellowship in Christ. Christians cannot stand just as isolated individuals. . . . They must support one another."
- ". . . the experience of the power of the indwelling Holy Spirit and a deep reliance upon prayer."
- ". . . an understanding of the true nature of the church and the priesthood of all believers."

- "... the recognition of the Lordship of Christ over every area of life..."

Fast forward to 2004. Around the world, church-multiplying movements were exploding. Not the old paradigm of planting individual churches or even planting reproducing churches, but movements of rapidly reproducing house churches that envelop a whole people. Every movement was unique, diverse as snowflakes. Were there any common characteristics? In 2004 David Garrison published the results of thorough research on the common indispensable characteristics among those movements.[2] Without them, no movement. And what were those characteristics? Two were not found in our pouch of five smooth stones, two elements peculiar to church-multiplying movements: (1) local, not foreign leadership, and (2) very rapid reproduction of many churches. I noted that those two characteristics were in fact working, but I could find no theological basis for them. Otherwise, it was plain enough that all the rest of the indispensable characteristics were the same as those we shall examine in the pages that follow!

Here's how I describe the basic biblical principles for doing ministry:

1. The Bible: making it the functional authority
2. The Congregation: aligning it with the biblical purposes
3. The Spirit: releasing his energizing power
4. The Plan of Redemption: the mission of every disciple
5. The Lord Jesus: gauging servant leadership

You may say, "That's so simple. Everyone knows that!" Then why do we flounder and miss the way? Could it be that we simply don't make the commitment to evaluate our work relentlessly by these standards? Or could it be we don't work hard at ferreting out the implications of these principles? I invite you to join me in deep reflection, honest evaluation, and courageous integration of each of these principles into the practice of every aspect of ministry. It will also take commitment to change whatever is necessary to experience the kind of life God intends.

My purpose in writing the story of my pilgrimage? An invitation for you to join in that quest! To give you a preview of what lies ahead in that quest, here's a summary:

- The *Bible* only and the whole Bible our only final authority for life and ministry
- The *Church,* central to all God's plans for redeeming a world
- The *Holy Spirit,* his energizing power indispensable to all life and ministry
- *God's Redemption Plan,* the mission of every disciple
- The *Lord Jesus Christ,* sovereign in every believer and in his church

---

2. *Church Planting Movements: How God Is Redeeming a Lost World* (Midlothian, Va.: WIGTake Resources, 2004). Summary of characteristics may be found on p. 172.

The Bible. To get anywhere with God's purposes through his church, the leaders and congregation must take seriously the responsibility to bring every aspect of the ministry under the functional authority of Scripture—every new idea, every old tradition, every activity, every plan. Otherwise it will fail. It won't be easy. Diligent, objective, thorough Bible research combined with determined full compliance and eternal vigilance are the essentials.

The Congregation. Don't forget that a congregation weak in even one of the purposes of the church is crippled by so much, falls short of full obedience. Remember, too, that for a parachurch ministry, concentrating on some specific purpose of the church, to be biblically authentic it must flow into and/or out of the local congregation.

The Holy Spirit. His energizing power in a congregation is seen primarily in the supernatural abilities he gives each member. The church is responsible to make sure every member fully uses his or her gifting—discovering, developing, deploying and, when a purpose of the church is weak, united in desiring earnestly the gift needed to lead the church in fulfilling that purpose. But the Spirit does so much more—guiding, providing. All this activity of the Spirit, however, is released only as we connect with him in prayer. A praying church is a growing, victorious church, fulfilling all the God-designed purposes. A prayerless church or other ministry is limited to what can be achieved by purely human wisdom and power.

God's Redemptive Plan—The Mission of Every Disciple. Beyond the varied callings and enablings of the Spirit is the first and paramount calling of all—to complete what Christ began, to fulfill Christ's last mandate, to participate fully in redeeming a lost humanity. Near-evangelism for all as witnesses and far-evangelism specialists sent by the church to enable it to reach its goal: every person on earth hearing with understanding the way to life and a congregation of God's people established in every place. Until that task is complete, the primary assignment of the church remains unfulfilled. And for that every member must accept the Spirit's call.

The Lordship of Christ. For any of this to happen, of course, Jesus Christ alone must be absolute Lord of his church. First he must be Lord of each member, but for him to actually function as Lord of the congregation or ministry, the leaders must embody the leadership model of God himself. To the extent he is Lord in their lives and ministry, to that extent will the church be united and pure, bringing about the fulfillment of all the purposes God has for the congregation.

Now it's time to begin a study that I pray will be as exciting, life-molding, and ministry-transforming for you as it has been for me. But first . . .

Question for reflection:
Is it God's intention to see ministry driven by biblical reflection?

Unit 1:

THE BIBLE

MAKING IT THE FUNCTIONAL AUTHORITY

The Bible alone, the whole of it,
is our ultimate authority for faith and practice.

I'd finished college and entered seminary where I promptly lost my faith. It wasn't the seminary's fault nor my undergraduate education. Sigmund Freud did it. Only later in life did I learn that the father of modern psychiatry and psychology was far more a philosopher than a social scientist. But I assumed his scientific credentials were valid, and he influenced me to reject any idea that couldn't be proved scientifically. By "scientific" he meant limiting one's investigation of reality to the natural realm. Following that path, the first casualty was the Bible. How could I test and prove the miracles of Scripture and all the teachings that contradicted contemporary scientific theory? Doubting the trustworthiness of Scripture, soon there was another casualty: God. I was smart enough not to become atheistic. That seemed a bit arrogant—how could I assert a denial, unprovable by definition? But I was definitely agnostic. I thought nothing was certain that could not be demonstrated scientifically.

It proved a lonely journey. So much of importance to me couldn't be proved "scientifically"—love, for example. And I was madly in love. It was a deep darkness, to be shorn of all confidence in the validity of human relationships or anything else immaterial. Then there was the confusion of trying to work out the impossibility of that modern oxymoron—absolute relativity. The thought came to me, *If you're so scientific, McQuilkin, why have you ruled out in advance the possibility of God?* So I concluded to be consistent I needed to include that possibility in my investigation of reality. I prayed, "God, if you exist, how about proving it in a way I can test, prove?" An arrogant prayer, demanding that deity meet me on my terms! But he is gracious and he answered by something I could hold in my hand, the very

1

thing I had stumbled over into agnosticism—the Bible. I was studying the higher critics and knew the doubts shed on Old Testament prophecy; but discounting all the passages that were challenged, I still found the residue of miracle in my hand—prophecies of the Messiah, for instance, in great detail predicting events hundreds of years before they happened. I say I returned to faith. But only partially. Still doubts flitted around the edges of my mind, but faith in the Book was strong enough to continue my course into Christian ministry.

Several years into ministry I had had it. Enough of these doubts. In or out, McQuilkin. So I went away for a three-day retreat on a lonely beach. There I read and re-read the Gospels. After two days walking with Jesus through the Gospels, even deleting the events and words that scholars had challenged, a historic person emerged, towering over history. Towering over me. Here was a person who couldn't be explained in naturalistic terms. On the third day, as I stood gazing over the Pacific there was a presence, almost physical, where Jesus seemed to put his hand on my shoulder and say, "Little brother, are you smarter than I?" In that moment a brilliant light flashed through my bewildered mind, "Oh, no, no. I'm not smarter than you, nor are all these critics who have tried to eviscerate you across the years." From that moment I embraced him with my mind, accepting what he said as my authority—he's smarter than I! Especially, what he said about the Book. If he affirmed its utter trustworthiness and authority, who am I to question it? Problems remain for me, but always I return to Jesus. He's smarter than I. He believed it; he obeyed it.

From that moment I've been passionate about making sure I understand and follow Scripture. If God said it, I'd better trust it! If God said it, I'd better obey it! To do this faithfully, there are several steps in laying the foundation. These we assume as prerequisites for this present study:[1]

- Determining what the text actually said. This is known as textual criticism.
- Determining the meaning the original author intended. This is hermeneutics.
- On the foundation of making sure what the text said and what it meant, we now search for answers to what it means for us today. There is no discrete discipline nor general agreement on principles for determining the intent of the Spirit for application of the text. That is the task of our present study, focused on ministry.

In preparation for this I spent a lifetime of seeking to do it. After years of teaching hermeneutics in English and Japanese, in college and seminary,

---

1. The approach of this book, assumed by most church scholarship for two thousand years, is now challenged as modernistic rationalism by the postmodern. We shall consider those claims in unit 1, chapter 2.

in lay institutes, gradually this book emerged: *Understanding and Applying the Bible.* That was the foundation. Then, putting those principles into practice in life and ministry became a driving force—*How Biblical Is the Church Growth Movement? An Introduction to Biblical Ethics, The Great Omission, Life in the Spirit.* All of those are the "third step," how do we apply Scripture in fidelity to the Spirit's intent? And now, *Essential Principles for Biblical Ministry.* How should we go about bringing all of ministry under the functional authority of Scripture? That is what we now pursue.

In this study, then, let us assume confidence in the trustworthiness and authority of Scripture and devote ourselves to the application of Bible teaching. How do we go about bringing every facet of ministry under the functional authority of Scripture? In unit 1, chapter 1, we will construct a grid for evaluating every concept or method for its biblical fidelity. Then we will illustrate the approach with two major contemporary challenges to the Bible's authority: harnessing postmodernism to biblical ends (chap. 2) and therapeutic theology speaks to a therapeutic society (chap. 3).[2] A third major contemporary issue, cross-cultural communication, may be found in the appendix. The crossing of generational and cultural boundaries in ministry is an ever-increasing challenge, so we will refer to that appendix at appropriate points throughout our study. These studies in Unit 1 should give us a sense of how to go about bringing concepts and methodologies under biblical authority and clear the road of contemporary obstacles to biblical obedience. In subsequent units we will apply this approach to evaluating the local congregation, participating in the ministry of the Holy Spirit, discovering the place of every disciple in God's plan of redemption, and the implications for ministry of Christ's lordship.

At the beginning of each chapter, I will provide a question for self-evaluation. The question will mark in advance where you should find yourself at the end of that chapter. Please don't take the reflective question lightly. The depth of your initial evaluation may determine how beneficial the chapter is to you.

---

2. In this unit, as we track with my pilgrimage of discovery I will share some previously published journal articles, edited for our use in this context.

CHAPTER 1:

MAKING THE BIBLE
THE FUNCTIONAL AUTHORITY

*All Scripture is inspired by God and is useful for teaching
the truth, rebuking error, correcting faults, and giving instruction
for right living, so that the person who serves God may be
fully qualified and equipped to do every kind of good deed.*
(2 TIM. 3:16–17 TEV)

**Question for reflection: Is every new approach proposed or every
tradition challenged, thoroughly evaluated by the entire group through
rigorous examination of all biblical data, bringing all church doctrine
and practice under the functional authority of Scripture?**

When I came back to faith from my sojourn in agnosticism, for me the
question of authority was settled. Or was it? Actually it's been a lifelong
pilgrimage of discovery. How does one make this God-breathed-out book the
actual functioning authority? Those who declaim most vigorously the inspiration and authority of Scripture may in fact actually revere it as a constitu-
tional monarch, celebrating the glories of the monarch while true authority is vested elsewhere. Often the actual authority is a tradition or system of
traditions handed down, but for many it's the opposite—the latest innova-
tion exploding across the contemporary scene. It may be the mind-set of a
therapeutic society for doing church, or the dictums of cultural anthropology
for doing mission. Probably, whatever else the functioning authority may be,
there's the ever-present stealth takeover of postmodern ways of seeing or feeling. And thus in one way or another the full authority of Scripture—designed
to determine what we are to think, what we are not to think, how we are not
to behave, and how we are to behave (2 Tim. 3:16)—has eroded, and we are
no longer well equipped and qualified to do God's work in God's way.

In this unit, then, we will first construct a grid for sorting out those
enduring principles of Scripture that should sit at the controls of our entire

ministry. Then we'll use the grid, by way of example, to work through some of the contemporary challenges to biblical authority: postmodern thinking and the therapeutic captivity of sanctification. After laying that foundation, in the balance of the book we will use the same grid to sort out God's enduring principles for doing ministry. We will look carefully at the purposes of the local congregation; discover how to release the energizing power of the Holy Spirit; examine how the congregation can identify, develop, and release each person's ministry calling; and, finally, engage the leadership of the church in the quest for unity and purity.

Functional Authority: Constructing the Grid

To ascertain God's revealed will for any concept or activity of ministry—or to make sure he has no preference in the matter—certain steps must be followed:[1]

- Identify the issue so precisely that both advocates and opponents will agree with the identification.
- Identify all Scripture that might bear on the issue, both pro and con.
- Determine if any given passage cited is addressed to the present church.
- Exegete the passage carefully to determine the meaning intended by the original author.
- Test for biblical emphasis and balance with other teaching.
- Implement, if demanded by Scripture, and exercise freedom to implement if the concept or activity is not in violation of Scripture and judged desirable.

To illustrate the use of this grid or matrix, I've chosen the "seeker friendly" concept of doing church. We will not try to fully analyze, much less establish conclusions, but in this chapter we will simply use one issue to demonstrate how to use this approach to knowing God's revealed will for ministry in the chapters and units that follow.

Identify the Issue So Precisely that Both Advocates and Opponents Agree with the Identification

Pastor Bridgebuilder has just returned from a conference where hundreds of pastors gathered to hear about an exciting and successful approach to doing church: "Seeker Friendly." The congregation's leaders gathered to hear his report and decide whether to make the radical changes needed to implement the approach.

---

1. For a more thorough presentation of the principles outlined in this chapter, see Robertson McQuilkin, *Understanding and Applying the Bible* (Chicago: Moody, 1992), especially chaps. 19 and 20.

"Sounds like what I hear at my American Management Association conventions, Pastor," said chairman of the board, Solomon Highcastle. "We can't just commercialize this operation, can we?"

"Where's the cross?" said elder Peter Steadfast. "Jesus threw up roadblocks, you know. If you don't take up your cross, forget it. That was his message. Doesn't sound exactly 'friendly.'" He flipped through his concordance in the back of his Bible and found Luke 14:25. "Listen to this, Pastor. Notice it was a huge crowd of seekers he addressed." Steadfast read the entire passage and closed at verse 33: "So likewise, whoever of you does not forsake all that he has cannot be my disciple" (NKJV). He quickly checked his marginal note on that passage and commented, "I count four more occasions just like this" (Matt. 10:34–39, 16:24–25; Mark 8:34–35; Luke 9:23–24).

"Quality, not quantity, I say," Deacon Dorcas chimed in. "Sounds to me like you've bought into the devil's old line about nothing matters but numbers. Besides, you bring in some new-fangled idea every few months. I get weary. . . ."

Pastor Bridgebuilder was taken aback. "Dorcas, it's true. I keep seeking for a solution to our big problem: plateaued growth. I promise this will be my last try for now. But all I'm suggesting is that we try to create a program and an atmosphere in at least one of our Sunday morning services that doesn't put off interested non-believers, but rather attracts them to give the gospel a hearing."

They began at the right place—defining the issue. Precisely what is being advocated? Until that is settled, there is no need to proceed. In fact, you can't proceed. At least, not very far.

Identify All Scripture that Might Bear on the Issue, Both Pro and Con

It won't do for Pastor Bridgebuilder simply to appeal to the incarnation as God's model of becoming seeker friendly. He can't just ring the changes on the apostle Paul's approach, becoming all things to all people in order to win some. He has to deal honestly with Peter Steadfast's problem. The hard sayings of Jesus have to be fitted in. After all, the seeker's cross was a major theme of Jesus' "evangelistic" messages, far more than his gentle invitation, "Come to me all who are worn down with heavy loads." They need to be sure they've evaluated all Scripture has to say on the subject—both pro and con.

If there isn't exhaustive Bible knowledge in the group, they can begin with a concordance or topical reference volume, or a Bible computer program. When it comes to a theological issue, good sources are systematic theology texts. For the "seeker friendly" issue, they could check out "soteriology" or "Christology" or "ecclesiology," not merely for arguments pro and con, but for identification of relevant biblical texts. Then of course, in this case at least, there are many books both for and against. The local church may not have time to read all of them, but it is important to check out an authoritative treatment that holds a position opposing the one advocated. That tends to keep everyone honest and pinpoints Scripture that might correct or balance the position advocated.

What then, should they look for in approaching this subject?

Are there any direct commands that demand this change? Assistant pastor, Junior Bookman, raised that question. "I can't find any command in Scripture that demands we do that kind of evangelism, Pastor. Where does it say, Go into all the world and preach seeker friendly messages?"

"Well," responded the pastor, "you're not saying there must be a direct command for everything we do, are you? After all, the principles of Scripture are just as binding as the direct commands."

"I'm not so sure," said Bookman. "There are over six hundred commands in the Old Testament and six hundred commands in the New. Are you saying they don't count?"

"No, I'm not saying they don't count. They do count. In fact, no direct command can be invalidated by some principle we derive. But we must obey the principles, too, and what could be of higher priority than God's own example in the incarnation, and Paul's example in doing evangelism?" Failing to find a direct command doesn't end the matter. They're pushed to the next level of inquiry.

Are there any principles that demand this approach? Pastor Bridgebuilder needs to give attention to how he establishes a principle from Scripture. Of course, principles may be directly stated in Scripture, such as, "It isn't good for man to be alone." If the principle is directly stated, the principle is just as binding as a specific command and it is our responsibility to aggressively seek out how God intends us to apply the principle. Principles, unlike specific commands, have a universal application and are thus very powerful. But principles can also be derived from direct commands. Nowhere does Scripture condemn pornography or voyeurism, but forbidding them on the basis of the command, "You shall not lust," is not only acceptable. It is a principle demanded by the command.

And then there is historical precedent. But as a source of deriving authoritative principles, that's tricky. Historic precedent was the basis of Pastor Bridgebuilder's argument. But just because Paul did something or even because God did something doesn't necessarily mean that we are bound to do the same thing, or even that we are permitted to do the same thing. History is recorded in Scripture on purpose and we do well to attempt to identify that purpose. But if Scripture itself does not identify the action or event as an example to follow (or avoid), we may not use it to derive an authoritative principle. Sometimes the historical context commends or condemns the action reported. Then we have a clue as to God's intent for his people.

Sometimes another passage will point out the good or bad in what was done, as in the case of the deception of the Egyptian midwives. If they are commended for their lies, we are pressed to search for the reason. But if we are not told in Scripture why an action is commended or condemned, we are still left with the dilemma of figuring out from other commands or principles whether or not the action illustrates an abiding principle. Pastor Bookman made this point.

"But," responded Pastor Bridgebuilder, "I'd say God's own example has to be good."

Yes, if Christ or God does something, it can't be wrong. At least for God! But that doesn't mean everything Christ did is an example we must follow. For example, his remaining in Israel for his entire ministry. Is that the example we should all follow? Christ commanded his disciples to do the opposite. Or the example of his cross. We're commanded repeatedly to follow that example. But then debate rages in missiological circles over how his atoning death can be an example without undermining his unique role in our salvation. Historic precedent, then, must be handled with care. Look for confirmation in direct teaching, principle, or command before seeking to establish principle from history. Even with biblical confirmation of a principle, the history is better used as illustration than prescription.

For example, Pastor Bridgebuilder might argue the fact that Paul adapted his message to suit his audience as evidence that Christ's incarnation model is for us today. Impressive as part of a larger biblical argument, no doubt, but of itself not conclusive.

Worst of all is the notorious argument from silence on which so much debate over ministry is based. If the argument from silence were valid, how do we justify church buildings, denominations, praise bands, children's work, and youth ministry? None appear in the New Testament church. No, Pastor Bridgewater, you can reject out of hand Junior Bookman's objection that he can't find a seeker-friendly command in the New Testament. He'll need to find teaching against it. Silence alone can't decide an issue.

Thus there are acceptable ways for establishing what a biblical teaching is, whether direct command or derived principle. The church board should do its best to ferret out all the Bible has to say about adapting the message of the gospel to specific audiences.[2] But there's more.

Determine If Any Given Passage Cited Is Addressed to the Contemporary Church

Once the search for God's will in a matter moves to specific passages of Scripture, the first thing that must be ascertained is whether the teaching was intended for all people or just for some. How do you go about deciding?

2. Unit 1, chap. 3 examines this in some detail.

The context itself may indicate a limited audience: "Blessed are you poor," said Jesus. Are all poor of all time blessed? He addressed a particular audience. The context may not clearly limit the audience, but other Scripture may, as in the case of Old Testament ceremonial law, set aside by Jesus or the apostles (Heb. 9–10).

Since Pastor Bridgebuilder did not appeal to any direct commands, his appeal to historic precedent assumed that Christ's example of becoming incarnate among us and Paul's example were universal in their application to all believers and all churches. Certainly Bridgewater's opponents assumed that their arguments were from universal principle as well. In this particular church conflict, then, this step did not settle the issue, but we shall find it essential in future chapters and units of our study.

Exegete the Passage Carefully to Determine the Meaning Intended by the Original Author

We shall risk going far astray if we impose meaning on the text. Most often this has happened historically by imposing a predetermined doctrinal structure on a given passage. The only way "God so loved the world" can be interpreted as "God so loved the elect" is to have already decided from other Scripture a doctrine of the atonement that requires setting aside the plain meaning of the text. More recently, cultural norms have been given greater authority than the text.[3] But our goal is to determine what the author of any given text had in mind when he wrote it. Establishing those principles of interpretation lies far beyond the scope of this book, but this step may be the most important of all. Pastor Bridgebuilder and his leadership team will need to examine all relevant texts in this way. For example, 1 Corinthians 9:19–23 where Paul explains in detail his policy of becoming all things to all kinds of people in order to win them to faith would need thorough examination. But in their case, something more is needed, something very confusing in this case.

Test for Biblical Emphasis and Balance with Other Teaching

There is no question but that Peter Steadfast is right to point out the pervasive "hard sayings" of Jesus, his constant confrontation of would-be seekers with the demands of the cross. On which side does Bible emphasis lie? Since all Scripture is our authority, how can these two apparently diverse teachings be reconciled without discounting either? This step requires that

---

3. Principles for making certain culture does not supersede the authority of Scripture have been thoroughly explicated in several journal articles and a book chapter by the author. These may be accessed on the Columbia International University Web site: "Problems of Normativeness in Scripture: Cultural vs. Permanent," *Hermeneutics, Inerrancy, and the Bible*, Radmacher and Preus, editors (Grand Rapids: Zondervan, 1984), 219–40; "The Behavioral Sciences under the Authority of Scripture," *Journal of the Evangelical Theological Society* (March 1977); "Limits of Cultural Interpretation," *Journal of the Evangelical Theological Society* (June 1980).

we bring into harmony, as best we can, all that Scripture teaches on the subject. Only then are we ready to launch, modify, or dismantle the approach—launch the new program or ministry, or dismantle the old. We may need to adjust the approach to bring it under the functional authority of all the teaching of Scripture.

Implement If Demanded by Scripture

We are free to implement the principle if it is not in violation of Scripture and it is judged desirable.

How do you think the "seeker-friendly" proposal will fare if the entire group in humility (each recognizing his own finitude and fallenness) gives faithful diligence to search the Scripture (2 Tim. 2:14–16), and love one another, each preferring the other more than themselves (Phil. 2:1–4)? My guess is that they will decide Peter is on the side of biblical emphasis but that the pastor's proposal is not prohibited by Scripture and that they could move forward, being careful to safeguard their implementation from violating any basic biblical principle. It's hazardous to guess, however, since (1) we're dealing with human beings and (2) we haven't done our own homework on the disputed subject yet! Making changes is never easy and must be pursued with great care, especially if the initial investigation yields a "free to implement" conclusion. In that case the debate shifts to pragmatic concerns. That shift must be carefully noted and observed, with neither side claiming to be on "God's side"! We will revisit the dynamics of change in unit 5.

In this brief outline of the steps needed to bring proposals under the authority of Scripture, rather than examining the issue to a conclusion, we have mined a popular concept for illustrations of how the steps could be implemented. As we move forward it might help to expand these steps into two exercises: checklist for insuring the functional authority of Scripture, and checklist for applying a Bible passage.

Questions to Ask for Evaluating the Biblical Authority of a Doctrine or Activity

1. What is the basic idea (presupposition, objective, etc.) behind this plan (program, method, activity)? A way to state the basic idea often involves defining terms being used.

2. Is this activity or objective commanded in Scripture? Is there an explicit declaration of the will of God?

3. If not commanded, is it obviously required by clear biblical principle?

4. If not required, is it permitted by scriptural teaching, compatible with Scripture?

5. Have I brought this activity into alignment with all biblical data that might be related, whether directly or indirectly?

6. Does the emphasis represented by this activity maintain balance with all other related biblical truth in such a way as to maintain the biblical emphases?

7. If this activity is extrabiblical, am I careful to make this fact clear and divest it of ultimate authority both in my own thinking and in the way it is presented?

These diagnostic questions can be put in the form of a flow chart for ease of use.

BIBLICAL
AUTHORITY
FOR A DOCTRINE
OR ACTIVITY

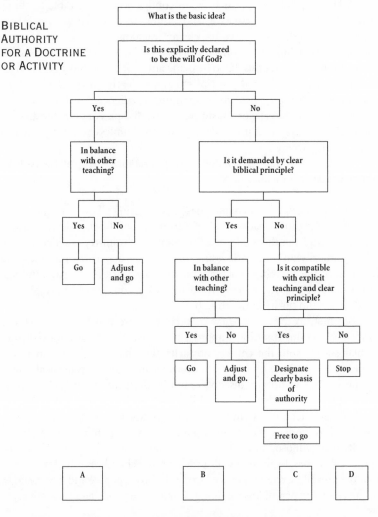

Questions to Ask for Applying a Biblical Passage

1. Does Scripture itself, either in the context of a teaching or in subsequent teaching, set aside or disallow a given teaching? Jesus set aside the Old Testament ceremonial law. Jesus later rescinded his own command to take no money or change of clothes.

2. Is the command or teaching addressed to an individual or specific group? If so, it is not binding on the contemporary Christian. God's command to Moses to take off his shoes was not intended as a universal requirement, for example.

3. Does a teaching appear to be in conflict with other Bible teaching, especially later, more persuasive, and clearer teaching? If so, preference should be given the later, pervasive, clearer teaching.

4. Is the teaching based on a historical event or example? This does not have authority in and of itself. To be made authoritative it must be based on direct commands or stated principles that are clearly universal. Only then does history set a precedent for demanding obedience. Much of Acts, for example, falls in this category. Just because the disciples or even apostles did something doesn't make it mandatory for others unless Scripture either in context or elsewhere says so.

On the following page is a flow chart to graphically display the path set out by the diagnostic questions.

The approach of this chapter, designed to bring all doctrine and practice under the functional control of Scripture, will be the "default mode" for all our study. In this wedding of theology and ministry practice, we will focus primarily on pragmatic issues of ministry such as the purposes and function of the church, the activity of the Holy Spirit in ministry, the role of the believer in God's redemptive plan, and the quality of leadership that yields unity and purity in the church.

But first, in the twenty-first century there are two main obstacles to implementing this traditional approach—obstacles that have moved from secular society into the church, obstacles that increasingly dominate the thinking and practice of those who consider themselves evangelical. These two pervasive assumptions disallow or inhibit the historic approach to Scripture of granting it independent and final authority over doctrine and practice. So, before looking carefully at ministry options in the light of Scripture, consider postmodern assumptions and therapeutic approaches.

If such "philosophical" issues don't excite you, feel free to skip to the "practical" issues, beginning with unit 2 on the church. But be forewarned that the prevailing contemporary mind-set of your people and, increasingly, of the emerging paradigms for doing church, could well derail any efforts to bring your church and ministry under the authority of Scripture. So in the balance of this unit our aim is to clear the roadblocks for a confident journey down the path of fidelity to Scripture in church and ministry.

APPLYING
A BIBLE
PASSAGE

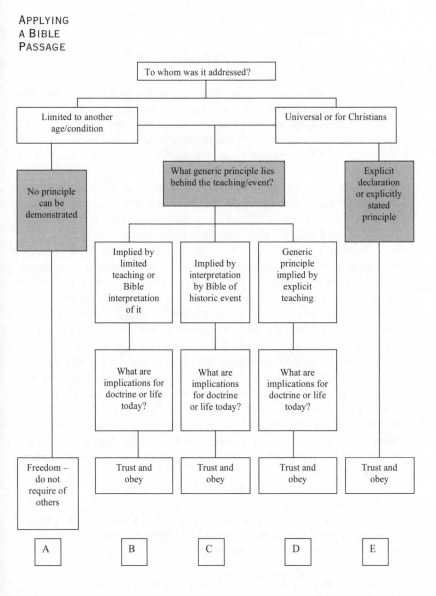

CHAPTER 2

POSTMODERNISM

Question for reflection: Does the church leadership strive to stay current on societal shifts toward postmodern assumptions and take appropriate action to distinguish among those concepts to be adopted, adapted, and rejected? Is the membership regularly alerted to the emerging societal shifts in education, entertainment, and media?

Postmodern assumptions, of course, invalidate the entire approach we offer for doing ministry. We assume that words convey meaning that can be understood. We claim that the Spirit of God chose to inspire the words of biblical authors with the intent that they communicate truth, that the Bible is the reliable and final source of all the truth God intends his church and his people to believe and live by, and that it can be understood. All of this is denied by postmodern thinking. But surely evangelicals, of all people, adhere to the Bible's view of itself and the church's historic position on that.

In the early nineties when a colleague and I revised the textbook, *Understanding and Applying the Bible*, we reviewed all books on Bible interpretation produced by evangelical scholars during the eighties. We were startled to discover that virtually all were relying to a greater or lesser extent on postmodern assumptions. These were the kinds of thinkers who lay the foundation for theological reflection and reformulation in each generation. Our first response might have been knee-jerk—this ungodly departure from biblical truth must be rejected! But I had long concluded that the "modern" culture we grew up in was no more wholly sanctified than the postmodern rejection of that modern rationalism. It might even have some biblical insights for us.

So, in 2000 when invited to address the annual meeting of the Evangelical Homiletics Association on Spiritual Formation Through Preaching,[1] I chose to include in that series, "Connecting with the Postmodern." I found elements in postmodernism we should adopt. Why? Because they were more biblical than our modern assumptions. Of course, I discovered elements

---

1. The series was published the following year in *Preaching Today*, an online journal published by *Christianity Today*, then as a chapter in *The Art and Craft of Biblical Preaching* (Zondervan, 2005).

which Scripture would have us modify and some that Scripture would insist we reject. But the effort was to bring these assumptions under the functional control of Scripture.

Transformational preaching must be audience-connected. *Hold on, you say. You're getting ready to compromise the truth if not actually betray it.* May I suggest that not to translate the message into contemporary language and thought forms is the real betrayer of truth? *But isn't our message totally counter-cultural?* you might ask.

That was the thesis of a practical theology professor I spoke with recently. We were discussing, over lunch, a colleague who has a powerful, life-transforming ministry to teens and young adults all over the world. Jack is past retirement age, but does he ever connect! He was just back from a weekend with four hundred collegians who'll never be the same. Talk about "spiritual formation"! As we talked about the impact of this old man, my lunch mate launched into a strong speech about how Jack belies all this talk about a generation gap. "You have to understand the postmodern mind and connect with them? Rubbish!" I was astonished to sense the intensity of his feeling about the error of trying to be "relevant" in different ways to different audiences. Especially from one charged with training preachers and teachers.

I was also bemused to think that this represented Jack's thinking, so I paused to call him and find out. He laughed. "Just the opposite," he said. "I study and work hard to understand postmodern thinking, how to connect with a totally different mind-set." In fact, he teaches this. He announces to his class they will be tested on the comments he is about to make and then proceeds to talk in Swahili. Then he tells them there's no point in talking your own language to someone who doesn't understand it, and he helps his students analyze the postmodern mind.

The responsibility of the preacher, then, is to get inside the head, indeed, inside the heart of his audience and communicate in thoughts and words that can be understood. More than that, thoughts and words that move to action. That's what Jesus did. He didn't drop in for a few weeks in a celestial bubble and talk celestialese. He became one with us. Incarnation, we call it. Today I plead for incarnational preaching. True, much of Jesus' teaching was counter-cultural because he was out to replace first-century Jewish culture with God's own way of looking at life. But he came not as an erudite professor to hammer into their heads an alien philosophy, not as a Roman emperor to impose a foreign culture but as a babe in a stable, an artisan in a shop, a strolling storyteller in the dusty paths of Palestine. And he spoke their language in the categories of thought they could understand clearly.

And so with us. We must understand and connect with the postmodern in categories they can understand and feel. No need to hide behind the walls of eternal, unchangeable truth, pronouncing theological jargon with precision and pitching Bible text grenades over the wall into the audience. Spiritual formation flows from audience-connected communication.

During my twelve years in Japan I didn't merely study the language; I studied the values of the culture. In fact, I wrote a journal article on using Japanese values in preevangelism, even when those values weren't particularly valuable to us missionaries as Westerners. I had to publish in the ecumenical journal because the evangelical journal wasn't interested! As a result of this immersion in cross-cultural thinking and communication, when I returned to the United States in the midst of student turmoil in the late sixties, I was prepared to study carefully to understand what was going on in their heads that wasn't going on in mine. I developed a message on "The Ten Commandments of America," and youth leaders requested that I preach it again and again.

But those verities were changing, and I almost got caught off-guard. In the eighties, I began to study postmodernism and, with a colleague, developed a journal article on "The Impact of Postmodern Thinking on Evangelical Hermeneutics" (*JETS*, March 1997). The growing capitulation of evangelical scholars to postmodern paradigms must be exposed and opposed, lest the authority of Scripture be eroded by contemporary ideas. And yet, how do we communicate the ancient truth to a generation immersed in postmodern thinking from its infancy? Our audience today is primarily made up of those whose entertainment, education, and culture have been pervasively postmodern.

For several years now, I've studied postmodern thinking as it is worked out in popular culture, and it gradually began to dawn on me that in my preaching I was vainly trying to sell typewriters to the computer generation! If you don't relate to that analogy, maybe you're trying to sell typewriters too.

Much of my preaching is for missions conferences. I was in a small-town Mississippi church that was weak from its untimely birth. Circulating among the early arrivers before the first service, I met a bouncy little lady who announced that she was the church organist. "Oh," I responded, "and how long have you been organist?" "Fifty years!" she said with a bit of well-earned pride.

"Fifty years! That's been a time of great change in music. It must have been quite challenging."

"I do not change," she stated, jaw firmly set. Then she continued, "If they want Bach and Mendelssohn, well and good. If not, they can get themselves another organist."

In an instant I changed the metaphor about my ministry from frustrated typewriter salesman. Here I am, constantly crisscrossing the country offering Bach pipe organ recitals to an audience dancing to the music of electronic praise bands. I preach commitment, sacrifice, and incarnational investment of life to reach people living and dying out of reach of gospel witness. It's like I'm from another galaxy! They're interested in sending their members on two-week junkets to exotic places, sending their money for nationals to do the job, and staying put in their pews, praising God. And not with a pipe organ!

What to do? I was fearful of the direction our young mission/anthropology professor was moving when he kept making positive sounds about postmodernism. They had told me you can't trust those behavioral scientists! But then he gave me the essence of an explosive paper he had read at a national convention of missiologists. He told them we are not of the kingdoms of this world. To be true to Scripture we must allow it to stand in judgment over all human constructs. Modernism? Of course, we oppose the naturalism of scientism, but we must be careful not to jettison the good. Don't we believe in propositional truth? Yet, as missionaries, we may be in danger of listing toward enlightenment rationalism because of our Western heritage. Then he moved on to postmodernism and suggested that there are evils to be exposed but goods to be exploited. Many in his audience were scandalized. How could there be some good fruit in postmodernism?

Since his thesis is the essence of my advocacy of audience-connected preaching, let me cite a few examples of what it might mean to connect with the postmodern. Let me suggest that there are elements of postmodernism: (1) we should adopt, (2) elements we should adapt, and (3) elements we are duty bound to oppose, to compensate for. But be forewarned, each category may well bleed over into the other, and don't think I'm willing to fight and die for the correctness of my analysis. I'm simply seeking to point the way for bringing these concepts under the functional authority of Scripture, not to settle all the issues!

Postmodern Elements to Adopt

1. The spiritual trumps the material. Well, hallelujah! Of course, we have to help define spiritual, but isn't it great we can champion the prevailing view that the unseen is the important part of our lives? From there it may not be so difficult to move on to the idea that the unseen is the real, the eternal.

2. Reality must be experienced. True, my experience doesn't alter reality and there is objective reality that can be known, but when we offer vibrant, living, experiential salvation and sanctification we're on solid biblical ground.

3. How I feel is more important than what I think. More important? Well, actually you can't really have one without the other, can you? And which comes first? But we do a grave disservice to this generation if we don't speak to the heart, stimulate feelings, godly feelings. Postmodernism

17

has recaptured the heart, opened us to our emotions, and for that we must be grateful, since it leads toward greater biblical reality than we knew as enlightenment moderns.

4. Relationships are paramount. What more could you ask? Not only human relationships which some preachers slight, but we must lead on to the ultimate relationship—created, as we were, God-compatible for the very purpose of loving companionship with him. And restoration of the image— to what end if not for loving oneness with God? Intimacy, you might call it, a favorite word to the younger generations. In fact it isn't too much to say that a person's main purpose is to love God and be loved of him forever. Relationships are, indeed, paramount.

5. Hope is in short supply. But desperately wanted. So we offer hope. But we mustn't offer megahope too soon. Better to offer modest hope, at least to begin with. The young person may not be able to change the course of history, but, we may assure them, "You can make a difference!"

Postmodern Elements to Adapt

1. Anti-intellectual. It is the renewing of our minds God is after, and transformational preaching certainly can't bypass the mind. But we can use the contemporary anti-intellectual mood to dethrone scientific naturalism and a materialistic mind-set. We may harness the mood to demolish that deadly enemy of spiritual reality.

2. Propositional truth is a fiction, the only reality is a fusion of what may be "out there" and my personal perception of it, postmodernists contend. Don't hammer me with Aristotelian logic, they say. Yet the Bible is full of propositional truth, and the faithful preacher will proclaim it. But we can capture one element of this mood, since narrative truth, not propositional truth, is the preferred mode, whether for hermeneutics or communication. The twenty-first century belongs to the storyteller.

3. Tell me a story, they say. Story? That has a familiar ring, doesn't it? Sounds like the Bible! The stories of ancient Israel, the stories of Jesus—in fact, he didn't speak at all except in stories (Matt. 13:34).

I've been asked to speak quite often on the Holy Spirit. I've found excitement and response among the younger generation when I offer to tell them the story of the Spirit. Jesus' story they know, but the Spirit's story? He's a doctrine at best, right?

I told that story in Denver. The pastor came weeping to the podium and invited those who wanted to renew their marriage vows to the Lord to come forward. They didn't have public invitations much in that church. After all, it was an upbeat, postmodern crowd who isn't into commitment. Half the congregation surged forward, many broken over the failed hope of an intimate love relationship with God. The power of story. God's story. I received an e-mail from the pastor. He wanted me to know that after the service a couple had come to him with a request: Would you give the opportunity next week to come forward? Now we're ready to become Christians, they said.

4. Radical individualism. If the only reality admitted is composed of what's out there with my perception of it, everyone's "reality" differs. And that's cool. When I was researching on what made the X and Y generations tick, I asked a powerful youth evangelist to give me some time and educate me. He said, "No need to spend time. I can tell you in one word." Then he shaped his two thumbs and forefingers in the shape of a W. "Whatever," he said with a shrug. Now I tell young people that "whatever" is an OK feeling, but point out the difference between an ungodly whatever that doesn't care and a godly whatever that lets God have his way. We co-opt a basic error for channeling it into a godly response.

5. Personal fulfillment is the goal of life. No, no. God's fulfillment is the goal! But when we chart the way to God-centered living we do no wrong in pointing out that as the only path to personal self-fulfillment. Try to fill up on stuff, sex, and significance—on self, that is—and you'll get ever more empty. On the other hand, work at emptying out life into God's purposes and you'll discover your "self" is filling up, fulfilled.

6. Personal freedom is the sine qua non of finding fulfillment. Why aren't we the chief champions of freedom? Of course, we point toward freedom as power to do what I ought rather than license to do what I please. For the seventy-fifth anniversary of Columbia International University, the president asked me to compile a book on our historic theme, the victorious Christian life. So the tentative title was "Victorious Living in the Twenty-First Century." An alumna in California wrote a strong protest. "That's so militaristic, so triumphalistic, it really turns off my generation." So we reworked the title and came up with "Free and Fulfilled." How could we express the promised abundant life more perfectly? When we asked our alum how she felt about the new title, she wrote back, "Great! My generation really resonates with that."

7. Celebrate diversity. The only sin is intolerance. I can attack this error head-on. And lose my audience. Or I can celebrate unity in diversity among God's people, in God's creation, while flashing the caution light of biblical limitations to the concept. If I champion unity in diversity, it won't be quite so easy to dismiss me as a hard-nosed right-wing obscurant.

Postmodern Elements to Oppose

1. Absolute relativism. Not only must we point out the absurdity of this ultimate oxymoron; we must show graphically how it is not a liberating concept as they had supposed, but how it leads to dreadful bondage. This is not hard for me to communicate because I have a story to tell—my own. In the dark tunnel of agnosticism I discovered how absolute relativism is narrow, not broad as they claim, constricting, not liberating, and not enlightening as they suppose, but very dark.

2. Self sacrifice is bad. It's dishonest, a betrayal of self, destructive. The God-story, the story of Jesus, is our ultimate weapon to destroy this perversion of Satan. We must hammer away at the theme of love and the joyful fruit of love. We must demonstrate powerfully how self-orientation is in the end destructive; how self-denial is the affirmation of our true self, the ultimate healing power.

3. Commitment is stupid. We should find it easy to demonstrate from marriage stories the end results of non-commitment vs. commitment. And we can demonstrate from all of life how commitment is the glue that holds together that ultimate desire of the younger generations—relationship and bonding. With one's fellows, yes, but above all with God. You might even persuade them to hope for an ultimate love relationship.

I have hesitated to be specific about possible responses to postmodern thinking because, in the nature of the case, so complex a set of issues can't even be accurately named in so short a space, let alone adequately explored. Besides, I myself am on pilgrimage in these matters—developing a whole new generation of messages and revising old faithfuls in my personal attempt to connect more effectively with the postmodern generations I have opportunity to address. So I'm reluctant, but I overcame my reluctance with the thought that I might be able to set a few markers toward harnessing the all-pervasive postmodern engine to drive spiritual formation.

In that article I addressed the pragmatic question of what a preacher should preach if he is to bring the content of his message under the authority of Scripture. But in addressing the entire scope of ministry in this study and in seeking to do it all under the authority of Scripture, the problem becomes broader and deeper.

Do we use the historic hermeneutic approach in Bible interpretation or the emerging postmodern hermeneutic as our control? For example, is there objective truth? Increasing numbers of evangelicals would hold there is enduring truth only in the major doctrines of Christianity, that beyond that we arrogantly go astray when we seek to establish "biblical authority."

Again, does God even have a will for us in matters of ministry or do we simply use Scripture as a source of historic reference, sort of a case book of stories for reference? God's stories, to be sure, but not intended by him to make normative demands on those at another point in time, living in another culture?

Does "meaning" exist objectively? And if so, does it reside in the text or in the mind of the interpreter, bound as she or he is by their culture? And is the Reformation dogma valid that holds the perspicuity of Scripture and the priesthood of each believer, capable and responsible to understand and obey Scripture? Or are the doctrines and practice of the church created from our own cultural understandings combined with the historic interpretations of the universal church?

The historic response to these questions among evangelicals until the 1980s would have been: The Scripture and the Scripture alone is the final authority for faith and practice. Words do convey meaning, and in Scripture, it is God's meaning, objective and unchanging across time and culture. Further, it is fully adequate to teach us what we must believe and not believe, how we are not to behave and how we are to behave. The text is the bearer of objective truth, and the meaning intended by the original author is accessible to the diligent student. Our responsibility is to understand and obey that truth. That is the foundational presupposition of this study, so we must begin with an honest confrontation of the insidious inroads of postmodern thinking.

Taking our tools of Bible interpretation, we now use them to evaluate another contemporary assumption: a therapeutic society. After clearing our pathway of these major roadblocks we will invest the balance of our study in using the Word of God to evaluate the major aspects of ministry with the confidence that God has a will and that we can discern it.

CHAPTER 3:

THERAPEUTIC THEOLOGY

Question for reflection: **Are all psychological insights
and popular assumptions consciously and constantly brought
to the bar of Scripture to evaluate the validity of church-based
counseling and preaching/teaching?**

In the mid-seventies I spoke to the Evangelical Theological Society on the
theme "The Behavioral Sciences Under the Authority of Scripture." I told
the delegates that while we sat and debated the finer points of theology, the
pastors and missionaries had left us for the psychologists and anthropologists. To illustrate I told them of two recent classes at our school, Columbia
Biblical Seminary. A small upstairs class of twelve students met with the dean
of evangelical theologians, Carl F. H. Henry, while downstairs in the audito-
rium 120 students met with a newly minted psychologist, Larry Crabb. That
was a paradigm for the future, I told them. And so it proved to be.

A quarter century later I was in a conference of several hundred pastors where I shared the platform with a world-renowned psychotherapist.
In the breakout sessions he would deal with psychological issues for several
hundred pastors and I would, by request, introduce the study course *Life in
the Spirit* to a handful of pastors. As I taught, my mind wandered. I contemplated what psychology could do and what the Holy Spirit could do. What
is the difference between psychotherapy and psuche-therapy? I reflected on
the parallel with medical science. We accept with gratitude every advance of
medical science and celebrate the ways in which our bodies feel better and
last longer. But we don't expect the doctor to give us eternal life. We have
to go to the evangelist for that! But when it comes to counseling, somehow
we tend to forget that deep and permanent healing and health of our inner
person ultimately awaits the work of the Holy Spirit. Instead, we see more
hope in the professional counselor to fix us than in the miracle work of the
Holy Spirit.

Pragmatically, the results on each side sometimes seem to bear out the
contemporary intuitions of our therapeutic society. People are enabled to
cope through psychotherapy but don't improve much through preaching.

Why? We'll think about the failed preaching part in later units of our study, but the fundamental problem with much of our counseling and therapy, whether on the couch or in the pew, is theological. For the most part, we aren't doing our behavioral sciences under the authority of Scripture.

During that interval between the meetings of theologians in 1975 and pastors in 2003, at Columbia Biblical Seminary we needed to find professors of counseling/psychology who were actually doing their work under the authority of Scripture. The search was not easy. I developed a checklist of key questions to test the extent to which a prospective teacher did his work under the authority of Scripture. What follows is not intended as an analysis of each issue but as illustrative of what the issues are in applying the Bible authority grid to a specific discipline: psychotherapy. Please do not assume that the common assumptions here noted are restricted to professional therapists. Most of them can be heard any Sunday from pulpits throughout the land and in classrooms of Christian institutions for the education of our young and of our not-so-young. Yes, even for the training of our pastors.

1. Who needs professional counseling? When the response is that the majority of people have their "trusters" or "choosers" broken so they cannot obey the injunctions of Scripture until the professional "fixes" them, I think, *It's too bad the Holy Spirit didn't know that and made provision in Scripture.* When the candidate responds that he does his work on the assumption that, with the Holy Spirit's enabling, anyone can understand, trust, and obey Scripture, unless there are organic reasons for the dysfunction, I know we have a candidate who attempts to do counseling under the authority of Scripture.

2. What are the major causes of dysfunctional attitudes and behavior? If the answers are limited to early environment and present circumstances, and sin as the root cause is left out of the equation, I know we have a therapist who doesn't do his work under the authority of Scripture.

3. What are the major factors in what a person becomes? Here I'm fishing for the four basic factors Scripture teaches, not the single factor of environment, especially not environmental determinism. True, early environment is recognized in Scripture as a factor, as is the impact of inherited factors such as a sinful disposition. But far more than heredity and environment, Scripture emphasizes from start to finish two factors—human responsibility for choices made and the intervening grace of God. If these two factors do not dominate therapy, how can it be said to be under the authority of Scripture?

4. Are feelings morally neutral? One therapist puts it this way: "It does mean confronting our feelings honestly—all of them. It means accepting our feelings as neither good nor bad. Feelings fall outside the realm of value judgments. It is only the things we do as a result of our feeling that can be judged."[1] A good thing the authors of that line were not applying for a position at Columbia! If the candidate holds that anger and lust, for example, are morally neutral until acted out, we know to look elsewhere for a candidate. Of course, the therapist should not go to the other extreme and promote false guilt, when the subject is fighting off temptation, not sinning; and he should certainly promote honesty about one's feelings. But to make all feelings morally neutral is to undercut a major emphasis of Scripture. The Bible holds the basic problem to be of "the heart," and the victory promised is not just for bad actions but a bad heart—yes, for wrong feelings.

5. What do you as counselor do about guilty feelings? If all guilty feelings are treated as part of the problem to be counteracted and not part of God the Spirit's gracious work of redemption, how can it be said the counseling is biblical? "I won't put you on a guilt trip" is the mantra. But the Spirit was given specifically to put people on a "guilt trip," Jesus said. Of course, the counselor's special tools may be able to ferret out guilt that is unbiblical and work to eliminate that and, if so, they operate under the authority of Scripture.

6. What is the goal of therapy? If the goal is diagnosis and developing coping strategies to modify behavior, and no hope is offered of supernatural transformation by the power of the Holy Spirit to ever greater likeness to Jesus, to a restored image, how can the therapy be of deep and lasting value? Naturalistically based psychology can help in diagnosing the problem and helping develop strategies for more healthful attitudes and behavior, but it is impotent to transform the essence of human nature. Restoration of God's image isn't an objective of most practitioners, yet that is the core message of Scripture.

7. Is a person responsible when unable to change behavior? The Bible holds us responsible for our choices and what we become, but it does much more. It offers to change the "unable" to "able."

8. Are any common counseling or therapeutic techniques unacceptable for a Christian therapist? Many hold that none are off limits if they work. Express your anger because it's unhealthy to hold it in; use pornography, if necessary, to improve your marriage; lie if it's the loving thing to do. But Scripture makes no such allowance for breaking ethical standards.

9. How important is self-love to wholeness?[2] This usually lies at the core of therapy, but to be under the authority of Scripture one must delve into two other loves: love for God and love for others. My wife and I were reading a devotional book that insisted we are commanded to love ourselves.

---

1. Raymond R. Mitsch and Lynn Brookside, *Grieving the Loss of Someone You Love* (Ann Arbor: Servant Publications, 1993), 102–103.

2. An analysis of the fundamental teaching of Scripture on love lies outside the purview of this study, but a thorough analysis can be found in the first chapter of *An Introduction to Biblical Ethics* (Tyndale, 1995) by the author. At this point perhaps it should be noted that misplaced love of self is not a slight aberration but lies at the core of dysfunction in persons and in relationships, as viewed by Scripture.

I asked for the references and she read them off. All were repeats of the command to love others—"love your neighbors as you love yourselves." That's no command to love self; that's an observation of fact—we do love ourselves and so, say Moses and Jesus, "get on with it and love your neighbor with the same commitment and care." I'm unaware of biblical teaching that would advocate self-love as a strategy, but self-acceptance for who I am in grace is certainly a biblical theme and of utmost importance to spiritual/emotional/psychological health. A "high" or "good" self-image is good only to the extent it is realistic. Otherwise it is ultimately destructive, according to Scripture. The biblical therapist, then, will work toward helping counselees view themselves realistically: who they are by nature and who they are and can be by grace. That's a healthy self-image.

I make no attempt to examine these critical issues in depth, of course, but simply offer them as pointers toward what it means to do therapy under the authority of Scripture. But lest you dismiss my concern as that of an ignorant non-professional, let me quote some of the words of one of America's premier authorities in psychology, Paul C. Vitz, senior scholar and professor of psychology (emeritus) at New York University.[3]

> After a hundred years of trying to understand human problems it is time to study human strengths or positive characteristics. . . .
>
> The almost exclusive emphasis on negative psychology has had undesirable consequences as well. For one thing, it has contributed to the widespread victim mentality characteristic of today's American society. Psychotherapy has been one of the most influential of the modern disciplines: directly or indirectly, it has changed the way most of us think about ourselves. The general perspective provided by negative psychology is that we are all victims of past traumas, abuse, and neglect caused by other people. . . . Many of us can see ourselves as victims—that is, as sinned against—but fewer of us recognize ourselves as victimizers, as sinners. In many ways this victim mentality is a consequence of the very structure of traditional psychotherapy, which can only identify your hurts and problems and their possible sources. Therapists report that it is uncommon for anyone to present to the therapist a problem that he or she has caused for another.
>
> A further disturbing consequence of this mentality is the widespread belief that we are not responsible for our bad actions, since they are caused by what others have done to us. . . .
>
> What is needed to balance our understanding of the person is a recognition of positive human characteristics that can both heal

---

3. Excerpts here describe the new directions in psychotherapy, spotlighting weaknesses of traditional approaches. The entire watershed article can be found in the journal *First Things* (March 2005), 17ff.

many of our pathologies and help to prevent psychological problems in one's future life. Positive psychology therefore emphasizes traits that promote happiness and well-being, as well as character strengths such as optimism, kindness, resilience, persistence, and gratitude. . . .

The previous model for negative psychology was based entirely on the traditional scientific worldview of a deterministic past causing the present. In moving to positive psychology, the discipline has moved not only from science to philosophy, but also from the past and its effects to the future and our purposes, from mechanical determinism to teleology. . . .

This has happened in part because research has demonstrated that seriously religious people tend to be happier, healthier, and longer-lived. . . .

Psychology, as it has become aware of the virtues and the need to recover them, has begun to develop an important virtue of its own—humility. . . .

The majority of psychologists have now recognized: that although psychotherapy is helpful, it rarely provides life-transforming insight or happiness.

This appraisal makes me bold to present to you what I attempted years before I heard of "positive psychology." It was a layman's effort to capture the positive possibilities of a discipline that has had such pervasive deleterious effects in our society. I present this with a measure of confidence because these concepts seem to be acceptable at least to some professionals. The following was first published in the journal *Christian Counseling Today* (1999, vol. 7, no. 2); reprints and translations appeared and some professors of psychology distributed them to students as a paradigm, I assume, of how theology and psychology might interface.

Therapeutic Theology

I arrived just as Virginia was lifted from the ambulance, strapped to a metal stretcher. When she saw me, her greeting was simply, "God has abandoned me." Maybe you'd feel that way, too, if your husband had died an agonizing death from cancer less than a year before and this was the second automobile accident since then, the one you knew intuitively had ended your driving forever. But her voice was flat—no wail of self-pity or angry accusation against God. It wasn't the first time my sister felt God had abandoned her. Actually, she's felt that way periodically over the past twenty years since Margie, the joy of her life and only daughter, was brutally killed. It didn't help that the killer had done it before and had just been released from prison on the advice of a court-appointed psychiatrist. It didn't make sense that a young woman who loved God and people so intensely should be snuffed out by a madman. Perhaps God abandoned Virginia's daughter too.

I thought to myself, *Why do I never feel that way?* Some judge that I have cause enough, but I never had those feelings. This started a train of thought about other things I've never felt: despondency, depression, anger with God, for example. Then I began to think of feelings I have had that I wish I hadn't: unforgiveness, impatience, and numbness of spirit. Why the difference? Perhaps theology has something to do with it.

Theology? More likely heredity or environment. Except that Virginia and I sprang from the same gene pool, were raised by the same parents. In fact, we're much alike in personality. As I thought about my inner responses to external circumstances I was drawn irresistibly to the theology factor. What I truly believe seems to have set me up—both for success and for failure.

When asked to share some of my life experience for an audience of professional counselors, I thought, *I'm no counselor. What could I contribute? I've spent my life at theological reflection, not psychological.* But then I realized my life story might point up some of the interface between the two, an interface theologians seldom consider and an interface a counselor might be tempted to bypass. So without trying to explicate how that interface should work for either theologian or psychologist, let me tell the story.

Consider a few positive examples from my life, then a few negative examples which seem to support the idea that theology played a major role in who I have become and continues to play a major role in what I am yet to become.

Theology Provides Protection

More than therapy to heal the broken, perhaps, theology builds an immune system to keep a person from breaking in the first place. Here's how it worked for me.

I Believe I'm Finite

I didn't always believe that. Oh, I would have admitted to finitude if asked, but my youthful self-confidence led me to believe I had a corner on the truth. Then, in my early twenties I entered the dark tunnel of agnosticism—from knowing "everything" to knowing nothing for sure, especially about God and his Book. I wasn't arrogant, affirming that no god existed, just that I, at least, couldn't find him. When by God's grace I emerged from that dark tunnel, I had great confidence in the basics—that God is, that the Savior actually saves, that God has purpose for my life. But I was shorn of any pretense of infallibility about the details. My expectancies—for myself and others—were lowered to the realities of human finitude.

I exulted in the confidence of what God had revealed for sure—so sure that all believers of all time would affirm it. But I concluded that most things I would never figure out no matter how long I investigated and contemplated, things about God's infinities and things about my finitude—like the meanings of my past, the hopes for my future, the reasons for my circumstances, the goings-on of my inner self. I'm comfortable now with that ambiguity about life though I recognize others may not be. Some seem to need to have everything settled for sure.

For an inquisitive thinker and an intense activist, the realization of one's finitude can be a marvelous relaxant and stabilizer. Besides, lowered expectancies of oneself is a doorway to making room for others. Maybe they're finite, too—and in a different configuration yet! That realization could make a peacemaker out of a person. For example, when Mack set out to get rid of me as leader of the ministry, I didn't have to try to "be good" and not get angry, fight back, or hold a grudge against him. After all, he saw things differently than I. Besides, maybe he was right. I didn't think so, but neither did I conclude he was devilish. Our finitudes had clashed and we both thought we were doing God's service. My theology had protected me in the crisis.

I Believe I'm Fallen

And so are others. So I expect them to behave that way and that helps make allowances for their failures, which doesn't come to me naturally. What comes naturally is to be easy on myself and hard on the other fellow. So it's a trick to be realistic about my fallenness without justifying my own ungodly behavior because I've been easing off on the other fellow. I haven't figured out all the ramifications of the doctrine of the Fall for protecting me from wrong thinking about myself and others, but on the larger scale, that doctrine has been a powerful deliverer in my life.

Here's how. The whole of creation is under the curse of the Fall. I'm not exempt, because of God's love for me, from the consequences of living in a world of vicious cancer and violent winds. Nor from a world of finite and fallen people who inflict harm on me, wittingly or unwittingly. I expect the worst and rejoice when, by God's grace, it usually doesn't happen! Sometimes when I wake in the morning I muse, *Lord, lots of folks died last night. Why not me?* At my stage of life so many of my dearest family and friends suffer painful, debilitating illness and agonizing death. Why not I? That's the only reasonable "why" question for a person who lives in a fallen world.

I don't want to oversimplify the problem of evil; a whole complex of theological issues intertwine. For example, if God made his own people exempt from the human condition, who wouldn't become a believer?

But what kind of believer would they become? Again, when does God heal and to what end? For what purpose does God protect or remove the protection? The theological questions seem endless, especially when faced with personal tragedy, but the bottom line for me is this: I'm fallen and so is my world. Not, "why me, Lord?" when trouble strikes, but "why not me, Lord?" when it so often misses.

Muriel was blessed with eternal youth—looking forty when she was actually fifty-five. But that's still far too young to fall before Alzheimer's, the disease of the old. "Early onset" they called it in clinically sterile terminology. Early onset of what? Of grief for me who must watch the vibrant, creative, sparkling person I knew dimming out. No grief for her, however, except for momentary frustrations quickly forgotten. She never knew what was happening.

So, why us, Lord? There are various theories. One alumnus said it was God's judgment on me for allowing contemporary Christian music on our radio station. I don't feel guilty about that, but I do know circumstances contrary to our desires are always intended to make us more like Jesus, and God has surely used those two decades of lingering grief to develop in me more Jesus-like attitudes and behavior where there are deficiencies. Perhaps God wanted new leadership at Columbia International University, though the board and administrators didn't buy that theory. Of late I've begun to wonder if the Lord put me under "house arrest" so I'd do something my busy life didn't allow much of—writing books and articles. Of course, whatever other purposes God has in sending or permitting adversity, there is always the purpose of bringing God glory, either through his mighty deliverance from suffering or his mighty deliverance in suffering. And that he has done in wonderful ways I'll never fully understand. So it's obvious I have contemplated the "why?" question.

But why have I not fretted over the answer? Why have I not demanded healing from God or frantically pursued the many cures friends and strangers have suggested? The bottom line is this: we live in a fallen world—what else did you expect? Theology protects from destructive inner turmoil and allows me to accept reality.

I Believe I'm of Value

I live with the acute realization of my own finitude and fallenness, but the contemporary assures me I cannot be truly free and fulfilled if I put a low value on self. A low self-image will ruin it all. But "low" and "high"—who decides? Where is the price list? We need a reality check, because only recognizing true value will liberate and open the way to fulfillment. An inflated view or a deflated view, distorting reality, will surely tie me up tighter than ever and shut out the possibility of fulfillment. But if I measure my worth by what I own, how much fun I'm having, and how successful people recognize me to be, I've given in to the world's value system and have doomed myself to bondage and unfulfillment because those things—no matter how abundant—cannot liberate me or fill me up. If a therapist persuades me I really am significant, no matter what those around think about me, such counsel can be permanently liberating only if it's true. And the truth is that I'm worth a lot!

I'm a designer brand. I'm valuable not because of what I own or have done but because of how God designed me. He created me on his pattern. I have his insignia stamped on me. I'm an image bearer of the Infinite One and that's impressive, no matter what others may think of me.

I have a very high sticker price. God himself valued me so highly he paid an outrageous price to buy me back from my slaveholder, my bondage to stuff, fun, and an inflated self-image. I'm of infinite worth to God, not for my achievements or possessions, but because he invested in me the life of his own Son.

Those values are shared by all believers, but I have a value no one else shares. I have a unique destiny. God not only created me to bear his family likeness, he not only purchased me with the life of his only Son, but he did so on purpose. He has a purpose for me, something he wants to accomplish on earth through me. No matter how the world or the church may evaluate my contribution, the grand designer valued me enough to plan my unique role to bring him the greatest possible honor. That's why I'm proud to be a homemaker. I try to be the best cook, housekeeper, gardener, and nurse I know how. I'm not the best at any of those, to be sure, but I give it my best because it's my assignment, God's purpose for me. And I greatly enjoy it and never fret about what I'd rather be doing, about what might have been—much less compare my "value" to others with higher callings and greater gifts.

And there's something more. Worth is often judged by the company a person keeps—royalty, skid row, whatever. And I'm a member of high society—the highest! Incredible as it may seem, God has planned my life around him, uninterrupted companionship with the greatest lover who ever lived.

Talk about self-worth! If that knowledge of who I am in Christ doesn't liberate and fill life to the full, what will?

- Created on the pattern of God, not a monkey
- Purchased by the most precious commodity this world has ever known, the blood of God
- Living a life planned by the master designer of the planets, the suns, and every atom
- A constant companion of the King of kings

Indeed, theology can liberate and fill a person full.

I Believe in God

But what kind of God? In my thirties, I discovered three stories in the Bible that focused on the kind of God I didn't have. The hired mourners knew the child was dead, so they ridiculed the God-man who said it would be all right. The distraught father, finding Jesus' disciples failing of the press releases, said to the all-powerful one: "If you can, please heal my son." The disciples, veteran sailors, despaired of life as the winds howled, and wakened the sleeping passenger, "Don't you care that we're dead men?" Some doubted his wisdom—they knew better. One doubted his power—"If you can," he said. And some doubted his love—"Don't you care about us?" When this snapped into focus, I realized that when I worried about my impossible circumstances—death, illness, and storms—I was calling into question the character of God. Am I really smarter than God to know what is best? Is he truly impotent in the face of my impossible circumstances? Or maybe he just doesn't care that much about me? What blasphemy!

Muriel was a chain worrier. One stormy night she was totally stressed out about her three teenagers who were out in the fringes of the hurricane. She was just as distraught over the last two when the first arrived in good cheer, unscathed, and still immobilized by fear for the third after the second appeared. As she writhed in an agony of worry on her bed, harassing the Lord with her unbelief, he seemed to say to her, "Do you want to spend the rest of your life living like this?" Startled, she cried out, "Oh, no, Lord! I truly don't. Please deliver me!" And, as she never tired of testifying, he did. In an instant. For most of us it takes a bit of growing, but not for Muriel. She just quit once she got focused on who God really is. Later she wrote this couplet:

> Anything, anytime, anywhere,
> I leave the choice with you.
> I trust your wisdom, love, and power,
> What e'er you say I'll do.

I may not know what God's purpose is in sending or permitting difficulty in my life, but that he has a purpose I am confident. And a God with wisdom to know what is best for me, love to choose that best, and power to carry it through, I can trust. I can never be a victim, except a "victim" of God's love. Self-pity can't even get a hearing! Shake my puny fist in the face of God, as some testify? They must not fear the infinite, holy one. Or perhaps they've not watched the agony of the Father's face as his only Son hangs helpless, crying out, "Why have you abandoned me?" Why indeed! For my sake it was! That's how much the Father and the Son love me. How often, when I've tried to untangle the reasons God seems to have abandoned me, have I returned finally to Calvary and whispered,

"Dear Jesus, how could those hands pierced for me ever allow anything truly evil to pass through to touch me? Help me trust you when I can't figure out the why."

Theology does indeed protect from the ravages of ungodly responses!

I Believe in Love

"How does God enable you to love Muriel when there's so little left to love?" I was being interviewed on camera, but I knew the young anchorwoman didn't make up that question. She'd been given it by the production manager who had asked me similar questions during the last twenty-four hours. I waved for the cameras to cut.

"I'm sorry, but I don't know how to answer that question," I said to the producer. "How would you feel if I said you were very difficult to like but that God was giving me supernatural ability to like you anyway? Not much of a compliment! I know that anything of merit in me comes as a gift from God. So perhaps his gift to me was by creating in Muriel a wonderful person who to me was totally irresistible. So I love Muriel because she's altogether loveable. I can't not love her. She's my precious."

"OK," the producer responded, "that's fine. Just say that." And the cameras rolled.

She loved me passionately for forty years and stored away countless memories that still flood me with joy. And in the morning when our eyes connected and she flashed that glorious smile for a fleeting moment, my heart would leap. All those years abed, she was so gentle and contented—oh, I can't explain love. But I believe in love.

Theology seems to have built up my spiritual and psychic immune system. But when that immune system fails, I've discovered theology also has the power to heal, to correct wrong thinking, to renew.

Theology Rehabilitates

I Believe in Grace

But I haven't always. Some would say that's because I had a strict, old-fashioned mother who periodically chastised me with a bamboo cane. Or perhaps they would point to my parents' philosophy of life—never compliment the boy lest he be seduced by pride. I can't remember a single affirmation. Show of affection? I never saw my parents embrace. Furthermore, my father would today be called "absentee," he was so busy and so often traveling. And my mother also was often teaching the Bible in some distant place when I returned home from school. Yet I knew they loved me dearly, believed in me. I don't know how, but I guess you could say they somehow built a "strong self-image." So I've never bought into those theories about my parents banging up my little ego. Furthermore, I understood grace from that day at age six when I was delivered from the fear of hell—well-deserved I was certain—and ran to embrace Jesus. Guilty feelings—except when there was some unresolved guilt—were never a problem. But somehow I had a lot of growing to do in understanding grace. Two areas come to mind: lack of passion in my love for God, sort of settling for a formal correctness, and forgiveness—not God's forgiveness of me, but my forgiveness of others.

I don't like to admit it, but it was two decades after my salvation encounter before I ever shed the first tear over my own sin. I was reflecting on Calvary and suddenly realized it was my sin that nailed him there—not Hitler's, not Stalin's, but mine—my very own sanitized, civilized, damnable sin. And it broke up the hard granite of a semi-grateful heart. Then, for the first time, I exulted in his grace.

A few years later the ministry for which I was responsible was not doing well. I cried out to God for deliverance and victory, but it seemed my prayers weren't getting through. So I went out on the mountainside—perhaps with no ceiling those prayers would rise higher! But still the line was dead. Then a thought broke through—try praise. I was so out of practice in praise that I ran out of thanksgivings and praise in five minutes! But my soul was uncaged, and I discovered that the weary spirit rises on the wings of praise. And no wonder. To focus on God sets me free from my own finitudes and fallenness. I say I learned it, but I have often had to relearn it.

My beloved was being taken from me little by little in the eighties, and then the blow fell; my eldest son was killed in a diving accident. All accidental deaths are tragic, but this one was so preventable. Two years later I resigned the presidency of Columbia International University to care for my beloved, leaving my life's work at its peak. I was numb under the blows of life. Not angry, not despondent, just numb. My faith might better be described as resignation, as Kierkegaard once said. The passion in my love for God had evaporated, and I was left with the residue of a sure but formal relationship. This was a call to do what I learned early in ministry—off to a mountain hideaway to be alone with God. There, as I focused again on him, I discovered that indeed the heavy heart lifts on the wings of praise. Theology helps rehabilitation.

One of the greatest pains in life is betrayal. To discover a trusted friend scheming to bring you down can unleash all kinds of ungodly responses. But I who had experienced forgiveness was ready to make allowances and forgive—not holding against him what I considered evil and he considered good. But it took years to face the fact that though I wanted to forgive and forget, I didn't want God to! I found no echo in my soul for the gracious response of Jesus on the cross or Stephen under assault. I might not seek retaliation or even rejoice in some trouble in the life of my nemesis, but God surely will bring justice. Don't let him off the hook, God! I realized that I wasn't so Christlike after all and asked God to cut out the cancer that was eating away at my soul. The healing began when I noticed what the disciples asked for when Jesus told them to forgive the same offense 490 times. They didn't ask for more love; they asked for more faith. I was doubting God's ability to handle the situation properly. When I turned it all over to him, asking him to let my "friend" off the hook, healing began. But I hadn't yet gotten the theology of forgiveness worked out.

Years later when a ministry for which I had great hopes was deliberately snatched from me by nefarious scheming, I was consumed with the inner struggle to forgive. I discovered my "rehabilitation" wasn't complete. So I turned to the Bible and made a thorough study of forgiveness in Scripture. Once again I found that theology does indeed rehabilitate. It taught me of grace. God's grace, yes. But also how I also must grace my brother.

I Believe in Victory

When I became a new person in Christ, I was given new potentialities. Whereas before I could do right but couldn't consistently choose the right, the new me can choose wrong but need not. Besides, the Holy Spirit took up residence and in that new relationship I'm empowered to win out in the battle against temptation. Oh, I'll not be sinless until I meet him in person, but in the meantime I have power to say yes to God and no to sin whenever I have the conscious choice. But then there are those involuntary sins and my uninterrupted falling short of God's glorious character. In those areas the Spirit promises to change me, to grow me up more and more into the likeness of Christ, if I only let him. I believe this because Scripture teaches it but also because I've experienced it in my life.

Take patience, for example. As a teen I'd shoot from the lip and occasionally settle things with my fists. But gradually I came to abhor this and by the age of eighteen I began to ask God daily to deliver me and give me patience. I saw a remarkable spurt of growth and thought I'd been delivered. Until, following marriage, my wife and I disagreed on how our first child should be disciplined. I didn't say anything in anger, but I seethed inside for days. Three days, to be exact. When I could stand it no longer, I confessed my attitude to God and asked him to deliver me. This happened three times during the first decade of our marriage until finally I had a showdown. "Oh Lord," I said, "how can I give these Japanese people the hope of salvation when you haven't saved me from my own temper? If you don't deliver me, I'm out of here."

God knew I meant it. He heard and delivered. Never again did that evil spirit intrude into my relationship with Muriel. But God wasn't through with me. Our children became teens, and I found that patience was not yet the natural fruit of my spirit. After that it was a board, then certain faculty. Next I entered a graduate program in patience with a beloved wife who lingered for more than a decade in the advanced stages of Alzheimer's.

God didn't give me the instant deliverance from impatience I longed for and begged for. But he did do what he promised and transformed me "from one degree of glory to another, for this comes from the Lord, the Spirit" (2 Cor. 3:18 NRSV). I believe in victory. I'll never settle for lockdown into some intractable dysfunction of spirit.

That's the way I sought to demonstrate a legitimate interface between theology and psychology, not systematic and comprehensive, but personal and representative. And that is what the Christian counselor must do with every aspect of his discipline when he makes therapy personal to each client. And that's what each church must assure for its approach to human dysfunction. Counseling and preaching must be done under the authority of Scripture. And for both counselor and preacher the goal must always be spiritual transformation by the power of the Spirit.

Psychology and Bible truth have been in conflict from the beginning, when the most powerful shaper of Western culture, Sigmund Freud, gave birth to a new "science" and called it psychotherapy (from the Greek for "soul," *psuche*). Militantly atheistic, he ruled out any consideration of anything beyond the natural as he sought to understand the human soul and how to rescue it. Since the nature of humans and the way they may be rescued from their dysfunctions is the theme of Scripture, conflict was inevitable. The "book of nature" and the "book of revelation"—we're called to study both and both yield benefits. But in this chapter we have sought to illustrate how essential it is to keep fallible insights into human nature under the authority of revealed truth about the human psyche. Psychological counseling is useful for diagnosis and developing coping strategies, but it is helpless to transform. That takes Holy Spirit miracle power. Even in its often useful diagnosis, however, without biblical definitions of the problem, psychology can lead far astray.[4]

In this chapter I've shared a sampler from my life in an effort to demonstrate how theology works to help hurting people see themselves and their world more nearly from God's perspective. That viewpoint protects from wrong feelings and attitudes and heals when I fail. I call it "therapeutic theology."

This is our second illustration of how I've faced in my own life a contemporary assault on biblical authority that has virtually redefined Western culture, and indeed the entire ministry of the church, at least in

---

4. A book that seriously attempts to and usually succeeds in doing psychological counseling under the authority of Scripture is *How People Grow* by Henry Cloud and John Townsend (Grand Rapids: Zondervan, 2001). A practical guide to doing therapy under the authority of Scripture is *Darkness Is My Only Companion* by Kathryn Green-McCreight (Grand Rapids: Brazos Press, 2006).

North America. We can—we must—bring our psychology and psychother-apy in the church under the full functional control of Scripture.

There is a third megashift in our society. The impact of cultural anthro-pology is not confined to cross-cultural missions, important as that is. Actu-ally all ministry is cross-cultural—crossing over from a heavenly culture to our human one. But ministry in American culture of the twenty-first cen-tury is especially cross-cultural, not the least of which is cross-generational. We consider the implications of this for biblical fidelity in the appendix. But for now we turn to more pragmatic concerns. How do we do church under the functional authority of Scripture?

Conclusion to Unit 1

In unit 1 we have tried to establish a grid for discerning biblical author-ity in an issue, applying that approach by way of example to two major con-temporary issues. We now turn to the direct consideration of the remaining four principles for doing God's work under the authority of Scripture: the purposes of the local congregation, the role of the Spirit in ministry, the plan of redemption as the calling of every disciple, and Christ as Lord of the church.

Unit 2:

THE CHURCH

ALIGNING THE CONGREGATION WITH
ALL OF GOD'S BIBLICAL PURPOSES

I will build my church.
(MATT. 16:18 NIV)

*The whole Church. . . . now enjoyed a period of peace. It became
established and as it went forward in reverence for the Lord and in the
strengthening presence of the Holy Spirit, continued to grow in numbers.*
(ACTS 9:31 PHILLIPS)

I was born and raised parachurch. My father was president of a transde-
nominational theological training institution (Columbia International
University) and conference center (Ben Lippen) from before my birth until
he died in my twenty-fifth year. Our lives centered on those ministries. Oh,
we were always church members, but church life was at the periphery of my
life. I would never even have conceived the theme of this unit of study. But
I had a conversion.

When I enlisted my graduate students in researching how God intended
ministry to be done, the beginning of my attempt to wed theology and practice, we soon discovered there were no theological training institutions in
the New Testament. And we found no evangelistic organizations, no welfare
or relief organizations, no "parachurch" at all. Not even a mission board,
though there was a missionary team. Even it, however, flowed out from and
into a local congregation, was accountable to the sending church. Of course,
argument from silence or from what was not done in New Testament times is
notoriously weak. So what was done? Does that give a clue to God's intent?

The New Testament record of the apostles—who heard Christ say, "I
will build my church," and who heard Christ's commission to them on at

least four or five occasions following his resurrection—makes very clear what they took him to mean: they started local congregations. Their example is hard to explain away. It defines what Christ intended to "build."

God had built a nation where worship centered on law, lived out in the temple sacrifices and priesthood. In the New Testament, the words of Christ between the cross and the sending of the Spirit indicate that God was building something other than a nation. The church that emerged could exist under any political rule, be translated into any cultural setting, and it required only twice-born, Spirit-indwelt disciples to exist. But across the centuries, the term "church" has become fuzzy in its meaning.

One confusion about "church" is the way the term is used. It can mean a denomination (the Roman Catholic Church); it can mean the universal people of God of all ages, living and dead; it can even mean a church building (the church at First and Main). But the New Testament use of *ecclesia* points to another meaning. True, nineteen times it refers to the universal body of all believers, the church at large, or at least to multiple local churches. But ninety-one times it refers to a local congregation.[1] It is clear that in the minds of the apostles, the local congregation was central, was indeed God's appointed means for accomplishing his redemptive purposes.

Sheralee didn't buy into that. She insisted, in our seminary course on the theology of doing church, that "church" meant universal and that the purposes I outlined for the local church were actually intended for the church at large. Each local congregation has its own calling, its own profile of responsibility. For example, her church did evangelism, not foreign missions. And that's OK. "That's our calling." Just as no individual Christian, not even the pastor, has all the gifts—the Spirit distributes as he wills—so the local church has a particular calling or gifting. I couldn't persuade her otherwise.

On the way home from the city where Sheralee and I discussed the issue, I formulated an answer. She had not been convinced by the exegetical answer outlined above, so I told a story. Here is part of what I wrote:

> If a local congregation has its own profile (like individual Christians) and is responsible for less than all the purposes, what if a person goes to a church and finds no singing, no worship, just offerings and prayers and preaching. "Oh, you want worship? Well, you'll have to go down the street to New Life Charismatic Fellowship." You go there and find great worship but very little solid Bible teaching from the pulpit, so you ask when they do that. They say, "Oh, if you want Bible content, you'll have to go over to Calvary Bible Church." So you head down there and like it for a while, but then discover a lot of hypocrisy, leaders living double

---

1. In this study we will customarily use "local congregation" rather than "church" since there is less ambiguity.

lives. You ask why they don't have any discipline and they say, "You want discipline, accountability? You'd better try First Fundamentalist Church over on Main Street." So you go there and wow! how you begin to long for some caring help, some sense of family belonging, but all you get is hard-edged discipline.

I've been to many churches that are great on evangelism and keep growing and growing, but they don't have two thoughts or care two dimes' worth about the billions living in the spiritually dark one-third of the world, outside gospel light. And I've been to other churches that send lots of folks to the mission field and have big missions budgets but it's the same crowd year after year. No evangelism at home, no growth. So what is the motive that drives them to all local evangelism and no missions or to all missions and little local evangelism?

Sharalee responded graciously: "That scenario helps me to sort this out much better in my brain. I think your example is an excellent one! I believe you have made me see clearer why every local congregation should be doing everything God has commanded us to do." Sheralee experienced the same conversion I had experienced years before. The local congregation is God's appointed means for achieving his redemptive purposes, and he expects the full prosecution of all the purposes he has established.

I call her former position the suprachurch viewpoint. It is dissimilar, but in a way quite like my own original parachurch orientation. The parachurch organization chooses one of the purposes of the church, perhaps one inadequately pursued in local churches, and that's OK. OK, that is, if it meets two criteria: does this specialized ministry, focusing on a single purpose of the church, flow out of and into the local congregation? If not, its validity should be questioned and adjustments made. To "flow out" means it is sponsored by or at least accountable to one or more local congregations. To "flow into" means the product of the ministry must reinforce a local church or churches in their prosecution of all the God-given purposes.

Consider Paul's missionary team, called by some a "sodality" of the local church. The local congregation at Antioch sent the team as their representatives and the team reported back to that church periodically. That's accountability. Furthermore, the missionary team was engaged in more than evangelism; it was in the business of establishing local congregations. So their activities flowed "into" church in two directions: they functioned as part of the congregation's worldwide outreach, enabling Antioch to fulfill one of its major purposes, and they "flowed into" the creation of many new congregations.

All the purposes, then, for each congregation. And what are those purposes? We must admit up front that the Bible doesn't give us a list. As a consequence, leaders have outlined anywhere from a few to eight or more purposes. But I've discovered a remarkable similarity. Though the purposes are divided and grouped differently, the same themes recur in virtually all the listings I've seen. How could that be? Though the New Testament never says, "Here are the essential purposes of the church," the emphases are so clear that all who analyze the biblical data converge in affirming the purposes God has in mind for his church, the local congregation. Here's the way I list them:

1. Worship *(proskuneo)*
2. Make Disciples *(matheteuo)*
   a. teaching/learning
   b. accountability[2]
3. Member Care *(koinonia)*
   a. family solidarity
   b. healing, caring, providing
4. Evangelize *(euangelizo)*[3]
   a. witness (by all)
   b. gifting (of some)
5. Ministry of Compassion *(splanknizomai)*
   a. justice
   b. mercy

We turn, then, in this unit, to examine the purposes of the church, using these criteria to evaluate the health of any local congregation.

---

2. Accountability, including unity, conflict, and discipline, will be considered in more detail in unit 5.
3. Evangelism, near and far, will be considered in greater detail in unit 4.

CHAPTER 4:

WORSHIP

*True worshipers will worship the Father
in spirit and truth, for they are the kind
of worshipers the Father seeks.*
(JOHN 4:23 NIV)

Questions for reflection: Is worship
defined biblically in terms of whole-
life worship? Is the music ministry
God-focused, not man-focused, and
developed in a way so that all can fully
participate emotionally and spiritually?

T he year was 1636, and Black Death or bubonic plague was sweeping
Europe once again. Pastor Martin Rinker that year buried five thousand
parishioners, an average of fifteen a day. As he heard the cries of the bereaved
and dying outside his window, he wrote these words:

> Now thank we all our God with heart and hands and voices,
> Who wondrous things has done, in whom his world rejoices;
> Who, from our mother's arms, has blessed us on our way
> With countless gifts of love, and still is ours today.
>
> O may this bounteous God through all our life be near us,
> With ever joyful hearts and blessed peace to cheer us;
> And keep us in his grace and guide us when perplexed,
> And free us from all ills in this world and the next.
>
> All praise and thanks to God. . . .

Now that's worship. It's the kind of worshiper God seeks—one who
worships "in spirit." Focus is wholly on God, not on the "flesh" or visible
world which was for Rinker full of dread beyond comprehension. And it

was "in truth"—genuine, no fakery. As leaders in the congregation, it's our responsibility to see that God finds among us that kind of worshiper.

But what is worship, after all? After all the centuries of tradition and reinventing, after all the definitions and redefinitions, what is it we are supposed to help our people do? In Hebrew and Greek the word meant to prostrate oneself before someone or something—a god, for example, or an important person. In ancient days it often meant to kiss the feet of the person worshiped. It still does in some places. Far out in the desert of Tanzania I was waiting at a lonely telephone outpost when a young man approached. He bowed and began to kiss my feet. Embarrassed, I tried to prevent this "worship," but the missionary, culturally attuned, told me not to resist, that he was simply showing respect. When the Israelites used the term, gradually the kissing part disappeared because their God was invisible.

What do you think of when you see a picture of Muslims at prayer? Maybe they're on to something we may be missing. The chief word in the Old Testament for a right relationship to God is not love or faith, but fear— you prostrate yourself before deity in humble awe. We like to think of the "man upstairs," the lover, the friend. We seem to have lost the majesty, the grandeur, the holiness—the wholly otherness of our God. Most of us never prostrate ourselves before his majesty.

Since to prostrate oneself was a way of showing honor and the highest honor was reserved to their God, Jewish people gradually began to include, along with the idea of prostration, the inner spirit of it, the fealty, the adoration. So when the English translators looked for the right word to translate the Bible term of prostration, they came up with "worth-ship" because bowing down to express fealty is what you did before people of worth.

Gradually the term "worship" came to mean not only the praise and adoration of one's heart but all the outward evidences in religious symbols and rituals. A "worship service" we called it. One of those worship activities is music; so gradually, in twentieth-century America, "worship" came to mean praise and adoration in song. So we no longer speak of a song leader but of a worship leader, and we mean music.

But not just any kind of music. We invited Phil, a graduate who had returned to faith through the Jesus movement in California, to lead our "worship" in a conference on the campus of Columbia International University. After a day or two of contemporary praise songs, one of the faculty members approached me. "Would it be possible to sing just one grand old hymn of the church?" I passed this request on to our worship leader and he exploded. "I thought you wanted worship!" Thus, in the last quarter of the twentieth century, "worship" came to mean not just music but a certain kind of music. This newer definition of worship fits well the contemporary psyche since music, more universally than anything else, defines contemporary youth. At least Allan Bloom in his influential work *The Closing of the American Mind* says so.[1]

But what *is* true worship? To answer that question biblically is important because Jesus told the religious debater at the well that God is searching for a specific kind of worshiper (John 4:23). There are two qualities of true worship, he taught.

In Spirit

The loose woman, when she thought *water,* well, she thought *water.* And when she thought *worship,* she thought the same way—physical, outward, the location. Jesus said, "You've got it all wrong. The kind of worship God is after is of the spirit." It's not where, it's not how—either the traditional mode of the Jews or the revised mode of the Samaritans—but an interior, personal connection. What might that interior, personal connection look like?

The Old Paradigm

The Westminster divines, who understood the grandeur and sovereign rule of God, came up with the formula, "Man's chief end is to glorify God and to enjoy him forever." That fit with the theology of a sovereign imperial deity who is in full control of everything all the time.

When our son Kent was six years old, one evening he was doing his best to impress our guests. I called him aside and said, "Kent, it's not polite to show off." He acquiesced but must have spent the night thinking about it. The next morning he came to me with a profound question, "Daddy, why does God tell us to brag on him?" He had a point I didn't discover for years. Finally I decided to investigate. I found in the Bible more than four hundred appearances of "glory" and its cognates like "glorify." Most of those speak of the glory of God, though there are plenty of references to glorifying humans, in a positive sense, and even to the glory of important bad people. The astonishing thing is this: I could find only a handful of commands given by God to glorify him. It's true, many of his prophets exhort us to do so, and it is obvious that God expects us to glorify him and says so at least once (see Lev. 10:3). But if glorifying him is the main thing he has in mind, why didn't he say so? Still, he is obviously pleased with being glorified by us.

But why? Why does God want us to "brag on him"? What is God after? Is he on an ego trip, wholly self-serving in his purpose for humankind? I think not. Jesus, the full revealer of God in all his glory, didn't fixate on demanding

---

1. Allan Bloom, *The Closing of the American Mind* (New York: Simon and Schuster, 1987), 73–75.

praise as his chief objective. I think what God is after is for us to recognize and acknowledge truth. When we give him the glory due his name, we line up with reality. When we fail to recognize his glory, especially when we take some of his glory to ourselves, we break with reality. Any break with reality is destructive, but to break with the ultimate reality—our God in all his full splendor—is the ultimate destruction. He loves us too much to allow us to self-destruct with a too-low view of him or a too-high view of ourselves.

But the "glory" paradigm has been changing.

New Paradigm

With the narrowing of the concept of worship to mean mostly singing or listening to someone else sing, worship has come center stage as the primary way to glorify God. John Piper has worked hard at bringing the glorifying and the worship together in what he calls Christian hedonism. A person's chief end, he says, is to glorify God *by* enjoying him forever.

There's a problem, however, with both the old paradigm and the new. It's quite possible to glorify someone you despise, especially if the pay is right. Ask any press agent. And you could worship a god you feared or hated. Millions do.

So there's a third paradigm about what is ultimate in our relationship with God. And it's older than the other two. In fact, we don't have to speculate about what is ultimate because Moses told us. And Jesus affirmed it.

Jesus' Paradigm[2]

When a Bible scholar asked Jesus what was the most important thing, the ultimate, he replied, borrowing from Moses, "You shall love the Lord your God with all your heart, with all your soul, with all your mind, with all your strength. This is the Big One, the great commandment." Then he added, the whole teaching of our Scriptures hangs on this. Sounds like you might say, "A person's chief end is to love God and be loved of him forever." It's so beautiful—if you truly love a person you will glorify him or her, keep the spotlight ceaselessly on the true worth of the beloved. If you truly love a person and he is God, you will honor and glorify him so highly that you will worship him, you will bow down in humble adoration, you will sing to high heaven. So to glorify and worship God doesn't automatically lead to love. But to love God, to truly love him, will always bring praise and worship.

So to worship him "in spirit" is to love him with all your heart. To pursue a lifetime of loving intimacy with him. But it's not just a worship in spirit, a tight connection spirit-to-spirit. What God is looking for, said Jesus, is people who will worship him not only with that intimate, love-intoxicated inner connection, in spirit, but also "in truth." No fakery.

---

2. For a more complete exposition of this, see "Ultimate Purpose," an article of mine that can be found on the CIU Web site: www.ciu.edu.

In Truth

The old German stood to tell his story. During the Nazi regime, the railroad running through his small town began to transport Jews to the death camps. When the trains would pass through town and the Jews, peering through the cracks in the cattle cars, knew there were people who could hear, they began to cry for help. His little church was right by the railroad track, and a train would always pass through during the worship service. The members knew the schedule, the old man said, and they planned hymn singing for that time. Perhaps they could drown out the cries for help. When the cries could be heard above their singing, he said, they would sing louder. Then, voice cracking and tears streaming down his face, the old man said, "Sometimes in the night I can still hear those cries."

The proof of love is not in how loud you sing but in how well you obey. Sing your heart out to Jesus. Enjoy the rush of corporate celebration. But above all, to truthfully worship, obey. That's how we most truly spotlight his worth. That's how people see and understand our God's true value. He is seeking those who worship in truth. That's why the racism, the cowardice, the self-deception of that little congregation repel us. Ungodly choices give the lie as to who God truly is. That's why the religious arguments of the woman who had no trouble hooking up with men didn't make the grade with Jesus.

If you love me, Jesus said, you will—what? Feel that affection deeply? Say and sing it with fervor? But of course. Yet what he said was, "If you love me you will keep my commandments." That's to worship in truth. Our whole lives demonstrating his worth, extolling his virtue. "Godly" we call it—in some small way, a godlike life. That's to worship.

I have before me a church bulletin where I read, following the order of worship, "Our worship has ended, now our service begins." No, no! "Our corporate worship in words has ended and our worship in action—service—begins." That would be nearer the truth—true worship, that is. To worship in truth is to worship God with our lives as we put his glory on display. True worship is to love with intense passion and to express that love with words of adoration. Sing your heart out! But to love is to obey. That is true worship, the kind God seeks.

Worship flowing from love begins on the "inside," then "in spirit," and becomes visible and audible in obedience, praise, thanksgiving. So "worship in truth" is to have our lives so aligned with his that truth is demonstrated, but it also includes truth in our thinking. Truth can never be found apart from revelation, God making known to us what we cannot bring up from inside ourselves alone. Truth (revelation) flows from the outside into a trusting, loving heart. Thus both "spirit" and "truth" are needed. Some Christians study truth but do not allow it to penetrate the motives, values, and priorities of the heart. We can ignore feeding on truth, and worship then becomes a heart filled with empty words, and that projects a distorted image of God.[3]

Our charge, then, is to lead the people of our congregation into true worship, in both spirit and truth.

Consider the implications of this biblical definition of true worship as applied to the congregation gathered in worship: the content of corporate worship and the most controversial aspect of that worship, music.

Content of Corporate Worship

The older understanding was nearer the truth about worship: it should be all that takes place during the "worship service," not just the music. That view must govern our thinking and planning if we are to worship in spirit and in truth. For example, to give generously in the offering should be to worship God most authentically. And the sermon, above all elements of worship, should point people Godward, put his glories on display, enable people to live out their lives in the coming week as true worshipers. So every element of the time when God's people are gathered should be worship.

Having said that, however, the directly spoken worship of God—prayers and singing—is essential to true corporate worship. And it needs to be monitored carefully to see that it incorporates all biblical elements of verbal worship: thanksgiving, praise, and adoration. These certainly may blend, but if care is not taken to ensure that each element is fully expressed in corporate worship, we will come up short in pleasuring our God.

- Thanksgiving. Thank him specifically for what he has done for you.
- Praise. Praise him for who he is. Tell him what you like about him, each glorious characteristic.
- Adoration. Tell him how you feel about him. Love talk.

Here's a sample from my own experience. When on my annual retreat alone with the Lord, the following worship overflowed. It's not immortal prose, to be sure, but it gives some indication of what these essential elements of worship might mean.

> Thank you, Father, for your marvelous gifts: salvation and hope,
> the Savior's loving presence within and about, the blessed Spirit
> who transforms and empowers, your friendship, incredible as
> that is. Thank you, thank you, for the wonderful Book. And
> thank you for the gift of such a magnificent world: the flow-
> ers, the grass and trees, the lovely birds and wondrous beasts,

---

3. First Timothy 6:6–10 and Matthew 6:19–24 illustrate a negative example of a heart loving, serving, and desiring something other than God (money) that becomes the master, actually, the object of worship.

mountains and seas, streams and mighty rivers, rocks and sands and all things beautiful. And food—what a delightful way to survive and thrive! And what a glorious idea marriage was! And family. Friends so loyal and loving and bountiful. And human-kind, displaying your image-imprint, creating magnificent art and literature and music. I love fine architecture and astounding technologies. You've given me work to do that counts for eternity. The gifts of health and abilities and, especially, my wife. Thank you.

I praise you, Father, for what you have done, your mighty acts. You saved me and continue to save me and will save me, and a world of men and women besides. Creation that seems almost as infinite as you, the invincible church, made of impossible building material. Your incredibly complex and wondrously beautiful plan-ning and your meticulous execution of every intricate part; your sustaining power for all the worlds and for each sparrow. What a wonder you are! Hallelujah!

My adoration, Father, above all is for who you are. Every char-acteristic speaks your majestic godhood. But from among them all, in splendid array, I focus often on your wisdom, power, and love. Wisdom to know all things, power to do all you will, and love to count me in. What more could I ask? I could ask for holiness, for what kind of God would we have if he could figure everything out, accomplish anything and felt affectionately toward us, but were crooked, no model of right and dispenser of justice? And what if you were unpredictable and given to change? How inse-cure we would be! And what if you had a beginning or—worse—an end? That would be the ultimate insecurity. But no, you are all there is of perfection, beyond all imagination. And today I bow in humble gratitude.

Note that the thanksgiving, praise, and adoration interplay throughout. It isn't necessary to make each part of worship a discrete element, but only to be sure all elements are present when we lead the congregation in worship. We can't express our love for him too extravagantly, just as two young lovers find praise and adoration exploding beyond containment.

Music[4]

When the music wars exploded in our midst at Columbia International University in the early seventies, we did what any educational institution

---

4. Rather than attempt a detailed study of this critical issue, I refer you to the most thorough and balanced analysis I know: Steve Miller, *The Contemporary Music Debate* (Wheaton: Tyndale House, 1993). Miller examines the history, psychology, biblical evidence, and practical approaches to music in ministry.

would do—appointed a faculty study commission. Perhaps a church in conflict would benefit with the same approach! The assignment was to study Scripture for teaching, or at least clues that would help us resolve the conflict between traditional and contemporary. After thorough investigation the committee reported back. They could find nothing in Scripture that would help identify "right" and "wrong" kinds of music.

If a style of music is conditioned in a given culture to be associated with some bad thing—like drugs or promiscuous sex or idol worship—that style of music might be unwise to use for godly purposes. If the lyrics are not the sole determinant of the message, that is, if the music itself by association communicates an ungodly message, it should not be used. That principle, however, is tricky since it may be hard to prove a secondary message. And furthermore, as in the old bar room ballads that were "baptized" by Luther and others for church use, the style itself may be redeemed.

But the cultural factor is strategic.[5] The object is worship. If the participants are not aided in worship by a particular style of music, the purpose of worship is aborted before it begins. That is why so much of missionary hymnology is ineffective. In most lands evangelized from the West, the music is imported—both music and lyric—translations foreign to the culture. How much more worship-enabling if the music were indigenous. And remember, there are cultures within a larger culture, as in the United States. The music wars are a direct result of this, a generational cultural divide. Not to mention personal taste. The thing to remember in sorting through this divisive issue is the objective—to worship in spirit and in truth. If a segment of the congregation cannot do this well through the music provided, they will either miss out on true worship or leave. If many leave at once, the music has produced a church split. If a "blended" music approach does more than enable each culture to tolerate the other, the split may be avoided, but the basic question remains: does this music enable true worship? Culture isn't wrong. To ignore it is. That's because we're talking about the core of each person who would worship, and to ignore that core is a grave dereliction of pastoral duty.

Then there's the question of seeker-friendly music. To sort this out we must come back to the basic premise. If the purpose is worship, the music must be God-oriented, not human-oriented, especially not unregenerate-human oriented. If the worship music appeals to some people who don't know and love God, well enough. But they could hardly worship. Does this mean that music to attract the unbeliever is wrong in church? Not at all. It's just not worship. It might be entertainment, good, clean, spiritually oriented entertainment. With that I have no quibble. Can worship and entertainment be combined? Tricky. I wonder. But the objective of the music provided and

---

5. See the appendix, "Cross-Cultural Communication," for a more extended consideration of a biblical approach to crossing cultures.

the venue in which it is provided must always be controlling in choice of music.

One ameliorating factor: culture is rarely static. So new cultural forms gradually become accepted and then a broader spectrum of people can participate in spirit and in truth.

In considering the purposes of the church, we begin with worship, because worship is the Godward function of the church and thus of paramount importance. The responsibility of the leadership is to ensure that each member is enabled to worship in spirit and in truth, both in the "worship service" and in the "worship life." We move on now to the other purposes of the church, which, unlike worship, are better done on earth than in heaven.

CHAPTER 5:

MAKE DISCIPLES

Foundation:
Prophets & Apostles

Go, then, to all peoples everywhere
and make them my disciples. . . .
[T]each them to obey everything
I have commanded you.
(MATT. 28:19–20 TEV)

Question for reflection: Is the teaching
ministry of the church multifaceted,
including small group accountability,
and the results in spiritual
transformation and growth evident
in most members?

In Japan, they tell us, 80 percent of those baptized disappear within a decade. For over a century, Christian missionaries have obeyed Christ's commands to follow his example in going (John 20:21), to witness (Acts 1:8), and to preach (Mark 16:15; Luke 24:47–48), but it doesn't appear we have followed the mandate given on the mountain in Galilee (Matt. 28:19–20). We obeyed Christ and went to the people of Japan, witnessing, proclaiming, preaching, yes, evangelizing and starting churches, but apparently we didn't do a very good job of making them into disciples.

I take it this command was to make disciples in every nation rather than to make a disciple of each nation, since I can't figure out how we are to disciple a nation as such. Perhaps he intended to imply that the entire nation was to be moved Godward by the impact of many disciples? I can't say with confidence. But what Jesus meant by making an individual disciple is clear enough. And it was not, "Teaching them all that I commanded." No, it was, "Teaching them to observe, to obey, to practice everything I have commanded." That would be a disciple, a true follower of Jesus, would it not?

In our ministry in Japan the average attrition rates didn't hold. Why? Perhaps it was because we focused on teaching until observance emerged. So when I returned to visit the little congregations, now grown large, twenty-five years later, fifty years later, I found far more than 20 percent of those early disciples continuing on with spiritual vigor. How did it happen?

Of the many facets of discipleship and disciple-making which we will explore throughout this entire study—and particularly in this unit on the purposes of the church—we now focus on two. These two are of critical importance for fulfilling the congregation's responsibility to make disciples: teaching and accountability.

Teaching

In the congregation there are two levels of teaching, so in the typical growing American church this may mean that two services become necessary.

"Church" or "congregation" in Hebrew, Greek, and English refers to the gathering of people who belong together, to congregate. Often Jesus taught the gathered disciples, which became a large number indeed. But he also taught "the multitudes." That included the inquisitive, the inquirers, the seekers, the semi-followers. Following Christ's example, then, the leader needs to speak to the entire gathering the words of truth. But if his Sunday morning messages, for example, are evangelistic, seeker-oriented, or inspirational rather than expositional (teaching the Word), the preacher should follow Christ's example and proactively plan another venue to instruct the entire congregation of "belongers." That's what seeker-friendly Willow Creek Church, for example, does mid-week.

In our church start-ups in Japan I began with the new group of seekers and finders with topical messages on key doctrines. But as soon as we were growing and reaching a discipleship level with significant numbers of congregants, I began to preach through John, written specifically that "believers" might truly believe. In other words, to establish faith. Following this, in each church plant I would preach through Romans to establish a solid doctrinal foundation. Then I would leave and start over again.

Preaching the word is not only central in Protestantism, it was a central facet of Christ's ministry and Paul's. So it must be in our own.

Small Is Essential

Jesus not only taught the thousands (as in the feeding of the 5,000), the hundreds (I assume the "disciples" to which he addressed the Sermon on the Mount may have been the first fruits of the "more than 500" to whom he appeared after his resurrection), and the "seventy" he sent on mission. He also planned time to be with the Twelve and the three, Peter, James, and John. Something happens in disciple making in small group encounters that can never happen in the congregation gathered. Small is essential not only for disciple making, but the small group is essential for fulfilling each of the purposes of the church, though we will not be able to explore all the implications for all the purposes of the church.

If "small is beautiful," what of the large church? The megachurches, though high profile and the dream of many American pastors, even in aggregate actually account for a small fraction of disciples in America. But there is excitement in the "full-service" ministry of the megachurch, providing many services that the typical congregation cannot. And if the church became "mega" through evangelistic rather than transfer growth, like the famed million-member Yung Nak Church of Seoul, Korea, the very size and excitement can be a powerful "draw" for evangelism. There are other benefits as well. But one of them is not disciple making. That requires "small."

Of course small in and of itself doesn't produce disciples, but it's in the context of small group learning, caring, and accountability that disciples grow best. Even Bill Hybels, who epitomizes the megachurch phenomenon, says, "Most lasting changes in our life occur within three feet of another person."[1] McLean Bible Church, a megachurch with more than ten thousand members in the suburbs of Washington, D.C., understands this:

> At McLean Bible Church, we try to create this kind of caring
> community in a variety of ways. But the primary way we seek to
> achieve it is by helping every person to get connected to a small
> group. We have thousands of people in a wide variety of groups.
> But we believe that our job is undone until we get every person
> who calls McLean Bible Church their home church into a small
> group where they can be loved, cared for and supported—and
> where they can do the same for others (McLean Bible Church,
> Core Values, p. 13).

That's a church serious about discipleship. But the vast majority of congregations in the world don't need to structure small groups; they are a small group. For them the challenge is to transform that great asset into a disciple-making relationship! Also, it seems that the way to actually fulfill Christ's command is to intentionally multiply small congregations. Consider what is happening around the world in the burgeoning church multiplying movements.

> The churches in Church Planting Movements begin as small
> fellowships of believers meeting in natural settings such as homes
> or their equivalent. . . .

---

1. The pastor of one of the first megachurches, Stuart Briscoe, tells the story of how Elmbrook Church gradually developed from traditional into vital use of the small group in an article first published in *Moody Magazine* (June 1978). He provides a fascinating account of the stages of transition which could well serve as a model for small or mid-size churches struggling with transition from traditional approaches.

Meeting in small groups certainly has economic implications. Liberating the fledgling movement from the burden of financing a building and professional clergy is no small obstacle to overcome. But there is more. . . . Consider the following benefits.

1. Leadership responsibilities remain small and manageable.

2. If heresies do occur they are confined by the small size of the house church. . . .

3. You can't hide in a small group, so accountability is amplified.

4. Member care is easier, because everyone knows everyone.

5. Because house church structure is simple, it is easier to reproduce.

6. Small groups tend to be much more efficient at evangelism and assimilation of new believers.

7. Meeting in homes positions the church closer to the lost.

8. House churches blend into the community, rendering them less visible to persecutors.

9. Basing in the home keeps the church's attention on daily life issues.

10. The very nature of rapidly multiplying house churches promotes the rapid development of new church leaders.[2]

Although these movements may be the most exciting development in the evangelization of the world today, the paradigm may not be established easily in traditional church contexts. But the benefits of the small group in any church context could hardly be more powerfully articulated.

Not only is discipleship best done "small," but the New Testament model would indicate it is normally best done in gender-specific groups, men-to-men and the same by implication for women. There are exceptions, of course. For example, there can be value in a mixed gender setting for couples just starting a Christian life; the support of the spouse can be very important. But in many cultures men hide their true feelings in mixed gender settings. They don't want to appear weak to the women. And women may tend to focus on topics they feel safe discussing. Furthermore, many topics essential for discipleship, such as dealing with sexual temptation, should occur only in same-sex interaction. I believe there is a strong need for single gender small groups, since that allows a transparency and depth seldom found in mixed gender settings.

Both teaching the congregation gathered and small group intensive discipleship were modeled by Jesus in his earthly ministry. But there is a further method of making disciples that neither he nor Paul are depicted as

---

2. David Garrison, *Church Planting Movements: How God Is Redeeming a Lost World* (Midlothian, Va.: WIGTake Resources, 2004), 191–93.

using—one-on-one. Just because they didn't seem to have used this method of disciple making doesn't mean it is not a worthy approach, only that it might not be essential. Yet in today's church context it does seem to be of great benefit.

Personal Is "In"

A personal mentor is often considered the fast track to spiritual growth. In recent decades, borrowing from the Roman tradition, one type of mentor has been increasingly called a "spiritual director," considered essential to "spiritual formation." Though the more recent articulation of that role has become quite specific, the more commonly used paradigm since the mid-twentieth century is the "counselor." If the professional counselor actually aims at spiritual development, then he or she would be participating in disciple making. Whatever the approach, clearly the concept of having someone gifted and called to the role of personally instructing believers and holding them accountable could indeed be a major source of spiritual development, of becoming ever more like Jesus, of having the lost image restored, of living out life in the presence and power of the Spirit. In short, of becoming a true disciple of Jesus Christ.

It is said that relationships occur at five levels: beginning with talking about inconsequential matters; moving to offering an opinion; then expressing a belief; listening to others share their dreams, fears, and emotions; and finally, sharing these things with others. Women seem to find it easier to share personal matters with others, but even for them a personal relationship that results in spiritual growth may need time to develop. That time may be shortened, however, when mentoring is intentional on the part of both mentor and disciple.

How does a typical mentoring relationship work? A minister asked me to mentor him and gave me a list of questions he wanted me to ask him on a weekly basis. Never having done this before, I was startled. "You want me to ask you these questions?" I asked. "Yes," he replied, "I need you to hold me accountable." His list of questions went something like this:

1. Did you have a daily quiet time every day? How long was it? What was the quality of the encounter with God?

2. How has your relationship with your wife worked out this past week? Any differences between you? How did you handle them?

3. What portions of food did you eat? Did you snack between meals? Did you make progress toward your targeted weight loss?

4. How did your relationship with your son go?

5. Did you watch TV? How much? What programs?

6. How did you feel about and relate to the pretty young secretary in your office?

Each week we would concentrate on one of his areas of concern, evaluating progress, planning a strategy for gaining ground against the Tempter. It was amazing to see the growth—until we reached what for him proved to be the Big One. So we developed a new strategy, tweaking the old, failed strategy. The following week it was the same—no progress. After several weeks I said, "Well, why don't we take a rest until you make up your mind whether you're going to actually implement what we agreed on?" He never came back. But what growth in discipleship while we tracked!

That's an example of a common approach to mentoring, but historically the one-on-one relationship has been much more informal, usually consisting of a regular Bible study together. However it's done, a personal relationship can prove very helpful in becoming a true disciple, obeying all that Jesus commanded.

Accountability

To really grow spiritually it takes more than a teacher teaching and a hearer listening. Ideally, for mind renovation and behavioral change to take place, accountability to another person or persons is essential. The small group and personal mentoring (above) are sub-authentic if they end in teaching/learning, let alone if they end in no more than warm fellowship and encouragement. Accountability within the group or in the mentoring relationship should be a part of the relationship if true growth and discipleship are to take place.

There is an important part of discipleship that must be present in a congregation whether or not personal accountability structures are provided. We call it church discipline. The church must faithfully deal with sin among its members if spiritual growth is to take place. How this is to be accomplished is so important that we will devote an entire chapter to it, but for now we must note that any serious attempt to "make disciples" must include holding all members accountable. When a member falls into moral dereliction (as in the church of Corinth), it not only means the sinning person becomes less than a true disciple of Christ, but his failure, unchecked by the body, affects all other members. This is a major theme of Paul in both letters to the church at Corinth. Again it is obvious that a person who teaches heresy is not a true disciple. But it must be emphasized that his teaching also holds back the rest of the body from advancing in discipleship, in right thinking and right behavior.

Responsible relationships in the congregation, however, go far beyond those two "disciplinable" behaviors—unrepented moral dereliction and teaching heresy. We must hold one another to the highest standards of Christian behavior, not just in those major matters that demand church discipline. For true growth in discipleship *all* that Jesus taught is included (Matt. 28:18). And for that we really do need one another.

It won't do merely to proclaim the truths of holiness from the pulpit. In some structured relationship, small group or one-on-one, all of us, including leaders, need to have accountability partners. That's what "small groups," "mentoring," and "pastoring" are all about!

In church discipline, when we are to take action and how it is to be done have everything to do with success in the making of disciples. We will return to this theme in chapter 20.

CHAPTER 6:

MEMBER CARE

A new command I give you:
Love one another.
As I have loved you,
so you must love one another.
By this all men will know
that you are my disciples,
if you love one another.
(JOHN 13:34–35 NIV)

Question for reflection:
Does member care reach
beyond spiritual pastoring to
full-service emotional, physical,
and material responsibility
for all members?

My seatmate on the flight into Atlanta turned out to be a high-ranking Air Force officer who had just returned from his third tour of duty in Viet Nam. He had flown more than three hundred sorties over North Viet Nam and had returned unscathed. The average hit on American planes was one every twelve sorties! I asked if it were scary when the ground-to-air guided missile came after him. "No," he replied, "those big ones are easy to evade. They're the size of a telephone pole. When they come up you just dive and they miss you."

"What about air-to-air missiles from behind—where you can't see them?" I asked.

"Oh, that's why we always fly in pairs. Your buddy alerts you. If he fails, you're dead meat."

So, I concluded, he wasn't the ace I thought—he just had a good buddy. That's why he came home safe every time. And so it is with church. The big ones you may be able to dodge on your own. But those that slip up from behind—you need a faithful buddy for those. And that's the theme of this chapter.

Family solidarity is the least experienced of the five God-designed purposes for his church, at least in American congregations. Of the six or seven congregations I have belonged to in all parts of America, not one had a program to monitor, let alone proactively care, for members' spiritual, emotional, physical, and material welfare. And that's sad because what's a family for? And family was God's design—the blood ties of Calvary binding us closer than human blood ties (see John 13:34–35; 15:12–13; Rom. 14:17–19; 1 Cor. 1:10; 13:4–8; Gal. 5:13–15; 5:25–6:10; Eph. 4:1–3; Phil. 2:1–4; Col. 3:12–15).

One exciting way to get an overview of what Jesus had in mind is to review the "reciprocal commands" of the New Testament. Bobby Clinton summarizes the work of Sue Harville.

Reciprocal Living: The One-Another Commands[1]

Reciprocal living refers to the mutual obligations and relationships which believers have as a result of their common relationship to Christ as members of his body. It may be defined as the outward manifestation of fellowship in which each believer puts all that he or she is and all that he or she has at the disposal of all other believers and that others do the same for him or her in order to enable one another in Christian living.

HARVILLE'S FOUR CATEGORIES OF RECIPROCAL COMMANDS
TABLE 1: SUMMARY

Commands	Number in New Testament
Inter-Relationships	9
Negative	7
Mutual Edification	5
Mutual Service	5

---

1. Sue Harville, *Reciprocal Living* (Coral Gables, Fla.: West Indies Mission, 1976). This is now out of print as is her small groups manual, *Walking in Love*, which was used as a simplified thirteen-part study of the reciprocal commands. I have copied directly Harville's definitions of each of the reciprocal commands.

COMMANDS BEARING UPON INTER-RELATIONSHIPS

Command	Biblical Reference	Explanation, Description, or Definition
Love one another	John 13:34	Love is an inward attitude of affection, expressed in benevolent behavior or action, which seeks the ultimate welfare of another. Loving one another is allowing this inward attitude to control our behavioral relationships with other Christians so that we indeed seek their ultimate welfare. (Also the basic idea occurs indirectly in John 15:12, 17; Rom. 12:9–10; 13:8; Gal. 5:14; 1 Thess. 3:11–12; 4:9–10; James 2:8; 1 Pet. 1:22; 3:8; 1 John 3:11, 23; 4:7, 11–12, 21; 2 John 5.)
Receive one another	Rom. 15:7	Receiving one another is taking to ourselves our brothers or sisters in Christ, freely and without constraint and reserve, in full recognition of our equal and mutual fellowship in Christ.
Greet one another	Rom. 16:16	Greeting one another is an outward acknowledgment of our mutual life in Christ and our brotherly love for one another (1 Cor. 16:20; 2 Cor. 13:12; 1 Pet. 5:14).
Have the same care for one another	1 Cor. 12:24–25	Having the same care for one another is showing an impartial care for another, equal interest in the welfare and ministry of every believer based on the full recognition and appreciation of that one's God-given position and function in the body of Christ.
Submit to one another	Eph. 5:18–21	Submitting to one another is inwardly considering oneself to be under the authority of fellow Christians and willingly complying with their decisions, instructions, or wishes.
Tarry one for another	1 Cor. 11:33	Tarry one for another refers to waiting patiently for people in order to partake together of a love feast (often associated with the Lord's Supper).
Forbear one another	Eph. 4:1–3	Forbearing one another is graciously enduring and putting up with the displeasing, offensive, or sinful attitudes and actions in others. It includes the idea that rebuke, discipline, or correction be delayed as long as possible in hope that the offender recognizes his or her offense and takes steps to correct it (Col. 3:12–14).
Confess your sins to one another	James 5:16	Confessing sins to one another is acknowledging to fellow believers one's sins as an outward sign of sorrow for the offense, intent to change, and desire for reconciliation. It presupposes a previous or simultaneous acknowledgment of the particular sin to God.
Forgive one another	Eph. 4:31–32	Forgiving one another is regarding a fellow believer who has wronged or offended you, not with contempt or resentment but rather with compassion, not holding that person accountable for the wrong or its consequences.

The Negative Commands

Just as the Scripture tells Christians how to relate to one another, it points out and forbids several sins that are destructive to Christian fellowship.

Command	Biblical Reference	Explanation, Description, or Definition
Do not judge one another	Rom. 14:13	Judging one another is reckoning one's own position on a disputed practice or doctrinal question as superior to others' positions and expressing criticism, condemnation, or displeasure at their disagreement.
Do not speak evil of one another	James 4:11	Speaking evil of one another is speaking of a fellow believer in such a way as to discredit, dishonor, depreciate, or belittle his or her character or actions.
Do not murmur against one another	James 5:9	Murmuring against one another is expressing discontent, impatience, or displeasure with one believer to other believers, usually in a secret or in a covert manner.
Do not bite and devour one another	Gal. 5:14–15	Biting and devouring one another is showing hostility and ill will to fellow believers through attacks on their character, worth, motives, beliefs, or actions in order to establish one's own advantage or superiority.
Do not provoke one another	Gal. 5:25–26	Provoking one another is challenging the work, reputation, position, or belief of a fellow believer by words or actions in an effort to assert oneself or gain recognition.
Do not envy one another	Gal. 5:25–26	Envying one another is desiring for oneself the position, ability, achievement, or possessions of a fellow believer, usually with a sense of resentment that the other has the advantages one desires.
Do not lie to one another	Col. 3:9–10	Lying to one another is telling as true that which is known to be false, distorting the truth in any way, or conveying a false impression of oneself or something, with the intent to deceive another believer.

Commands Bearing upon Mutual Edification

When something is edified, it is built up, strengthened, or fortified. The New Testament uses this term of building up and strengthening of believers in their faith so that they live lives that are pleasing to God in every way. One of the ways that God has chosen to edify his people is through the ministry of believers themselves. Christians are to edify one another. Mutual relationships of love form the basis for this ministry of edification. In fact, Paul tells us that love edifies (1 Cor. 8:1). But the Christian life is more than relationships. It is obedience to all of God's will which he has revealed in his Word. This mutual edification begins, but does not stop, with love. To edify one another in the biblical sense of the term, believers must also help one another to learn and apply the Word of God in their daily lives. And this task is not meant only for pastors and teachers. All Christians are to be involved. These mutual edification commands tell Christians how they can help one another, out of love for one another, learn and apply the Word of God in daily living.

Command	Biblical Reference	Explanation, Description, or Definition
Build up one another	Rom. 14:19; 1 Thess. 5:11	Building up one another is a process of interaction among believers by which they promote, by teaching or example, the development of Christlike character and behavior in one another.
Teach one another	Col. 3:16	Teaching one another is instructing, explaining, or exposing biblical truth to fellow believers in such a way that they may understand the truth and are enabled and encouraged to apply it in their own lives.
Exhort one another	1 Thess. 5:11; Heb. 3:12–13	Exhorting one another is a threefold ministry in which believers urge each other to action in terms of applying scriptural truth, encourage each other generally with scriptural truth, and comfort each other through the application of scriptural truth to their needs. The main thrust of the command is that believers should strive to help each other understand the implications of the Word of God for daily living.
Admonish one another	Rom. 15:14; Col. 3:16	Admonishing one another is a disciplinary ministry in which believers bring to each other's attention their sinful attitudes and practices or unmet obligations, and offer corrective instruction that will enable and encourage them to bring those areas of their lives into conformity with the Word of God.
Speak to one another in psalms, hymns, and spiritual songs	Eph. 5:18–20; Col. 3:16	Speaking to one another in psalms, hymns, and spiritual songs, or in singing to one another, is a means of teaching, exhorting, or admonishing others, and joining others in praise to God, in words set to music.

Commands Bearing upon Mutual Service

The thought of being a servant is not appealing to most people. Serving is a hard and sometimes thankless job. And servants must continually put the needs and interests of others before their own. But this is just what Christians are supposed to do: be servants to one another, not grudgingly, but out of love for one another. Because Christ loved us he made himself a servant to us throughout his life and finally in his atoning death on the cross. Because we love him and his people, we are to make ourselves servants—to him but also to one another.

Just as Christians who truly love one another will seek to edify one another, they will also seek to serve one another. These mutual service commands deal with ways that Christians can express their love to one another in practical and down-to-earth service.

Command	Biblical Reference	Explanation, Description, or Definition
Be servants to one another	Gal. 5:13–14	Being servants to one another through love is freely and voluntarily obligating oneself to undertake for fellow believers any work or task which may be necessary, helpful, or advantageous to their spiritual, physical, or mental welfare.
Bear one another's burdens	Gal. 6:2	Bearing one another's burden is taking upon oneself a fellow believer's difficulty, problem, or oppressive circumstance as it if were our own and taking any possible action to alleviate it.
Use hospitality to one another	1 Pet. 4:9	Using hospitality to one another is receiving into one's home fellow Christians, especially strangers and those in distress, and providing for their physical and material needs as for one's own.
Be kind to one another	Eph. 4:31–32	Being kind to one another is expressing love and benevolence to fellow Christians in gestures of generosity, helpfulness, and thoughtfulness, without regard to circumstances and expecting nothing in return.
Pray for one another	James 5:16	Praying for one another is making known to God the sins, needs, or concerns of fellow believers, asking him to act on their behalf so that his will might be accomplished.

The reciprocal commands form a biblical foundation for the whole life responsibility of the congregation for each of its members: spiritual, emotional, physical, and material/financial.

Whole Life Responsibility

Spiritual

The primary responsibility of the church body is to provide the context for each member to grow toward greater likeness to Christ and closer oneness with him. As Paul declared, "We are all one body, we have the same Spirit, and we have all been called to the same glorious future. . . . He is the one who gave these gifts to the church: the apostles, the prophets, the evangelists, and the pastors and teachers. Their responsibility is to equip God's people to do his work and build up the church, the body of Christ, until we come to such unity in our faith and knowledge of God's Son that we will be mature and full grown in the Lord, measuring up to the full stature of Christ. . . . Under his direction, the whole body is fitted together perfectly. As each part does its own special work, it helps the other parts grow, so that the whole body is healthy and growing and full of love" (Eph. 4:4, 11–13, 16 NLT).

So spiritual care is paramount, and that is what we have been emphasizing. But it isn't all. The two purposes of the church focused inward, on its own members (discipleship and member care), cannot be divorced. Each must be fully integrated with the other. We separate them in this study because "making disciples" is often the focus of the church and the member care element in the making of a disciple is neglected. Thus member care needs special attention.

But there's another reason to focus separately on member care. Spiritual welfare, though the most important (that's why we devoted an entire chapter to "making disciples"), is only one aspect of a person's life. And the congregation as family is responsible to care for the other aspects as well: emotional, physical, and material.

Emotional

I'm not sure how the emotional relates to the spiritual in the human psyche, but in our "therapeutic society" we seem to have emotional needs that go beyond normal spiritual care.

At the least, a congregation cannot concentrate on teaching biblical truth and monitoring godly behavior while neglecting how a person feels. The congregation needs to provide a safe haven where all people—the timid, the wounded, and the fearful—feel at ease. Church must be a fellowship that welcomes beyond warm greetings and "fellowship potlucks." It must be a place where everyone belongs (1 Pet. 5:2–5).

Studies consistently show that love expressed is more effective than professional therapy in the healing process. Perhaps that's why, in our church-starting efforts in Japan, those who were emotionally or relationally dysfunctional came to our fledgling church family in disproportionately large numbers. They found a nesting place, a haven of refuge, a loving family.

But more is needed than a loving, caring community. Many people need special help, and every congregation should have one or more people with a pastoring, shepherding gift (Jude 17–23). If the church is large, the senior pastor cannot possibly meet all the needs of his flock. Undershepherds must be discovered and developed. Also, if the leader is not gifted, supplemental help is needed in people who are gifted and trained to shepherd. In a large church, of course, this may be a professional. But in all churches people with a heart for pastoring or shepherding can be trained "in house" using mentoring, books, and seminars funded by the church. But no matter how gifted a pulpiteer, no matter how small the church, if the public leader is not gifted in pastoral counseling, he must swallow his pride and provide for this basic need through others.

The third level of emotional care is for those who require professional attention. If the church is able to provide this service in-house at no charge, that is ideal. But when this is not possible, the best possible Christian professionals should be identified for referral.[2]

Physical

Healing was even more prominent in Jesus' ministry than teaching. So if a member or members have the gift of healing, that's the place to begin. But it's not the place to end, since the more normal method of physical care is through medical assistance. The only caution for the typical American church, at least, is to stop the common practice of shunting off their poor to governmental provision through Medicaid. The church should be responsible to care for the members who cannot care for themselves. This care is often needed when the illness is long-term and financially draining. Sending the occasional hot meal is good, but not sufficient. The church is responsible.

I'm not sure of any biblical teaching or principle that mandates the programs of many contemporary churches to provide for physical fitness for the able-bodied, but by the same token I know of no principle that would forbid it. Bodily exercise does profit a little, the apostle John teaches (3 John 2).

Material/Financial

The ordinary way of financial provision is for each member to provide for himself or herself and for their dependents. "Nor did we eat anyone's bread free of charge, but worked with labor and toil night and day, that we might not be a burden to any of you. . . . we commanded you this: If anyone will not work, neither shall he eat. . . . work in quietness and eat (your) own bread" (2 Thess. 3:8–12 NKJV). "If anyone does not provide for his own, and

---

2. For cautions and guidance on how such should be chosen, see unit 1, chapter 2.

especially for those of his household, he has denied the faith and is worse than an unbeliever" (1 Tim. 5:8 NKJV).

That's the normal way of provision. But there are special circumstances. Unemployment, illness, or other crises call for intervention on the part of the congregation. It may be a famine in Jerusalem, so Paul was often gathering financial aid from churches near and far. It may be indigent widows who were enrolled in the official church program for their care (1 Tim. 5:1–16). A safety net is provided as part of the church's responsibility for its members (1 John 3:16–18). So the church may not simply refer its own to a government agency to do the church's job of member care.

In 2 Corinthians 8–9, Paul outlined principles for giving. As we stand back and look at this section, the following truths become apparent:

1. God is sovereign over what he allows to touch his people.
2. He is in control of the resources that he provides for those he invites to give at a particular point of need.
3. But he is also sovereign over the person in need. Part of his plan for the person with a need is for her or him to humbly receive.
4. In addition God also raises up leaders who have the ministry of asking.

So, in the flow of God's grace-filled provision in the body of Christ, he provides the giver (and the gifts), the receiver, and the "asker." For us to mature, God may give the congregation opportunity to practice all three ministries. Many congregational leaders find it easier to be the "giver" or the "asker," but they are not as adept at letting others give to them. Yet admitting need and receiving help can be the very classroom where God equips the leader with deep understanding of what people in need really feel and the level of humility it often requires to graciously receive.

Furthermore, it won't do simply to leave the financial needs to the haphazard provision of benevolent members of the congregation. A structured program such as the "roll" for widows in the early church should be provided. Crisis intervention, job placement, retraining for employment—whatever the need—if family should provide, so with God's family.

Most churches would be put to shame by the Jewish community of Venezuela or the Sikh community of north India. They guarantee the livelihood of all members. For example, when indigent Jewish immigrants arrive in Venezuela from Europe, the local brotherhood sets them up in a small business. If they can't make a go of it, they provide employment opportunities. Why cannot the church of Jesus Christ do as much?

A major purpose of the church is member care—spiritual, yes, but also emotional, physical, and material. This is the way of love. If we love as commanded in the reciprocal commands, it will work out in these pragmatic applications to church life. It is by such demonstrated love that people will recognize this group is different, indeed that it's a Jesus-fellowship (John 13:34–35). Such caring is more intense and comprehensive than care for the community at large, but when actually practiced within the congregation it will spill over into the community, and that is the next purpose of the church to which we now turn.

CHAPTER 7:

PURSUE WELFARE
OF THE COMMUNITY

You are like salt for all mankind.
But if salt loses its saltiness,
there is no way to make it salty again.
It has become worthless,
so it is thrown out
and people trample on it.
(MATT. 5:13 TEV)

Let us work for the good of all.
(GAL. 6:10 NEB)

Question for reflection: **Does the congregation have ministries
to promote the welfare of the community at home and abroad?**

The church by its nature as the body of Christ is the visible embodiment of his presence on planet earth. The local congregation needs to fulfill the purpose of being salt and light in the world (Matt. 5:13–16). Jesus spelled out his interpretation of "light"—that people may see your good works and glorify God. There could be an evangelistic purpose in that. But what is salt? Did he have in mind flavor for an insipid society that insistently stays flat in godless living? Or did he have in mind the preservative influence of believers in a decaying society? At least the concept of influence, of permeating one's environment with good, must be present.

The church is designed to be God's visible evidence of his design and desire for each person. The world is to see in the church God's own love and holiness. The people of God and the Spirit of God are in partnership to give the world truth (accurate definitions of sin, love, and righteousness) so that people can know of the freedom and life that is the opposite of Satan's kingdom (John 8:34–37; 10:10; 16:7–11).

In that responsibility, two things come to mind: ministering mercy and seeking justice. The religious leaders of Christ's day were strong on justice but weak on mercy. Jesus emphasized a major theme in the Good News of the kingdom of heaven. He desired mercy to govern our relationships (Matt. 9:9–13, 12:1–8). This difference in their understanding of God's priorities separated most of the religious leaders from Jesus. But God's plan is for his people to pursue both justice and mercy for the welfare of its community. Note, however, in our diagram of the purposes of the church, this outward-directed purpose is shorter than the evangelistic purpose. This is not by accident. The intention is to represent the emphasis found in the New Testament.

It is true that the record of Jesus' ministry gives more space to reporting his healing ministry than his teaching ministry. His acts of mercy were intended as "signs" validating who he was, but, unlike Moses' miracles, they were not merely signs pointing to God's power; they were very focused—healing a broken humanity. Yet his final instructions for what he wanted his disciples to do in "building his church" make slight mention of this purpose, and, in fact, the record of apostolic activity in the New Testament (especially Acts) emphasizes the purpose to win people to faith, disciple them, and build his church. To be sure, there was healing ministry, but it wasn't featured as the chief purpose of the church in the outside world.

Yet the balance between these purposes—evangelistic and healing, helping—is a perennial source of conflict, especially among missiologists.[1] The so-called "incarnational" approach cites Jesus' words in Nazareth (Luke 4:18–19) where he quoted from Isaiah 61:1–2:

> The Spirit of the LORD is upon Me,
> Because He has anointed Me to preach the gospel to the poor;
> He has sent Me to heal the brokenhearted,
> To proclaim liberty to the captives
> And recovery of sight to the blind,
> To set at liberty those who are oppressed,
> To preach the acceptable year of the LORD (NKJV).

This statement of Jesus' calling is taken as the model for the church today so that healing and seeking justice in society are on a par with "preaching the gospel." Indeed, since the prophet Isaiah specified the audience, "to the poor," even that hint of evangelistic activity actually tends toward the mercy/justice end of the spectrum.[2] In spite of this, we stand by the Great

---

1. See the appendix.
2. The battle between those who give priority to evangelism and those who give equal billing or priority to social action has continued without let-up throughout the twentieth century. Yet at the end of the century, in the year 2000, Engel and Dyrness proposed this as a "new paradigm" and named it "Incarnational Mission." (James E. Engel and William A. Dyrness, *Where Have We Gone Wrong?* [Downers Grove: InterVarsity, 2000]).

Commission as the mandate for the church and see the apostles in agreement with that understanding, acting out what Jesus intended—the evangelization of the world, making disciples, building his church. Nevertheless it's much easier to go to a consistent extreme than to stay at the center of biblical tension. Most of the evangelical church tends toward neglect of the social dimension of church responsibility.

So when congregations neglect reaching out in an organized way to the community, dispensing mercy and seeking justice, they seem to have biblical precedent of a sort. It would seem the biblical way is to emphasize evangelism and then, through transformed lives, transform the community. "Redemption and lift," Donald McGavran called the common phenomenon of societal reformation when large numbers become Christian.

But the purpose of promoting community welfare should not be amputated. And throughout history the church has indeed fulfilled this purpose, taking the lead in providing health care and education, for example. In the Western world for many centuries, the only hospitals and schools were Christian. The same was true in pioneer missionary penetration of non-Western societies. In fact, often the church became so involved in seeking the earthly welfare of the community that the evangelistic mission was eclipsed. Nevertheless, the church, if true to the example of its Master, will reach out in mercy to the surrounding community. The church presents the loving heart of Christ who came to seek and save by being a loving presence in the community. We are called to do this as a church, not merely through those members who do so privately from personal compassion.

Seeking justice through political activism as a church is another matter.[3] The fact that neither Jesus nor the apostles pursued justice through political action may not be construed as a prohibition of such activity. The argument from silence is notoriously weak. Simply because a matter is not mandated in Scripture does not mean we may not do it. Much less does the fact that some activity is not reported in Scripture have normative implications—that is, that since neither Jesus nor the apostles did something can hardly mean that we may not. If biblical silences were mandates, many good things could not be done. For example, church buildings, children's ministry, theological education, and many other things would be ruled out. On the other hand, since they are not forbidden in Scripture, polygamy, slavery, pornography, abortion, and a host of other things would be acceptable. Our conscience must be governed by the principles of Scripture, not historical precedent or scriptural silence.

One possible reason for the early church's lack of involvement in the political process might have been the impossibility of it. They could hardly

---

3. For a thorough examination of the relationship of the church and society, see my *An Introduction to Biblical Ethics* (Wheaton: Tyndale House, 1995), 447–506.

have done anything "political," since they lived under the rule of totalitarian Rome. Of course, they could have launched a revolution as many attempted. But Christ expressly forbade taking up the sword in his name (Matt. 26:52–53). His kingdom is not of this world (John 18:36). If the Crusaders had obeyed Jesus' teaching, perhaps the holocaust of the twenty-first century would not be upon us!

And yet, what a poorer world this would be if Christians had not become involved in the rough-and-tumble of politics to rid the world of slavery and other social evils. My judgment in the matter is, however, that seeking justice through the political process is better done by Christians as citizens when they live in a society where this activity is possible, rather than by the church. To enter the political arena as a church is hazardous because the chief purposes of the church can be eclipsed. Besides, neither Christ nor the apostles gave such a mandate nor did they state principles that would demand it. Thus, one way the congregations Christ is currently building differ from the nation God built in the Old Testament is that the people of God bound together in Christ's name can be "planted" in any political, economic, or social context.

To say that there is not a mandate for the church to always, in every context, take political action in seeking justice does not mean, however, that the church should not speak out on moral issues that have become embedded in the political process. For example, the social reformers in England brought about the end of slavery in that nation through direct political action. The social activists of America today rightly campaign to change the laws concerning abortion. The prophetic voice is not merely permitted, it is demanded. And racism. In a graduate class in ethics I would ask the entering students to list the most significant problems in society in order of priority. Consistently, black students put "racism" at the top of the list and white students left it off altogether. Strange for Christian people. But lest black folks feel smug about this blindness, they need to consider how racism is endemic in black thinking as well. It's just that the white racism has power to impose injustice and the black community does not. Surely the church should be active in healing racial divides and fighting injustice.

But more than seeking justice, the church follows Christ's example when it seeks to "do good to all." Ministries of mercy have been largely left to merciful governments—and thank God for merciful governments—but still, to be true to its character and to its Lord, the church itself must reach out to the poor, the grieving, the ill of mind and body, the disadvantaged in education, those trapped in addictions. Perhaps Rick Warren with his P.E.A.C.E initiatives launched in 2005 will bring renewal to the church in ministries of mercy.

Some dysfunctions in society require both political and mercy solutions. For example, the church that is active in anti-abortion politicking should surely minister to those with unwanted pregnancies and single mothers. Should not those who seek legal protection from the advances of homosexual activists or drug availability also reach out to provide hope for those who are trapped in damaging lifestyles?

Injustice in our society is pervasive, the needs almost without limit. No local congregation can heal all the hurts. But to shrug off all responsibility is surely not the way of Christ. Wise selection of what societal ills a church should address might be the starting point for the congregation that has done nothing for those outside the walls of the church. But start we must if we are to follow our Lord's example and commands.

To sum up this unit, the purposes of the local congregation fall under five headings: (1) worship, (2) making disciples, (3) member care, (4) evangelism, and (5) pursuing the welfare of the community.

Conclusion to Unit 2

These purposes will permeate the study of each of the subsequent biblical principles, just as the first principle of making biblical authority functional permeates the whole. Certain purposes of the church, however, will be considered in greater depth in later units. For example, the evangelistic purpose will be a major focus of unit 4 and the unity of the church will be explored in greater depth in unit 5. But for now, use the church purpose grid below as a template to evaluate your own church's ministry.

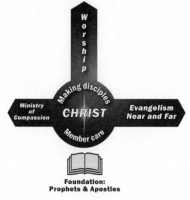

Foundation:
Prophets & Apostles

THE HOLY SPIRIT

RELEASING HIS ENERGIZING POWER

When He, the Spirit of Truth, has come,
He will guide you into all truth.
(JOHN 16:13 NKJV)

You shall receive power when the Holy Spirit has come upon you;
and you shall be witnesses.
(ACTS 1:8 NKJV)

The manifestation of the Spirit is given
to each one for the profit of all.
(1 COR. 12:7 NKJV)

Whatever the triune God intends for humankind, the Holy Spirit does it, whether creation, revelation (inspiration, illumination), redemption (conviction and regeneration), sanctification, or church (forming, energizing).[1] Since this study is concerned with ministry, in this unit we will consider what the Holy Spirit does to energize his people and his church and how we connect with him so that can happen.

Although the Holy Spirit alone can birth the church and he alone can empower and although he is given to guide each congregation, throughout much of church history biblical teaching on the Spirit has been marginalized. That, in spite of the fact that from Genesis' first chapter to Revelation's last chapter we meet the Spirit more than three hundred times! He is pervasive, even though his role is to keep the spotlight on the Father and the Son. Yet we neglect him.

Pastor Bill Barton, a church health consultant, visited me to talk about the Holy Spirit. He introduced the subject by saying, "We Presbyterians and

---

1. These activities of the Spirit are thoroughly examined in my *Life in the Spirit* interactive study (Nashville: LifeWay, 1997) and trade book (Nashville: Broadman, 2000).

Episcopalians believe in God the Father, you Baptists believe in God the Son, but if you want someone who really believes in the Holy Spirit, you have to go to the Pentecostals!" He knows what he's talking about. He told me that in 1645–47 the Westminster divines produced a magnificent statement of faith; but when the first draft of the Westminster Confession was presented to the Scottish General Assembly, there was nothing in it on the Holy Spirit! So the assembly sent the document back to committee to correct that error. Even so, when the United Presbyterian Church was revising its confession or constitution three hundred years later (1967), they made the same omission! They, too, had to go back to the drawing board.

Why does the church so frequently neglect the Holy Spirit? I asked a group of Baptist pastors and leaders that question when *Life in the Spirit* was first introduced at their conference center, Ridgecrest. They had several reasons: It's so spooky, said one, "we call him the Holy Ghost." "I've never heard it called 'him,'" said another. But the chief reason they all agreed on was, as one pastor put it, "There's so much wildfire around him we don't want to get close or we might get burned." And indeed there are aberrations in the twentieth century's "Second Pentecost," as it has been called.

Aberrations, yes, but the explosive growth of the church in the southern hemisphere, especially in Latin America, has been largely fueled by the revival of teaching on the Holy Spirit. The Pentecostal Movement was born in 1901 followed by the charismatic offshoot in the Roman Catholic and mainline Protestant churches coming at mid-century. In those years adherents of evangelical faith in the southern hemisphere exploded from three and one half million in 1900 to three to four hundred million in 2000. No wonder the twentieth century has been called the century of the Holy Spirit! True, often there was indeed "wildfire"—unbiblical and extrabiblical distortions. But the Spirit's power was unleashed as never before since the first century.

The influence of the charismatic movement was not limited to churches that emphasized speaking in tongues as the indispensable evidence of being Spirit-filled. Apart from the Pentecostal denominations, a strong prayer movement swept the churches of America, and what is prayer but an acknowledgment of how dependent we are on God and a seeking to link up with the energizing power of the Spirit? And there was another phenomenon: a great emphasis on the gifts of the Spirit. Since we are dealing in this study with biblical principles for ministry, it is those two emphases we will now consider: gifts of the Spirit and prayer in the local congregation.

CHAPTER 8:

DEFINING GIFTS

Question for reflection: **Has our church identified the roles and abilities (natural and spiritual) needed to accomplish each purpose of the church?**

One influence of the Pentecostal and charismatic movement of the twentieth century, reaching far beyond its own borders, was a focus on spiritual gifts. For decades, controversy over the phenomenon of speaking in tongues caused many evangelicals outside the movement to ignore biblical teaching on Spirit-given gifts altogether.

Many evangelicals, especially in the Reformed and Dispensational traditions, held that gifts were apostolic and ceased at the death of the last of the original Twelve. The problem with that position was lack of evidence in Scripture to indicate the Bible authors foresaw cessation. "Tongues . . . shall cease" (1 Cor. 13:8 KJV) was a last-ditch grasping for evidence, a passage clearly misappropriated to teach cessation. The context is "the now" with incomplete gifting and "the then" when all will be perfected in heaven. No amount of exegetical dexterity can claim this phrase for the cessation position, and that is the passage that is marshaled in evidence. As a consequence, the cessation position did not gain ascendancy.

Though some have denied that the activity of Spirit-gifting continued beyond the apostolic era, none have denied that the Holy Spirit is still operative. For this reason, we may assume that whether or not every gift named in the New Testament is operative today, certainly there must be parallels with the operation of the Holy Spirit today. If the church is charged with the same mission and responsibilities as the apostolic churches, the need for active participation with the Spirit must be normative. The New Testament teaching on gifts, then, was clearly not for the apostolic era alone but is for our edification today.

Because of the cessation controversy and because the biblical lists of gifts are not identical, some have tried to distinguish among them. Some speak of "gifts," "administrations," and "workings," making a clear-cut distinction. Others divide between motivational gifts, ministry gifts, and manifestation gifts. Others go for two categories: "sign" gifts and "ministry" gifts. Again, some interpret the passage in Ephesians to refer to the gifts of certain gifted people to the church and the gifts in 1 Corinthians 12 as gifts of certain abilities to individual Christians. All such distinctions, however, have failed to gain wide acceptance because biblical evidence for such divisions is totally lacking. For this reason, in our study we will consider the gifts more simply in a general way, seeking to discern basic principles for understanding and using whatever abilities the Spirit would give to a person to do a certain type of work in or through the local congregation. He wraps his gift in the personality of each member and then gives the gift of such a person to the church.

In spite of the challenge of striking a biblical balance on the activity of the Spirit, emphasis on spiritual gifting spread across theological and denominational lines in the last quarter of the twentieth century. Swiftly, the nation was blanketed with self-analyzing questionnaires, computer programs, and books. At first I participated but gradually came to have misgivings. If God intended to reveal such a full program of gifting, why didn't he give us a comprehensive list with precise definitions, things assumed by the phenomenon of gift-analysis sweeping the nation?

Since the Holy Spirit must do the work of ministry through us, if we don't connect and do it his way, there is no hope for accomplishing his purposes. Even those who teach cessation of the biblical gifts agree that the Holy Spirit must enable people to do God's work or it won't be done. So how can we discern what that gifting might be? Let me suggest three ways to align ourselves with what God intends: biblical lists and examples, tasks to be done, and purposes of the church.

Bible Definitions

In the New Testament there are several lists of gifts or abilities given by the Spirit to accomplish the work of the church in the world.

Romans 12:3–8	1 Corinthians 12	Ephesians 4	1 Peter 4:10–11
prophecy	wisdom	apostleship	various unnamed
service	knowledge	prophesy	speaking
teaching	faith	evangelism	serving
encouraging	healing	pastoring	
giving	miracles	teaching	
leading	prophecy		
showing mercy	discernment of spirits		
	tongues		
	interpretation		
	apostleship		
	teaching		
	helping others		
	administration		

Some of those seem to be clear in what the evidence would be if a person has the gift. The name tells you. Others are not that clear, so it's hard to judge whether or not a person has that gift. When it comes right down to it, we don't know for sure what most of those gifts will look like if a person has them. Therefore the meanings are hotly disputed. Some are clear, however.

Defining the Gifts

1. Teaching may be clear, but only if we define the outcome as a person explaining the Bible and spiritual truth in such a way that lives are consistently changed.

2. Healing would seem clear since a sick person would have to get well. I've experienced that. What the doctors described as an incurable disease kept me from becoming a missionary. A friend came and prayed for me and that night my pain left me. Forever! But to my knowledge, that's the only time that friend saw such dramatic results, so he could hardly be said to have the "gift of healing." What would it look like if he did? I get the impression that Jesus—and in the book of Acts the twelve apostles—healed everyone who came to them for healing. Can contemporary healers match that? But even if not, if people are healed often through the prayers of a person, I guess we'd have to say that this person has a gift!

3. Evangelism. If people often come to Christ through a person's witness, that would be the sign of God at work, and such a person could surely be said to have the gift of evangelism. By our definitions, however, we must not limit or distort what the full meaning is. For example, if we tend to identify the gift of evangelism with mass evangelism and fail to recognize there are many other ways to win people to faith, we limit what the Spirit intends by distributing this gift. That can skew training programs, for example, or cause needless frustration for those who have the gift to win in other ways or who desire the gift of evangelism.[1]

Thus, even those gifts that seem clearly defined by their name may not be so clear-cut after all. One danger is to take our church experience and read it back into the text. Even so, note that in all those lists, the three above are the only ones that seem to be clearly defined by the term itself. Some would add others, such as tongues or interpretation. They are clearly supernatural, but people disagree on exactly what those gifts are. So I left them off my list of those in which the exact meaning is evident just by the word used to identify the gift.

There's another one you may be inclined to include—prophecy. If by "prophecy" you mean prediction, that would be clear and the person with such a gift could be easily spotted. His predictions would consistently come

---

1. We shall examine this gift and the implications of correct definitions in unit 4.

true. But prediction is only one use of the term in Scripture and, in fact, other uses are more prominent. Basically, a prophet was a Spirit-ordained spokesperson for God. Sometimes a prophet would foretell future events, but that was not the defining activity. For example, in the Old Testament, musicians, even instrumentalists, were in the order of the prophets. "David . . . set apart for the service certain of the sons of Asaph, and of Heman, and of Jeduthun, who should prophesy with harps, with psalteries, and with cymbals . . . who prophesied in giving thanks and praising Jehovah" (1 Chron. 25:1, 3 ASV).

How could that be? No prediction there, not even words! But if those people officially represented God in leading his people in worship, that was considered "prophecy." If music among God's people leads to true worship, the leader may well have a spiritual gift, perhaps the gift of prophecy.

Thus, what a person was to say in a prophetic word and what the outcome was are not clearly defined by Scripture. I'm sure there are many people in our day who are authoritative spokespersons for God, so Spirit-anointed preaching could be defined as one kind of prophecy. But since Scripture is not clear I'll not be dogmatic about all that "prophecy" might mean.

In defining gifts from biblical lists, we should note that a person may have a gift without recognizing it as such, or he may have a gift without having a correct definition of it.

Although we've learned something about what the gifts are by examining the biblical lists of gifts, apparently the Holy Spirit didn't intend to give a clear-cut list of specific job descriptions. Was he just illustrating the kinds of things the Spirit wants to accomplish through his people? If so, there may be good reason for the imprecision. Perhaps he intended flexibility for us to see what needs doing in each situation and trust him to provide people with the abilities needed to do it. Perhaps being open to active partnership with the Spirit is more important than clear understanding of spiritual gifts.

Task-related Gift Definitions

We had just finished a faculty workshop on helping students identify their gifts when Kenneth Kantzer, distinguished theologian, seminary leader, and editor of *Christianity Today* at the time, took the microphone. "I've never known what my gift is," this multigifted man said, to our astonishment. "All my life I've seen a need, been asked to fill it, and trusted the Holy Spirit to enable me to do it." Maybe he's on to something.

As we've worked through possible definitions of spiritual gifts, you may have been frustrated that they are not more precise, especially if there is some favorite gift definition of yours I called into question. I felt that way for years. I read books filled with precise definitions and self-evaluating checklists, searching for my personal gift or mix of gifts. Could I ever really know my own gift for sure? When it finally came clear to me that the imprecision of Scripture was not by accident, and that I should focus rather on the tasks that needed to be done, it was truly liberating. Now all I need to do is ask God for his Spirit to "grace" me with the abilities necessary to accomplish what he has clearly told me to do. We can leave the combination of abilities, natural and supernatural, to the Holy Spirit to decide—"as He wills" (1 Cor. 12:11 NKJV). And we can thank him with confidence that the custom-designed pattern of gifts is from him—the supernatural source!

There's another reason I've concluded we should focus more on the needs and roles required than endlessly debate the meanings of terms the Bible didn't define for us. Each of the biblical lists of gifts is quite different, no gift appearing in all of them. Teaching and prophecy appear in three, apostle in two, and twenty-two gifts appear in only one list. So none of the lists is intended to be exhaustive; they're just representative or suggestive.

Perhaps there are other gifts not listed, tasks that need to be done in your church which Paul didn't include in any of his lists. For example, music, a major ministry of the church, isn't on any of the lists. So where does your "worship leader" fit? If your church uses drama, you surely don't want your dramatic efforts to be purely human talent. You want the strong anointing of the Spirit to produce eternal outcomes. There are no doubt other contemporary activities or traditional activities that don't clearly fit under any of Paul's categories, like children's work. If we thought it through, however, many of those other activities would be the ability to exercise "teaching" or "prophetic proclamation" with those of a specific age group or form of communication. Writing, for example, might fit under one of those.

And what of counseling? It may be on one of those lists. The Bible doesn't define "pastor," but the word literally means "shepherd." That sounds a little like counseling, doesn't it? Today we use "pastor" as the over-arching identification of the chief church leader, and certainly the shepherd was called to lead the flock. But the original idea was more akin, perhaps, to what today we call discipleship counseling, or nurturing. "Encourage-ment" in the Romans list of gifts might fit here, too. Many laypeople are like Barnabas, good at "coming alongside" and helping others through the tough times. Studies consistently show that such a loving relationship has more healing power than the professionals can provide!

Perhaps counseling often includes "healing" grace. The ancients called counseling the "cure of souls," or, to use the original Greek, the "cure (or healing) of psyches." Professional counselors who have the gift of curing the whole soul, who see supernatural results in life transformation toward like-ness to Christ as the outcome of their counseling, might be said to have the gift of "pastor." Others have the gift of pastoring or "curing souls," of course, but if the professional adds to his natural talent and training an anointing of the Spirit, he or she can be especially effective in healing the soul.

There are other possibilities for linking contemporary tasks with biblical gifts. "Leading," "administration," "wisdom," "discernment," or "helps," for example, are capable of wide application. Just be sure not to be too dogmatic in claiming that your understanding of a gift name is the only meaning it could have. And always identify the touch of the Spirit by spiritual outcomes.

Defining Gift by Purpose of the Church

Remember, in unit 2, when we studied the purposes of the church, there was an exercise in identifying the strengths and weaknesses in a congregation. If there is a weak or missing purpose in a congregation, it must mean some activity of the Spirit in gifting members is being neglected. So what gift do we seek for ourselves or for our congregation? Pause now and review the purposes of the church, noting on the graphic representation the names of the gifts from the biblical lists (see p. 76) that might be needed to fulfill those purposes.

After completing that exercise, check my suggestions:

1. It seems to me that the gifts of preaching, leadership, and administration are needed for the fulfillment of every purpose since those are gifts needed to accomplish the overall purposes of the church. For example, leaders are needed who are gifted to understand the way God wants the church to go and get people to go together in that direction.

2. The ability to lead people to worship in spirit and in truth is needed if the church is to bring God joy and honor him.

3. The ability to proclaim God's truth with life-changing authority is needed if the pulpit is to be more than an empty symbol.

4. The ability to teach the Bible in such a way that lives are changed is needed if godly learning is to take place.

5. The ability to discern a person's spiritual need and give wise counsel is needed if people are to be made whole and grow toward greater likeness to Christ.

6. The fellowship function of the church, the family solidarity, is something that is the responsibility of the entire church, each one caring lovingly

for the emotional, physical, material, and spiritual needs of other members of the family. It seems to be fulfilled more by people bearing the fruit of the Spirit than by any particular giftedness. But if the church is to function as a family well cared for, special abilities are needed to help out in practical ways like financial management, feeding people, seeing needs and meeting them.

7. The ability to win people to faith is needed if the church is to fulfill Christ's last command and grow as he promised.

8. The ability to minister to the physical and social needs of the community in such a way that people are drawn Godward is needed if the church is to fulfill the mandate of Christ. Actually, this would be a "gift" only for some who may specialize in social helping and healing, perhaps as a full-time ministry, such as a vocation in health care or politics. Otherwise it's the responsibility of every member, the fruit of the compassionate Holy Spirit, more than any special gift.

In defining the gift package for each believer, it helps to think of the purposes of the church as defined by Scripture. But there are other elements in seeking to define biblical gifts. How do supernatural Spirit-given abilities relate to natural abilities? How do "gifts of the Spirit" relate to "fruit of the Spirit"? And what is the relationship between gifting and church office? We turn now to seeking a biblical synergy among these issues.

CHAPTER 9:

WHAT THE GIFTS ARE NOT

B efore turning to the vital questions of discerning, developing, deploying, and desiring a gift, several further elements in defining the gifts must be considered. How does a Spirit-given supernatural gift relate to the natural talent a person has been given or has developed? And how do Spirit-given abilities ("gifts") relate to Spirit-produced personal characteristics ("fruit")? Do gifts differ in importance? And finally, what relationship is there between a gift and a church office?

Natural Talent as Part of the Spirit's Gift Package

Though my natural ability is certainly part of the life stewardship entrusted to me from God just as surely as my Spirit gift, a natural ability can be used without the Spirit's assistance. And God doesn't usually get the credit for that. So the first thing to note about a natural ability and a spiritual ability is that both are gifts from God, as in the case of Moses and Paul, for example. Therefore we must give God credit for whatever ability we have and we must use both natural and supernatural gifts for his glory, not our own. It's a terrible sin to use either kind of giftedness for our own glory.

The second thing to note is that the Bible nowhere spells out a clear boundary between the two, and it's often difficult to tell the difference. For example, a person may have great natural ability to lead or sing or preach or teach or manage money, so great that most of us would be unable to tell whether the Spirit is at work. Even activity that definitely requires the supernatural touch of God, like evangelizing, healing, and casting out demons can be faked if the person has enough personal charisma. But we're talking here about those who truly lead people to Christ, truly heal the sick, truly exorcise demons. Still, most of the activities of the church can be carried forward at some level of competence just with natural abilities. And that's scary! Who needs the Spirit?

But you can tell the difference. "The manifestation of the Spirit is given to each one for the profit of all" (1 Cor. 12:7 NKJV). Notice that the work of the Spirit is "manifest" or made visible. Apparently you can see the evidence and, furthermore, it seems to be our job to do it: "Beloved, do not believe every spirit, but test the spirits, whether they are of God; because many false prophets have gone out into the world" (1 John 4:1 NKJV). John gives the test of orthodoxy—is the message biblical? But when it comes to gifts of the Spirit, there is a corollary test that should be used along with the test of true words. Is there a supernatural touch on the activity, is it his activity that is clearly seen ("manifest")? For example, Paul wasn't a world-class public speaker. He agreed with the Corinthians in that judgment. But when he taught the Bible, lives were transformed. A popular Christian music group can entertain—a wonderful talent—but are people lifted to heaven in worship? Or, do they merely have an emotional high and applaud such great talent? Do sinners repent and saints consecrate their lives to God when they sing? That's the touch of the Spirit. Does the counselor merely help people change their dysfunctional behavior or adjust their attitudes to develop coping strategies, or does he also lead them forward in a supernatural, transformational pattern of life?

Whether God chooses to bypass natural ability or overcome inability or whether the Spirit lifts a natural ability to a higher power we may not always know, but if it's a Spirit gift, there will be the Spirit's miracle touch. We may not know for sure the relationship between natural and supernatural gifts, but several principles are clear from Scripture:

- God can and does work altogether apart from natural ability.
- Natural ability alone will not accomplish God's purposes. We are doomed if we rely on the natural (1 Cor. 1–3; Prov. 3:5–6).
- Often we do not know the line of demarcation or the interrelationship in many of the gifts, because Scripture does not address the issue. Apparently God did not think it would help us to know. Therefore it is not possible to divide between the mediate (when God uses human personality and talent) and the immediate (when he bypasses human personality). The bypassing is clearer in gifts such as tongues and healing than in other gifts such as teaching and administration.
- Sometimes God purifies and raises a natural gift to supernatural power. For example, a person may have a natural ability to make money, but he will certainly need a heavenly charisma to give generously and wisely or to govern the affairs of the church. This is true of other gifts noted in Scripture such as teaching, management, spiritual insight (discernment), hospitality, and assisting others (helps).

- Some people may have "visible evidence" resulting from the work of unholy spirits! For example, the magicians in Pharaoh's court managed to duplicate some of the signs Moses performed (Exod. 7:11) but certainly didn't do them through the power of the Holy Spirit.
- A person may have been given a gift and still experience a lack of evidence because of adverse circumstances. For example, Ezekiel was God's prophet, but the people were rebels and wouldn't listen (Ezek. 3). Paul was no doubt the greatest of evangelists, but in Lystra people stoned him out of town (Acts 14).

In general, however, if no evidence shows the Spirit at work, if the ministry makes no spiritual impact, we need to ask if the ministry is God's. On the other hand, when I fail to see evidence in my own ministry, I don't immediately conclude that I have no gift or that he hasn't called me after all. I ask myself the following diagnostic questions:

1. Am I harboring unconfessed sin? When I've preached my heart out and lives aren't changed, I first examine myself to see if something in me blocked the flow of the Spirit. Do I have some unconfessed sin, a wrong motivation (wanting "success" for human praise, not for "the profit of all" but for the profit of me), unbelief (not trusting God to do what only he can do), or lack of prayer preparation?

2. Do I need to be persistent? When I felt called to do missionary work, I kept asking God for the gift of evangelism. People came to Christ through my ministry only sporadically, and I longed for the ability to consistently win people to Christ. Eventually he gave that fruit I longed for, but note the principle. Keep asking until you see one of two things: "visible evidence" of the gift you long for, or the assurance that God doesn't intend that gift for you. Stop asking only when God shows you the gift is not for you.

3. Am I in the right place? In Japan, we discovered we were ministering in a very unresponsive area. We asked God if there should be a change of location to a place or people who would respond. This is what Paul did more than once (see Acts 13:46, for example).

4. Is God vindicating himself? Perhaps, on the other hand, God intends a gifted person to stand firm when there is no "fruit" or outward result, as his vindication among an unresponsive people (as in Ezekiel's case). Don't run to this as an excuse, however. The general principle of Scripture is to concentrate your efforts where there is response.

You can see from the above exceptions that a legitimate gift may be without "visible evidence" in some situations; but ordinarily the touch of the Spirit is the proof of his presence and power.

In identifying a gift or package of gifting by the Spirit, a related problem often pops up. Why do some people seem to have such a great gifting for ministry and such a deficit in the fruit of the Spirit? Is it possible to have true giftedness and not have a Christlike character?

Gifts and Fruit

How do "fruit" and "gift" relate? The Bible doesn't tell us. I can't find even a hint. We would like to think there's a direct correlation since both are the Spirit's activity. But we all know of those people who have world-class gifting, making a huge impact for God, but remain notably deficient in spiritual fruit. Perhaps the lack of fruit is seen in the selfishness of a very large ego or perhaps the lack of self-control in a major moral failure. How do gifts of the Spirit and fruit of the Spirit relate?

Certainly, as we have seen, the gifts are designed to produce fruit. We don't grow in isolation but as each part contributes his or her special ministry to the rest. In fact, that's one of the primary purposes of the gifting (see Eph. 4:7–16). Beyond that basic relationship between gifts and fruit, however, questions remain. Several answers have been suggested, but are they biblical?

1. The more fruit (the more Christlike the character) a person has, the greater the gift he or she will be given (the more results in ministry).
2. A person could have a godly life while having very little results in public ministry.
3. It's more important to have lots of fruit in our lives than to have a great gift.
4. All Christians should have all the fruit, but perhaps only one of the gifts.

In the most thorough discussion of gifts in the Bible, 1 Corinthians 12–14, the first thing that becomes immediately clear is that fruit, especially love, is more important than gift (#3 above). Right in the middle of his discussion of gifts, Paul breaks away from his theme to say, "Now I'm going to describe something far more important than all these gifts combined." Then he gives the magnificent "love chapter," 1 Corinthians 13. And what is love but a fruit? In fact, some say it is the summation of all fruit. If anything is clear from New Testament emphases, it is that God intends all his children to be like him, to bear all the fruit of the Spirit (#4 above) to the maximum.

The gifts are important, too, but the chief point of 1 Corinthians 12 and 14 seems to be that the Spirit does not give all the gifts to any one person. "To one there is given through the Spirit . . . to another . . . and to still another . . . Are all apostles? Are all prophets? Are all teachers?" (12:7–11, 29 NIV).

It's just as well the Spirit doesn't give all the gifts to one person. What a power trip that would be! Think of it this way. God wants everyone to be completely like him in character, to put his beauty on display; and the more like Jesus we become, the more glory to God. But what of likeness to him in his activity? He never had any intention that anyone be like him in infinite wisdom or power or other capacities. That would make them lust, like Lucifer, to displace God or at least to get along without his help. No one member can be godlike in capacity lest he or she be tempted to act like God in accumulating personal power. But the Spirit does want his church to be empowered, so his plan was to distribute the gifts among all its members.

In summary, fruit: everyone, always, to the maximum; gifts: some one, some another. But the exciting thing is this: every member is given at least one ability to serve God in the church. There's a real conundrum, though, in how the gifts and fruit relate. It's a puzzle because the Bible nowhere spells it out for us. We see a person mightily used of God who may be egotistical or quick-tempered and we see another who is very godly in character but is not gifted to serve in any conspicuous way (#2 above). How can that be? Here are some possible reasons:

1. Isaiah 55:11 promises that the Word of God will accomplish his purposes and God often blesses his Word in spite of the spokesperson, not because of him or her.

2. There is always a question as to whether or not the apparent results of a person's ministry are real results. God doesn't necessarily evaluate giftedness as we do. He alone is the judge, and the time of judgment is yet future (1 Cor. 3:10–15, 4:1–5).

3. Sometimes a person may exercise his gifts effectively because of the momentum of true anointing in days gone by.

4. It is often difficult to judge what is the result of a natural ability and what is the result of a supernatural gift.

5. Sometimes a person may minister in supernatural power but it is not the power of God, as the magicians in the court of Pharaoh (see also Matt. 7:17–23).

6. All of us have weak areas in Christian maturity, and the fact that we are effective in ministry should not make us complacent about the immature qualities of our lives. The fact that gifted people are sometimes immature spiritually should cause us to keep our eyes on Jesus, not on some gifted and adored leader. And we should constantly watch for our own blind spots. Our treasure is in clay pots that the glory may be the Lord's. This does not mean, however, that we may sin that grace may abound. Furthermore, we must not excuse ourselves because of some great man's weakness which is similar to our own. We must be gentle in judging others, severe in judging ourselves.

We tend to evaluate people, especially Christian leaders, in terms of their giftedness, but God is the judge and he has already passed judgment— fruit is more important! Note that rewards and recognition on the final great day will not be based on usefulness, but faithfulness, just the opposite of the rewards we hand out—rewards of fame and fortune, for example. And remember, faithfulness is a fruit, not a gift. Think about it. Some poor bedridden lady who spent her years in intercession for others, unknown and unheralded, will on that last day stand at the head of the line, while some world-renowned preacher will do well to get in the door. Why? Because rewards are based on faithfulness.

Notice another contrast between fruits and gifts. The Spirit intends to produce all the fruits in every believer and fully provides for that. And he wants us to pursue the maximum—God's own level of perfection. But no one is given all the gifts, says Paul, nor does he provide each gift to the maximum in each person. The Spirit distributes the gifts as he wills for the purpose of accomplishing God's purposes in and through his church. Are all gifts, then, of equal importance?

Importance of Each Gift

Are all the gifts of equal importance or are some more important than others? To get at the answer, it may be necessary to ask another question: important for what? I suggest three possibilities:

1. Important for the individual. The most important gifts for you or me are those gifts God has given us or would give us if we asked. The most important thing for us is to find that gift or pattern of gifts and develop them, use them to the maximum. We'll consider that in the next chapter.

2. Important for the church. We might say, "all of them" since Paul seems to be saying the Spirit puts into each congregation all the gifts (or gifted people) needed to accomplish his purposes in and through that church. So the most important thing for the church is for all the members to function in the way the Spirit designs. Problem is, in most churches about 15 percent of the members try to fulfill the functions of the whole body! No wonder so many congregations are badly handicapped, or even totally disabled. The Spirit's will for the church is for every member to function as designed because every member is needed to accomplish his purposes. That happens when all members are using fully their gifts.

3. Important to God. Surely all gifts are of equal importance to him? Careful! The central purpose of 1 Corinthians 12–14 is to get the church to understand that gifts are not all of equal importance for accomplishing God's will. There are some less important gifts, and the church at Corinth was majoring on one of those (speaking in tongues). Furthermore, there were very important gifts which the church at Corinth should have majored on but didn't—gifts like apostle, prophet, and teacher. Paul even numbered them 1, 2, and 3 (12:28) so they wouldn't miss the point. He didn't continue his numbering system beyond those three, so they may just be representa- tive. But they give a hint as to what he considered more important: roles which seem to have the greatest impact for God's purposes in the church and in the world. Since Scripture nowhere stops to define those gifts, we're left to study the terms in their use throughout the Bible. After years of doing that, my personal definition of his top three would be pioneer missionary evangelist (apostle), power-filled proclamation or preaching (prophecy), and Spirit-anointed teaching—important tasks indeed.

Don't misunderstand what we mean by importance. We're not speaking of one gift being more "spiritual" than another. "Spiritual" has to do with fruits of the Spirit, likeness to Jesus, as we've just seen. And we're not talking about greater rewards for greater gifts more greatly used. Reward is based on faithfulness, not outward results, as we have seen.

But to accomplish God's purposes, some gifts are more strategic. For twelve years I was a pioneer missionary evangelist, starting churches. A very high calling, according to Paul. Today God seems to be using me in itiner- ant preaching and writing, not pioneer evangelism. But I'm not arrogant, claiming that my role in life is as important as anyone else's. For example, my calling cannot even compare with Billy Graham's calling in terms of eternal impact. And I'm not envious of Billy! God expects only that we be faithful to our own calling. Then the whole body can function smoothly, we will find personal fulfillment and, best of all, God will be pleased. Having considered two topics related to our theme of defining gifts (the relationship of gifting to fruit bearing, and the relative importance of gifting), we return to our theme: how do we define gifts?

In defining what supernatural ministry abilities the Spirit stands ready to give, I have suggested it may be helpful to combine the hints given in the undefined and partial lists found in Scripture with the clearly revealed pur- poses the Spirit has for the congregation. Furthermore, in a way unexplained in Scripture he is free to incorporate in that gift package the natural talents he has engineered as he creates unique individuals. Thus he provides all the equipment needed to fulfill what he intends to accomplish through his people. There is one other thing a gift is not. It's not an office in the church, though certain offices require certain gifts.

Gifts and Offices

It's important to distinguish between a gift and an office. This is partic- ularly clear in the case of the gift of apostleship which must be distinguished from the office of apostle. We'll consider that in some depth in unit 4. A person should have the gift or gifts necessary to fulfill an office before being chosen for that office. For example, a person should have the gifts of pastoral care and teaching before being chosen as a pastor or an elder (1 Tim. 3:2). To be sure, most of the requirements listed by Paul center on fruits of the Spirit as prerequisites, but those two gifts are included in the biblical listing of qualifications for office. Unfortunately for the church, often neither the fruiting nor the gifting is heavily weighed when elections are held!

We've considered at some length (chaps. 9 and 10) how to go about defining gifts, but that is only to lay a solid foundation for the important matters to which we now turn. How does one go about discerning giftedness, developing a gift, deploying the gifts of all members in each congregation, and, when lacking, what it means to "desire earnestly the greater gifts."

CHAPTER 10:

DISCOVERING, DEVELOPING, DEPLOYING, DESIRING

Questions for reflection: **Does our church have a program
and leadership in place to help every member discover,
develop to the full, and deploy his or her gifting and calling,
and, when some purpose of the congregation is less than optimally
fulfilled, do the leaders and members actively "desire earnestly"
in prayer the Spirit gifts necessary?**

The whole point of the effort we have devoted to defining gifts is aimed
at one thing: discovering and using those gifts. Let's consider the steps
in order.

Discovering One's Gift

Believing that the Spirit has a custom-designed gift package for each
member of the congregation, how does one go about finding out what's in
the package? Make it more personal. How do I discover my own gifting?

I don't know any way other than trying it out. You see a need, ask God
to help you meet it, and go for it! Or you have a burning in your soul to do a
certain kind of work for God. Well, try it out and see! Don't be discouraged
if you stumble or fall short of expectations at first, but sooner or later there
will be evidence if it truly is a gifting from God. What kind of evidence? Why,
the touch of the supernatural, of course—evidence of God the Spirit at work.
What are some examples of supernatural evidence? You have the gift of evangelism? How many people have come to faith through your efforts during the
past year? The gift of teaching? Do people who receive your teaching show
evidence of spiritual growth? The gift of counseling? Are your counselees not
merely coping with their problems but growing in Christlikeness, through
gaining spiritual victories? Are you an appointed leader? Is there evidence of
God in action to heal conflict and grasp new opportunities? Whatever the
gift, if it's the Spirit at work, there should be evidence.

But it's not a solo activity. There's a second element in gift discovery: the church must affirm. In other words, the leadership of the church is required to evaluate each member's giftedness. Timothy had his gifting through the laying on of hands. Whatever else that may have meant, it certainly indicated the agreement and endorsement of the church leaders on what God was doing in the young man (1 Tim. 4:14).

After class one day, a student handed me a note: "A pastor believes he has the gifts of pastor/teacher. Church leaders unanimously believe he doesn't." At that point, the only question is whether the pastor has the humility to accept the judgment of others. Or consider the letter I received from the opposite side of the country, asking me to give the writer a reference as an evangelist. His church wouldn't give him such endorsement, so how was he to get engagements to hold evangelistic meetings? I had never heard of him, of course, but even if I had, how could I evaluate without personal inspection? Furthermore, even if I did watch him in operation and felt he was so gifted, I'm not his church; he's not accountable to me. No, the voice of the congregation is essential to discovering a person's gift.

Of course, many churches are not capable of such evaluation. They don't even operate in the mode of exercising such responsibility. Perhaps, if one does not have the responsibility or authority to change things, that would be the time to find a fellowship that takes seriously the responsibility of helping all its members identify the Spirit's gifting of each.

In exploring the role of the local church in gift discovery, let me share how one church did it—our own church-starting efforts in Japan. The churches we started were composed of people who had known nothing of the gospel and, of course, nothing of what a church is supposed to be. But we assumed that these newborn Christians would be given abilities to serve God, just as the Spirit promised. So we gave everyone a job. We even gave unconverted regular attendees a job—like cleaning up before and after services or serving tea and rice crackers. From the outset they felt part of us and people were born into the family serving. That is, they assumed that to be a Christian meant to participate in God's work. And the assignment must never be "busy work." As the churches grew, we had twenty-seven meetings a week. Obviously, many people had to function, covering all the purposes of the church, or the work would not be accomplished.

At first the assignments were housekeeping, nothing that would test one's spiritual giftedness, but would test one's availability and heart for serving the rest of the family. These family duties often become spiritual disciplines, partnering with the Spirit's work of shaping a humble and fruit-filled heart. Here is a list of jobs we gave, in the order of spiritual responsibility, beginning with the task requiring the least supernatural enabling:

- straightening the shoes or geta in the vestibule where they were left upon entry,
- greeting and seating guests,
- serving rice crackers and tea,
- playing the electronic organ,
- giving a testimony at an evangelistic meeting,
- leading the meeting,
- preaching to non-Christians,
- teaching a Sunday school class,
- preaching to Christians, and
- teaching Sunday school teachers.

We would train and coach each believer until he or she seemed ready for the next assignment, stopping when they wanted to stop or the leaders in the church felt they were not yet gifted for the next assignment. There are two reasons for this approach, as we have seen. First, how do you know whether you have a gift or would be given a gift until you try it out? Second, giftedness should be confirmed by the church.

It is important for each person to discover and exercise his gift or gifts. No one is a spectator. This gives a sense of ownership, of membership in the family. Furthermore, exercising one's gift is a major means of grace (Eph. 4:16). But there's more. As we have seen, if not all the members are functioning, not all the purposes of the church will be fulfilled. The body will be deformed, even becoming dysfunctional. Does your church have a systematic plan for helping people discover their gifts? Is every member expected to serve in some capacity? Are people encouraged to try out new roles and use their abilities to the maximum? If not, perhaps it's time for change—change in attitude to raise expectations, change in structure to make it happen. This approach to discovering one's gift leads to the next step: developing that gift.

By way of summary, to discover or identify one's gift:
- Define the gift (see chap. 10).
- Spiritual discernment. A personal burden increases to the point of conviction.
- Natural appraisal. We must have an objective evaluation of gifts.
- Confirmation by experience. Is there evidence that the gift is operative and of the Spirit?
- Confirmation by the voice of the church.

In preparation for the next stage—developing and deploying the gift—let me expand on this last item, church confirmation. Timothy received the gift through the laying on of Paul's hands (2 Tim. 1:6) and those of the elders (1 Tim. 4:14). It is very important that the local congregation be united in a conviction that God has indeed called the individual to the ministry he would attempt to perform, if the proposed role has an element of spiritual ministry. This does not mean that some friends or fans of an individual concur in this judgment but rather that the church in its official action concurs in assigning a person to the ministry for which that gift is necessary.

This is a crucial—and often neglected—element in discerning or identifying a gift. It means that the individualistic approach of a young person aspiring to spiritual leadership in the church is not biblical. He decides on his own what God wants him to do, then goes away for specialized training. Actually, the church should be involved in identifying those whom God is calling to special ministry. When this gift and calling are evident to the leadership of the church, then the training should begin there in the church. After that, the church may choose to send such a person away for training as the need becomes evident. Few churches have the resources to provide the full breadth and depth of exposure that is ideal for a major ministry role, though increasing numbers of megachurches seem to, and some smaller congregations make an attempt. Often, however, the result is a narrow focus and limited development due to limited resources.

Of course, a person may not abdicate his responsibility before God to do what God calls him to do. Sometimes, therefore, it is necessary to choose against what the responsible church authorities may have decided. This should be done only with great reluctance as a last resort, and with great care. Sometimes the church or its leadership may not be qualified spiritually or practically to make a particular decision. Sometimes the biblical truth concerning the lordship of Christ, for example, is not followed and the pastor or other leadership has usurped the authority that belongs to the Lord. In such a case, "we must obey God rather than man." This should, however, be the exception. When the ideal prevails and the church has participated in identifying a person's gifting and calling, it then must join in the development of that gift and provide opportunities for its full use.

Developing, Deploying the Gift

Some people say if it's a gift, it comes fully activated. You can't really develop a gift, they say. Paul didn't believe that. Remember what he told Timothy? "Don't neglect that gift in you, Timothy" (1 Tim. 4:14). "Stir it up!" (2 Tim. 1:6). Paul was even more explicit: "Make these matters your business and your absorbing interest, so that your progress may be plain to all" (1 Tim. 4:15 NEB). The responsibility of the congregation is not only to partner with each member in discovering her or his gift, but also to partner with the Spirit in nurturing and developing those gifts.

By way of illustration, certainly not of prescription, here's how we did it in Japan. In our churches in Tsuchiura, Japan, we used all the training methods I'll outline here, and the result was that we started three churches in five years and developed two other embryonic congregations. We could never do that if the "professional," in this case, the missionary, had to do all the important functions of the church. But because the people were freed up to use the abilities the Spirit was distributing and because I concentrated my energies on equipping them for their ministries (Eph. 4:11–12), we could move forward simultaneously in every outlying community. Here's the strategy we used.

Practice

We've seen how getting to work on a job is the one sure way to identify a gift. Don't give up too soon, though. If the kids throw spit wads the first day in class, don't conclude you're not called to teach! Work at it.

Contrary to the proverb, however, practice doesn't always make perfect. In fact it can make very imperfect—consolidating all the bad habits we practice. We need someone who's gone on before and knows how the job should be done to come alongside and help us grow.

Apprentice Mentor

Dan was to be envied. A handsome people-person with a gifted wife, he had just been called to his first assignment after graduation—associate pastor of a prestigious old church at the heart of a southern city. He was excited because the senior pastor was a remarkably successful leader and Dan intended to learn all he could. So he approached his boss, asking the pastor to help him discover and develop his gifts. The pastor—a self-starting, can-do man who had never asked anyone for help—said, "Who do you think I am? The Holy Spirit?" Crushed, Dan limped along for a few months, dropped out, and engaged in construction work for the next twenty-five years. He was, however, "recommissioned" for missionary ministry late in life. But I've often wondered, had Dan encountered a true mentor, might he have been in ministry all those decades?

If your church is structured so that everyone has a mentor, or, even if not, if someone has reached out to help another grow in ministry, how blessed! But if not, what can be done? The individual can do the reaching out, can take the initiative. For example, the fledgling (or veteran) teacher can ask for feedback on her or his performance. Have the best teacher you know sit in on the class you teach and talk with you informally afterwards. You have to really want candid responses and you have to let them know that, or the exercise will be a waste of your time and theirs.

Another way to get feedback is to distribute questionnaires to those who see you in action, the one to whom you are responsible, the students in your class—anyone whose evaluation might be helpful. If you don't feel competent to develop an evaluative checklist for the job you're doing, perhaps there's someone in the church who could help develop such a questionnaire or checklist. In ways like this, individuals can take the initiative and recruit their own mentors, but the best way is for the church to provide mentors to apprentice everyone who begins a new ministry.

Looking at it from the other end, however, perhaps there is someone you could help in developing his or her gift. Be careful, however, to pray for wisdom on the best way to feel that person out and see whether he or she would like such a relationship.

But perhaps God would use you in an even larger role. If you are in a leadership role in the church, consider what steps you could take to get the church into a developing-everyone mode.

Literature and Media

In our churches in Japan we gave everyone, along with the job, a page of simple instructions on how to do that job. But in America we are rich in resources: teachers' manuals or how-to books on virtually every task in the church. Be sure the church library has a good book on each task and that people are encouraged to read, read, read. For some of the key roles there are videos or series of audiotapes or web sites produced by people who are the best in that particular role. Resources abound and can be discovered on the Internet or at the local Christian bookstore.

Special Training Classes

We opened a mini Bible college on Tuesday nights to train people who were serving or wanted to serve in spiritual ministry. Here are some of the courses we taught: teaching methods, preaching, principles of Bible interpretation, Bible survey, church history, theology, various Bible book studies, principles of Christian ministry, and evangelism. We should have taught world missions but didn't.

Inter-church Seminars

Our "mini Bible college" was an inter-church project in that we invited people from other churches in the region to enroll. But one of the most popular means of learning today in America is the major regional event, seminars on Christian education, counseling, witnessing, apologetics, family life, political action, preaching, prayer, missions—the list goes on. World-famous teachers lecture, and specialists offer workshops on every conceivable topic. Does your church budget include funds for key people to attend such conferences? Have individuals or groups from your church attended such, whether under church auspices or independently? Which kinds of seminars should your church leadership consider making a major part of the church program?

Formal Training

Finally there is formal training available for those who have grown beyond what the local church offers or who feel the need for intensive study. From our fledgling churches in Japan, more than half a dozen went away to prepare for full-time ministry, and three have become pastors with a nation-wide impact. That, from churches which at the time totaled less than one hundred members!

In America today increasing numbers of mature adults are choosing to attend a resident program when one's life situation permits. Some Bible colleges (undergraduate) and seminaries (for college graduates) have one-year introductory courses to give a broad overview of biblical studies, and the full program is available for those who feel the Spirit's drawing toward full-time vocational Christian ministry. Furthermore, seminaries and Bible colleges offer studies in locations away from their home campus—perhaps near you—and a few have a highly developed home study curriculum, available through media.

I have shared something of my personal experience by way of illustrating the responsibility of the church leadership to help every individual develop the gift or package of gifts the Spirit is giving each member. But what if there is a gift deficit in a church? Are some purposes of the church going unmet or only minimally achieved? No one seems gifted in evangelism, for example, and the church is not growing, or the church seems to lurch from crisis to crisis because there is inadequate leadership or management skills, or many members seem retarded in spiritual growth because most of the teaching is so superficial, or … whatever. Maybe things are going well with many gifted people fully functioning, but perhaps you yourself have a longing, a burning in your soul to do something for God you don't seem equipped for? Can anything be done about it?

Desiring the Gift

Some say, "It's a gift. You don't ask for a gift." So I respond, "Is salvation a gift? Did you ask for it?" In fact, you don't get salvation without asking for it! Did you notice how it's easy to get more spiritual than the Bible? Paul declared that we should desire earnestly the greater gifts (1 Cor. 12:31). Let's examine three important things about this crucial command. It's an active command, a continuous action command, and a command for the whole church.

An Active Verb

The command to "desire earnestly" is not a description of the feeling you have when you sit in your recliner and watch a luscious slice of pizza, dripping cheese, move across the TV screen. The word used has the concept of action. "Go for it," we would say, or "get with it!" If you pick up the phone and order that pizza, then you've "desired earnestly" in the sense of this word Paul uses.

My mother wanted me to desire earnestly service for God, but I didn't. I had yielded my life to God, but it was a passive yielding. I wasn't excited about it. "God, you shove and I'll move," was my mode. I didn't add, "But I won't like it, I'm sure," even though that's the way I felt most of the time. I wasn't obeying the command. I wasn't desiring earnestly any gift.

But I was involved. Mother saw Sunday afternoons as a training ground. She arranged (I later learned) to have college students invite me, just a young kid, to go with them in their ministry to housing developments, for example. Flattered by the attention, I went with them—even helped start a little country church one year. I hauled wood for the potbellied stove in that one-room, ramshackle schoolhouse. Mother was "church" to me, my incognito mentor, helping me discover my spiritual gifts! But I wasn't desiring anything.

When I was eighteen, however, the desire began to stir. In fact, I began to desire most earnestly that my life should count to the maximum for whatever God designed me for. That meant getting involved. I joined other young men in preaching on the street corner. Folks didn't stop much, so we took up preaching in jail. No one walked away! I began to obey the command to "get with it" and "go for it."

Many Christians don't desire earnestly the jobs they hold in church— they have been drafted! Something like my mother drafted me. But whether or not one volunteers or is drafted, something like Paul drafted Timothy, each should be encouraged to look back and see if there was any role that really excited them. Then they should be encouraged to reflect and pray about the possibility of being used in a larger way, maybe even some other more important-to-God role. It isn't presumptuous to "go for it." It's commanded! Furthermore, the leadership of every congregation is charged with the responsibility to reflect constantly on the purposes of the church, staying alert to deficits in fulfilling God's purposes and spotting, recruiting, enlisting those who might fill those positions. Paul says, desire it earnestly, go for it vigorously. Perhaps an even greater responsibility is to constantly seek to ignite those desires in the people.

Seek and Keep on Seeking

Taking action, seeking to uncover the latent gifts by getting to work is important, but obeying the command to "earnestly desire" means first of all to tell God of that desire. Not just a one-time, timid request, either. The form of the verb means to pray earnestly and keep at it, to keep on desiring. Persistent prayer until God gives the answer! Here are a few possibilities to check out:

How many adult baptisms were there in your church last year? Is it growing in numbers, at least 5 percent a year in baptisms of adult converts? If not, your church may need more people with the gift of evangelism.

Or perhaps your concern is the lack of spiritual growth. Once a person joins the church, nothing much seems to happen in dynamic spiritual growth. Many gifts would help, no doubt, but how about Spirit-anointed teachers or counselors, disciple makers?

Is the church harassed with gossip, squabbles, in danger of splitting up? Is it stuck in the rut of some worn-out tradition? Maybe you need a courageous prophet or the dynamism of Spirit-anointed leadership. Are you asking God for that? Earnestly? Persistently?

Command for the Congregation as a Whole

The Spirit intends to meet all the needs of the church, so this "desiring earnestly" can't be an individualistic pursuit. The church as a whole must obey the command. Actually, the verb Paul uses is in the plural—"you all desire earnestly." If you can't inspire the church as a whole to focus on this kind of praying, some smaller prayer group could include this request on a regular basis. Certainly the leadership team must make this a major prayer focus. Such a prayer meeting must not be a thinly veiled invitation to criticism, focusing on the negative. It must spring from earnest desire for God's highest and best. Unitedly desire earnestly the greater gifts.

Translators seem to have difficulty getting just the right word in English to translate this command:

- "eagerly desire" (NIV)
- "covet earnestly" (KJV)
- "set your hearts on" (TEV)
- "try your best" (TLB)
- "be ambitious" (J. B. Phillips)
- "earnestly desire" (RSV)

There's something emotional about it, a deep longing that moves to action. That's what I began to experience in my late teens. And it never left me—a compelling desire to count to the maximum for God. Every possible gift and opportunity the Spirit would give to advance the cause of the gospel—that's what I wanted.

But some people are like me. For years I had heart trouble. I didn't see the needs or opportunities or, seeing them, didn't care that much. Notice that Paul doesn't say, wait around until the desire hits you. It's a command: set your heart on that gift that is so desperately needed by your church or by a dying world. Take the initiative, says Paul. Go for it! If you don't have a desire to be used more in God's service, that may be the place to begin. Instead of asking for a particular ability, as I have often suggested in this chapter, perhaps the request should be for the Spirit to ignite a great flame of desire in your heart. If you've got heart trouble like I did, why not stop now and tell him about it? And commit to keep on asking him every day until he lights the fire.

While you're seeking that gift, don't forget that the size of the gift differs with each person. It's highly unlikely that every person in your church will have the gift of evangelism on the scale of Billy Graham, for example. So we must not fall into envying, imitating, or comparing. Paul said, "Don't get the big head! Be realistic! Curb those expectancies." Here's how he put it: "For I say . . . to everyone . . . not to think of himself more highly than he ought to think, but to think soberly, as God has dealt to each one a measure of faith" (Rom. 12:3 NKJV). Then he presents a listing of some of the gifts the Spirit gives. So, just as in natural gifting or talents we all differ, so with the supernatural, the gifts of the Spirit. Be persistent, go for it, but don't have unrealistic expectations. And it is not a competition. There is joy in being the person God created you to be and celebrating the diversity that others contribute. This unifying spirit motivates me to make my contribution and to give what the Spirit is entrusting to me, and also that I must keep my life open to receive what God brings to me through others.

When my heart was ignited at age eighteen so that I wanted my life to count to the maximum for what God is doing in this world, I set my heart on the Pauline role, pioneer evangelistic church starter among those who had never heard the gospel. Paul said he made it his ambition to proclaim Christ to those who had not heard, where no other proclaimer had been (Rom. 15:20). He didn't wait until he was drafted; he didn't sit around until desire emerged; he says that he took the initiative in stoking the fire of passion, of keeping the vision bright. The word means he was honor-driven; he set his heart on this task; he made it his aim. And so did I. There were many obstacles, but I persisted through my years of teaching and school administration to desire earnestly this that I considered the greater gift. The biggest problem, however, was that I didn't have the gift of evangelism.

I had opportunity to speak to teens and sometimes there would be a great response. Often there would be none. I would return home in tears. "Lord, please give me the gift. How can I be a pioneer evangelist to start churches among those who have never had access to the gospel if I don't have the gift of evangelism?" So we persisted in making this our ambition until we reached Japan. There we discovered we had a truncated view of what the gift of evangelism was. To be sure, the American mass evangelists had the gift, but in Japan that didn't seem to be the best approach. We discovered we could move into a churchless community and love the people to Jesus. They came in ever larger numbers. The gift we pled for, God had given us. By a faulty definition we hadn't recognized it. But, in obedience to his command, we persisted in desiring earnestly this greater gift.

In these ways the individual and the church are to discover, develop, deploy, and desire the Spirit gifts God would give for the fulfilling of his purposes through the local congregation.

The indispensable Holy Spirit does other things besides giving gifts, of course. He guides, he provides material as well as human resources, he empowers. And he does all this in answer to prayer. That's how we connect with the power source. We turn now to consider that connection.

CHAPTER 11:

PRAYER CONNECTION

*Praying always with all prayer and supplication
in the Spirit, being watchful to this end with all perseverance
and supplication for all the saints.*
(EPH. 6:18 NKJV)

*While they were worshiping the Lord and fasting,
the Holy Spirit said . . . . So after they had fasted and prayed,
they placed their hands on them and sent them off.*
(ACTS 13:2–3 NIV)

Questions for reflection: Is corporate prayer pervasive in our church
(involving a majority of members, and in many formats), vital,
expectant (faith-filled), and focused on spiritual needs of the
congregation, the community, and the unreached of the world,
not just on the physical needs of the members?

The Holy Spirit is indispensable in accomplishing all of God's work, not the least his work in and through the church. The reason for this is evident. We cannot accomplish God's work without the Holy Spirit because he alone has the knowledge of all the factors involved in any situation, he alone has the wisdom to make the right decision, and he alone has the power to carry through the decision.

We are extremely limited in our knowledge, even after long study and careful investigation of all facets of any situation. We know only indistinctly the spiritual dimension, particularly what is going on inside other people involved in the issue at hand. We know only partially the historic context that led to the current circumstances, and we certainly do not know any of the future. In fact, we know only a fraction of all the infinite number of factors which bear on any decision that must be made. God the Holy Spirit alone has this knowledge, so he alone is adequate for evaluating the situation.

If we were infinite in knowledge and had access to all the information impinging on any decision, we would still lack the wisdom necessary to make the right decision. We are not only finite; our judgment is warped by sin. God the Spirit is the only one with wisdom sufficient to make the choices.

Finally, even were we to make the right choice, our power is totally inadequate to accomplish God's purposes. So God the Holy Spirit must empower us to do the work.

The good news is that all the resources necessary for fulfilling the purposes of the church have been provided in the person of the Holy Spirit, and in him alone. Indeed he is indispensable.

- The Spirit is indispensable for salvation. "Convicting" (John 16:8) and "regenerating" (John 3:3–8).
- The Spirit is indispensable for sanctification. "We are transformed . . . into the same image . . . by the Spirit of the Lord" (2 Cor. 3:18 NKJV).
- The Spirit is indispensable for renewal. "Can these bones live? . . . I will put my Spirit in you and you will live" (Ezek. 37:3, 14 NIV).
- The Spirit is indispensable for guidance. "The Spirit . . . will guide you into all truth" (John 16:13 NIV).
- The Spirit is indispensable for provision. "My God shall supply all your need" (Phil. 4:19 NKJV).
- The Spirit is indispensable for spiritual power. "The Spirit works . . . distributing to each one" (1 Cor. 12:11 NKJV).

If the Spirit's power is not freely flowing, there must be a disconnect. If salvation, sanctification, renewal, guidance, provision, and spiritual power don't seem to be flowing full force in your congregation or ministry, it could be due to the lack of prayer. The infinite knowledge, wisdom, and power of the Spirit does not flow through the people in the congregation without activity on our part. But not just any kind of prayer will do. The pray-er must be connected. All Christians, but particularly the leaders in the congregation, must have an attitude of faith and obedience. If there is an unwillingness to do the will of God or a doubting that it can be accomplished, the Spirit is not free to do what he desires.

Note, however, that it is not enough to have the right attitude; this attitude must be expressed, and the channel of expression is prayer. The prayer of faith is the connection with the Spirit that lets the wisdom and power flow. Believing prayer by believing Christians, however, is not sufficient. This conscious dependence on the Spirit in believing prayer must also be in prayer together. This is the way God's people may discern his plan (Acts 13:1–3; 16:6–10). It is the way they will be empowered (Acts 1:21; 4:23–24, 29, 31). There are special promises for the church at prayer: "Where two or three are gathered in my name" and "if two . . . agree on earth as touching any thing" (Matt. 18:18–20 KJV).

The Spirit works in response to the united prayer of faith by an obedient people.

John 13–17 is often called the Upper Room Discourse. It is the last block of teaching Jesus gave his disciples before going to the cross. The purpose of the teaching time around the table was to prepare them to live the Christian life without Christ being physically present with them. So how do we live the Christian life without Jesus being physically with us? Jesus told them that he intended to give them—and us—the gift of his presence in the person of the Holy Spirit, the Spirit who had been with them and would soon be *in* them. But he is not a silent, impersonal force within; he is as personal as was Jesus to the disciples. So we can converse with him. Prayer is the connection.

A few weeks later, Jesus left them. The disciples had experienced three years under the personal mentoring of the Son of God. They had witnessed his death and resurrection. They had received his commission four or five times, but still they weren't ready. They had the wrong goals because they misunderstood Scripture. They were trapped by traditions and misled by their own ambitions. So he told them to wait and pray. And they did—united prayer of faith by an obedient people. Then the Spirit fell (Acts 2) and Spirit power surged.

The Spirit had come, the commission had been given—Jerusalem, Judea, Samaria, the uttermost parts, every nation, every person. But they stayed in Jerusalem. True, they banded together in regular prayer (daily, we read) and crisis prayer. The Spirit filled them over and over with things like power in witness (Acts 2:41, 47; 4:4), courage (Acts 4:23–33), and provision through incredible generosity (Acts 2:45; 4:32–37). But they stayed in Jerusalem. So God created compelling circumstances, persecution. Then they began to obey the commission, but still they didn't go very far—until there was a concerted prayer time in a Gentile city (Acts 13). How do I know it was more than a thirty-minute prayer meeting? It was fasting and prayer! (13:2–3). That's when the Holy Spirit spoke in guiding them out to the Roman Empire's edge. The Spirit moves in response to the united prayer of faith by an obedient people!

Does this plan still work? The world watches in wonder as a tiny nation, South Korea, mobilizes a missionary task force of thousands to penetrate the dark places of the world. How did it happen? Historians point to a prayer meeting in 1980. The vibrant Korean church leaders called a missions convention and astonished the world with a gathering of 2.7 million believers! On the last day of the convention there was a great outpouring of life—100,000 offering themselves for short-term ministry, 10,000 collegians and 3,000 high school students offering themselves for career missionary service and—most astonishing—a million parents offering their sons and daughters for missionary service. How did it happen? The Korean church is world famous for its prayer base, but that convention surpassed even Korean-style prayer commitment. The night before that offering of life, 600,000 people spent the entire night in prayer. On the concrete. In the rain. God moves in response to the united prayer of faith by an obedient people. A decade later, more than 10,000 missionaries represented the Korean churches around the world.

When God's people pray, the Spirit gifts the church, guides the church, empowers the church, provides fully for all its needs.

Gifting

We examined the gifting activity in chapter 9, but here it is important to note that desiring the gifts that are needed to advance each purpose of the church, discerning and discovering the gift package of each member, developing the gift to its maximum potential, and deploying the gifts of all members—all take place only in the context of prayer. Believing prayer, united prayer, persistent prayer.

Guiding

The primary guidance is through the authoritative Word, and this we examined as the foundation of our study in unit 1. Note that in each of the prayer meetings reported in the early chapters of Acts, the disciples laced their prayers with Scripture. That gives authority in prayer, builds faith. Note how the united prayer meeting of the leadership at the church in Jerusalem found God's direction for the whole church in a disputed matter (Acts 15:28). "It seemed good to the Holy Spirit" it is recorded. And, yes, also "and to us." But note that the decision was based on principles they discerned in Scripture. When we align our requests with God's revealed will, our hope merges into expectancy.

But what of guidance in matters not revealed in Scripture? Though of great importance, consideration of individual guidance lies outside the scope of this study, though it does often overlap with guidance for the church.[1] One thing I might note, however, is that in guidance concerning my own ministry, I learned early in life to trust the hearing ability of the constituted authority more than my own individual perceptions of God's direction. The Holy Spirit speaks to and through his church.

Note that the New Testament churches found the Lord's direction in

---

1. For a thorough treatment of finding God's will in matters not revealed in Scripture, see chapter 11 in my *An Introduction to Biblical Ethics* (Wheaton: Tyndale House, 1995). For church guidance, the popular *Experiencing God* (Henry Blackaby, LifeWay) offers great insights. If fact, the book might well have been titled, *Finding and Following God's Will in the Church*. Some have taken the strong affirmation of divine guidance to mean our understanding of that guidance can be always infallibly understood, but Blackaby himself assures me that is not his position.

united prayer. It seems they concluded the Spirit had spoken when there was a united conviction about the course of action the church should take. Note also, however, that even for the apostles, such guidance was not infallible. In Acts 16, for example, two false starts of the Pauline missionary team are recorded. First they headed toward Ephesus only to be turned back by the Spirit. Then they turned north toward Bythinia, only to have the Spirit block the way. This kind of apostolic experience should give caution and inspire modesty on the part of church leaders today. I watched a pastor lead his church down a spiral to destruction with the constant affirmation from the pulpit that what he was proposing was directly from God. "God told me" was a constant theme. History bore out what I always suspected: whoever told him, it couldn't have been God! A highly visible church split took place over the question of infallibility in finding God's will.

The powerful "Jesus People Movement" that emerged as the Calvary Chapel movement under the leadership of Chuck Smith came to a parting of the ways with another leader, John Wimber. Wimber's disciples seemed to treat his gift of prophecy to mean that his statements of God's will were infallible, on a par with Scripture, it was alleged. This led to a parting of the ways. I mention this only to highlight one of the major difficulties in finding guidance for the church. The strong charismatic influence in which "words of prophecy" are standard procedure in the church must be balanced with the realization that such prophets can and do err. Thus the spirits are to be tested, Scripture warns. Having mentioned this caution, however, I return to our theme: the Holy Spirit does indeed guide individuals and, especially, the church. That guidance is best confirmed by the united voice of a church at prayer.

Empowering

The Spirit empowers, energizes, all ministries of the congregation, or they will make little impact of eternal value. I am so acutely aware of this that I never enter the pulpit without pleading with the Spirit to connect. Though I've been preaching for more than a half century and am rarely apprehensive about public speaking, I know full well if the Spirit does not intervene, nothing of eternal value will result. So I plead each time that he will move in with power. When the Spirit moves among numbers of his people simultaneously, we used to call it "revival."

Can you imagine the power that is unleashed when a group of Christians simultaneously yield total control to the Spirit, so much so that his work is plainly seen by everyone? What would a worship service be like with such a group? What would their prayer meetings be like? What kind of impact would they make on unbelievers and, indeed, on the whole community? Do you ever long to be part of such a Holy Spirit outpouring? You might call it "revival," to use the traditional term, or "an awakening," or more recently, "renewal."

Interestingly enough, the Bible doesn't use the term "revival." Why, then, have Christian people always talked of revival? Because the Bible repeatedly describes great movings of the Spirit, and the church has experienced such movings periodically through its history. Naturally we've called those times revival—"re" means again and "vival" means life. So we speak of a renewal of life that once was or ought to have been. With all that experience and the plain meaning of the term itself, however, revival doesn't seem to mean the same thing to everyone. Here are some of the experiences people have called revival:

- In the midst of the speaker's message students began to stand all across the college chapel and confess their sins, often with tears. The meeting went on until midnight and the movement continued on for days in the dorms and across the campus, with changed lives and spontaneous eruptions of joyful singing.

- At the revival meetings at Bent Creek Church an alcoholic, a business man and his wife, three teens, and a prostitute were saved.

- The "Evangelical Awakening," powerfully advanced by John Wesley, transformed the entire British social structure, leading directly to the abolition of slavery, for example, and revitalized the Christian community so that the modern Protestant missionary movement was launched.

- When the invitation was given, the leading deacon in the church came to the front of the church, asked for the microphone and, with tears, confessed that his opposition to the pastor had caused grief in the church. He asked the pastor's and the church's forgiveness. Then a stream of people came forward or went to others in the congregation, asking forgiveness, embracing, weeping, and laughing. Healing of old wounds began.

- Jan studied *Life in the Spirit*, sensed that something was lacking in her life, and turned her life over to the Spirit's control. There was such a surge of his life force that she found herself spiraling up toward greater likeness to Christ, began to see spiritual results from her work for God, and sensed God's loving companionship. She was puzzled that not everyone in the church seemed interested in her great discovery.

All of those examples could be called "revival," but they're so different, they may confuse instead of helping us understand the term. So let's try a few definitions I've gleaned from various sources:

1. Revival is a powerful activity of the Spirit in large numbers of people at the same time.

2. Revival is a quickening of believers to extraordinary levels of praise and prayer, of powerful witness, of loving concern for others.
3. Revival is a renewal of God's people in which lives are reclaimed and the dying embers of spiritual life are fanned back into a flame. It's a visitation of life where there had been signs of death.
4. Revival is an evangelistic campaign.
5. Revival is an outpouring of miraculous signs and extraordinary emotional upheaval.
6. Revival is a time when spiritual matters become the pressing and absorbing concern of many.
7. Revival is a time Christians are restored to their first love for Christ; when sham and hypocrisy are exposed; when bitterness and strife which exist in the body of Christ are revealed and repented of under the pressure of the Holy Spirit's convicting power; a time when such changes are effected in the lives of Christians that sinners are brought to Christ in great numbers.
8. Revival is a sovereign act of God that cannot be anticipated, let alone brought about by human effort.

Among these definitions that people have proposed, I like #7 best, though each touches on some aspect of what has been called "revival." Since the Bible doesn't use the term, but does report movements of spiritual renewal of various kinds, perhaps we are safest not to prescribe the details of what must happen to qualify as true revival. We can, however, discern some common features among these examples and definitions:

1. Revival is the work of the Holy Spirit.
2. He revitalizes or renews what already partakes of his life.
3. This renewed spiritual vitality is visible to others and leads to change in them also, seen both in a spreading renewal among believers and a turning to Christ among unbelievers.

This last characteristic would seem to rule out the idea of a "personal revival," which some use to mean a fresh encounter with God. Anyone can experience that renewal at any time he or she is prepared to acknowledge a need, yield to God's control, and trust him for revitalization. But since "revival" has normally been used of renewal among many of God's people simultaneously, it may be better to refer to personal renewal by other terms like being filled with the Spirit. But it is encouraging to know that I can experience the fullness of God's blessing whether or not others participate.

Does your church need revival? To help answer that question, here are some signs of revival:

• There is excitement in our times of worship, both for young and old.

- People often find Christ through our church, and baptisms of new believers are common.
- There is a feeling of family closeness among our people, a loving spirit of care for one another; criticism is virtually unknown.
- The people in our community who don't join us still know something is going on and have to admit we're alive; they can't spot many hypocrites, hard as they may try.
- When one member fails, the others reach out in love and restore the person; repentance, confession, reconciliation are common.
- Prayer meetings are vital, God is answering prayer for important requests like changed lives, and people often spontaneously cluster with others to pray.
- Our church has a heart to reach the whole world for Christ. Most members could be called "world Christians," and missions is strong in our prayer and giving—and in sending our sons and daughters into missionary service.

If you can't find more than two or three of those typical evidences of spiritual vitality in your church, how do you feel about it? Are you resigned to the status quo or hopeful of "showers of blessing" from the Spirit? Vern Strom was a wheat farmer in western Canada who tells of the "dirty thirties" when he planted one thousand bushels of precious seed and reaped barely one thousand bushels in return. On one thousand acres, that's a bushel an acre! Like many a church—hard, hard work for a "survival" harvest. But in 1942 the rains came and he averaged a crop of fifty-five bushels an acre! The silos and barns and garages wouldn't hold it all, so they stored it in piles outside, twelve thousand bushels to a pile. That's the kind of harvest when God sends rain. Wouldn't that be great for your church? What can you do about the drought, if that's what you're experiencing?

1. Be sure that you personally are experiencing the fullness of the Spirit as a continuing pattern of life and
2. Pray diligently for revival, recruiting others to join you in prayer. "If my people, who are called by my name, will humble themselves and pray and seek my face and turn from their wicked ways, then will I hear from heaven and will forgive their sin and will heal their land" (2 Chron. 7:14 NIV).

"We cannot legislate spiritual awakening, but we can set our sails to catch the wind," said G. Campbell Morgan. My son Bob and I were trying to cross a large lake on the boundary between the United States and Canada, but the wind kept driving us toward the shore long before we reached the end of the lake. We paddled our canoe with all the energy we could muster, like the poor remnant in a church that stays faithful and tries to move things forward. Also, like that remnant, we wore out, went with the wind, and beached our canoe. After a rest we started out again, but made little progress. Then Bob, the veteran canoer, told me to tie his poncho between two paddles, sit in the prow and hoist my "sail" to the wind, while he would relax in the stern and navigate. Amazing! We began to skim across the lake under full sail, much to the astonishment of other canoeists struggling vainly to make progress. So it is when the mighty wind of God blows through his people with renewing power.

So let us set our sails, let's covenant to pray and keep on praying until revival comes in your church; in the whole church of Christ. In the meantime, until God chooses to unleash a widespread renewal, each of us can make sure that we personally are eligible for revival and thus no barrier to what God would do. That's the first meaning of being filled with the Spirit—unconditional yieldedness to his will, making sure each day that he is the one in charge.

> O Holy Ghost, revival comes from thee
> Send a revival, start the work in me.

As the third millennium advances, I sense fresh breezes of the Spirit blowing through his church here and there, cleansing and empowering. I've seen it in pastors and lay leaders, weeping and confessing to the Spirit their sin of neglecting him. I see it in the vast prayer movement circling the earth, far wider—if not deeper—than anything known in the history of the church. And certainly the advance of the gospel is at flood tide—new believers coming to Christ in Asia, Africa, and Latin America on a scale the church has never seen. The wind of God is blowing. Hoist your sail and catch the wind!

Providing

Many churches operate their finances like corporations. So if they have good management and effective fund-raising consultants, they can get what those can produce. It's almost like they had never heard that "my God shall supply all your need according to His riches in glory" (Phil. 4:19 NKJV). It's not just the church that suffers impoverishment, but such earthbound methodologies do not disciple the members in the method of prayer and faith for their personal lives.

Columbia International University has said from its inception that its method was prayer and faith. Or, better put, perhaps, the prayer of faith. Part of this approach, and by no means a biblically mandated approach, has been to make the needs known to interested parties, but not to personally solicit gifts. A large portion of staff salaries must be provided through gift income. If it doesn't come in, salaries are cut by that much. Sometimes there has been a shortfall for several months consecutively, but when the funds come in, back salaries are paid up. For almost a century God has provided so that no deficit has ever gone unmet. It's true, God works in response to the united prayer of faith by an obedient people! Furthermore, the history of the school is replete with the lore of building projects where payments often were met at the last day or even the last hour as the funds were "prayed in." Imagine the impact on generation after generation of students, educated in an environment where God actually keeps his promise and supplies all needs!

The Holy Spirit, then, is pledged to meet all the needs of the church or ministry: gifting, guiding, empowering, providing. Our responsibility is to connect through prayer.

Conclusion to Unit 3

Unit 3 has focused on the ministry of the indispensable Holy Spirit in the local congregation. Just as unit 1 on the functional authority of Scripture must control all subsequent units of study, so unit 3 on the Spirit must infuse the last two units of study in this integration of theology and ministry. This is especially true of unit 4, The Plan of Redemption, as the calling of every believer, to which we now turn.

Unit 4:

THE PLAN
OF REDEMPTION

THE MISSION OF EVERY DISCIPLE

You will receive power when the Holy Spirit comes on you;
and you will be my witnesses in Jerusalem,
and in all Judea and Samaria, and to the ends of the earth.
(ACTS 1:8 NIV)

From Genesis 3 through Revelation 22, the overarching theme of Scripture is redemption. And the astonishing thing, after we recover from the shock of this unveiling of God's character and his own incredible actions in providing that redemption, is his plan for distributing that redemption. He has chosen from the beginning to mediate that redemption through humans. So much so that he chose to become human himself to provide the redemption. And then he created the most resilient and powerful human organization—the church—to partner with him in distributing that redemption.

Thus God's daring and incredible plan is to do his work in this world through mere mortals. Fallen, broken mortals are declared partners with the Creator. And when he transforms our finitude by the infinities of his own presence and power, what glory shines on him!

You may have noted that we considered at some length in unit 3 all the purposes of the church but one. At the time we said we would revisit the evangelistic purpose of the church in greater depth in unit 4. So now we fulfill that promise. I wanted to make sure the evangelistic purpose of the church and calling of the believer is set in the context of all the purposes and all the gifts. We have considered in some detail all the other ministry callings and enablings of each believer and left this particular believer-assignment until now so we could devote adequate attention to the paramount purpose of the church, this universal calling for every believer.

Is it too much to say the evangelistic purpose of the church is paramount? I trust in the chapters that follow we may discover this to be an accurate biblical assessment of priority. In summary, we hold that position because redemption is the theme of Scripture and the meaning of Christ's incarnation. God loved the world so much that he gave his only Son, and then his strategy was to commission all his other sons and daughters to complete the task he began at Calvary. All the other purposes of the church will be accomplished so much better in heaven, but this one can be accomplished only on earth! Thus I conclude this must be the paramount purpose of the church-on-earth. But even for those who cannot accept such an evaluation, surely it must be one of the chief purposes of the church. It is very sad that few congregations treat it that way.

In unit 4, then, we examine not the theology of provision but the theology of distribution: God's redemptive mission committed to his church and to every person who has received redemption. First, we'll follow the teaching of unit 1 and examine the biblical foundations for a "theology of mission," then we'll check out the dominant contemporary paradigms for doing mission, examining their biblical foundations or lack of them. Finally, in chapters 15 and 16 we'll look at two major elements in the grand mission of the church—prayer and financial support. The purpose of this unit is to establish the theology of mission and then to give a grid for evaluating the participation of each congregation and each believer.

CHAPTER 12:

Biblical Foundations of Mission

The students at a leading seminary wanted to examine the question of the biblical role of world evangelism in the life of a Christian and in the life of a church. Being seminarians, they staged a debate. They invited the most influential man in world missions at that time, Donald McGavran. I once heard McGavran say, "Missions is a most important purpose of the church." After the meeting I approached him, "Dr. McGavran, the last time I heard you speak you said it was the most important task of the church. Which is it, 'a' or 'the'?"

"Well," said the old gentleman, "if it's 'the' purpose, that includes 'a,' and some audiences are not ready to call it the purpose of the church." He obviously ranked world evangelism near the top of his agenda of what the church is about.

On the other side of the debate was a leading evangelical theologian. Before the debate began, the theologian said, "Dr. McGavran, before we begin I just want you to know that I believe in missions. It's even in my theological system. It's point number D-12 in my theology." That's not bad, since most theologians don't include it at all. They leave missions to the church history or Christian education departments! That set the stage, for missions was clearly A-1 in McGavran's theology. After the debate the theologian said, "Dr. McGavran, you're very persuasive and I admire you and your work. But I want you to know that missions is still point number D-12 in my theological system."

Where would you cast your ballot in that debate? For 90 to 95 percent of evangelical churches in America, world missions is point D-12 in the church program or off their agenda altogether. What about the handful that are gung ho for world evangelism? Are "mission maniacs," as the vocal minority in some congregations are called, misguided, or are they merely obedient to the Lord of the church?

Seeing Things God's Way

More important than where you or I stand in that debate on the importance of world evangelism is to discover where God stands! As an initial clue, notice that when the Holy Spirit was given, nothing is said of all the glorious truths about his gifting for ministry or his sanctifying power. The Spirit's coming focuses on something outside ourselves; you will be witnesses!

I believe God went to considerable effort to reveal exactly the way he thinks. If we'll look even casually at that self-revelation, the Bible, we'll discover that world evangelism is indeed central in God's thinking. When we do, I think we'll find that:

- God's character makes world evangelism inevitable,
- God's activity proves what his heart is like,
- God's promises assure a successful conclusion to his plan, and
- God's command means we must think the way he thinks, act the way he acts.

In this chapter, we want to get the big picture, reviewing Scripture from beginning to end to see the world the way God sees it; we want to discover a biblical theology of mission.

But first, let's pause and establish a working definition of what we mean by "evangelism." The nature of evangelism is the communication of the Good News in such a way that people have a valid opportunity to accept Jesus Christ as Lord and Savior. The goal of evangelism is the persuading of men and women to accept Jesus Christ as Lord and Savior and to serve him in the fellowship of his church. Extending such a definition to the world as a whole, the task of world evangelism might then be considered accomplished when every person on earth has heard with understanding the gospel, and a congregation of his disciples has been established in every community. With such working definitions in mind, consider an outline of the Bible basis for making this our goal.

God's Character

What characteristic of God do you like best? Perhaps you agree with John who said there is a certain characteristic of God so central to his nature you could even say he is that. John wanted us to be sure to get the point so he repeated himself a few verses later: "God is love," he insisted (1 John 4:8, 16). God didn't create love to give his creatures a target at which to aim. He's that way himself by nature, the blessed tri-unity, bound together in living bonds of love. Then, from the overflow of his loving nature, God desired a being to love him back. As a result, the Spirit created humans on the pattern of God,

God-compatible, if you please, so that he could love them and be loved of them—the goal of creation.

It was a risky proposition. If he created such a being, that person might not love him back, might choose to walk away from a loving relationship, might even defy that love. Which is just what our first parents did; as did every son and daughter of Adam since. But that didn't change God's character. He continued to love the world so much that he gave his own Son to buy us back for that love relationship (John 3:16). That's the express purpose for his invasion of our humanity—to seek and to save the lost (Matt. 18:11).

If love was the reason for Jesus' first coming, love is also the reason he hasn't come again! People keep resisting God's loving advances to them, keep perishing, and it breaks his heart. The brokenhearted God delays his coming for one reason, Peter tells us—because he doesn't want anyone to perish (2 Pet. 3:9). Consider the tension in the loving heart of God: longing to return to embrace his bride, the church, and set all the wrongs right in this old sin-cursed world, but, at the same time, distressed over the fact that so many people are still lost.

How many? Just to say a number doesn't reach our hearts since we don't have the capacity to love each one as God does. But he does love them, even the nine out of ten who don't know him. Although almost two billion people are called Christians, the vast majority of those are Christian in name only. For example, Europe could be counted almost wholly Christian because people are born into state or dominant churches, but in many of those nations no more than 2 percent even attend church. Ever. The most generous estimates are that active, Bible-believing Christians in the world number no more than six hundred million. If that estimate by the statisticians of "born-again" believers is anywhere near accurate, it means that more than five billion people today are lost.[1] It's difficult to grasp such numbers and even harder to love those faceless multitudes. But God does love each one; they aren't faceless to him.

It's not merely that so many are out of Christ, however. It's worse than that. At least two-thirds of those lost people have yet to hear with understanding the Good News and half of those are out of reach of any witnessing church. And it breaks God's heart. Because God is love, world evangelism is central in his thinking. So the question for every believer must be, Is world evangelism central in my thinking? What would the people who know me best say is the big thing in my life, the A-1 subject? If what is central in God's thinking turns out to be peripheral in mine, perhaps I have heart trouble. But God doesn't. God is love; so much so that he gave his one and only Son that none might perish.

---

1. Martin Robinson and Dwight Smith, *Invading Secular Space: Strategies for Tomorrow's Church* (Grand Rapids: Kregel, 2003), 148.

God's Activity

Someone said, "Every major act of God since the fall is a missionary act." That's quite a statement. I wonder if it's so. Let's look at some of those major acts.

Abraham wasn't called by God to shower all his loving attention on his descendants and let the rest of the world go to hell. God favored Abraham in order to bless the whole world though him (Gen. 12:1–2). God needed a people isolated from the moral pollution of the nations so they could receive a revelation of himself without distortion and be his messengers of God's saving truth.

The Exodus seems like it was just for Israel. It meant the destruction of Egypt's military power and the subjugation of the people of Palestine. But there was a larger purpose. God was reestablishing his missionary task force which had been in danger of extinction in Egypt.

But God's missionary task force itself became corrupt, running after other loves, other gods. The loving heart of God pursued them, called out to them through prophet after prophet. The prophets visualized God's heart as the rejected parent, the abandoned lover. So God disciplined them, sending them into captivity in order to purify them. It worked! Never again has Israel been idolatrous. God was creating the spiritual and social context into which he could himself come and find a foothold.

So the next major event was the greatest missionary act in all history—the incarnation, when God's only Son left his homeland to become one of us in order to save us (Matt. 18:11; John 1:14).

Then he sent the Spirit at Pentecost for the express purpose of establishing a new method to carry out his saving purpose for the whole world: the New Testament church (Matt. 16:18; Acts 1:8).

Such is God's activity. God's actions prove what his missionary heart is like. Perhaps our actions prove what our hearts are really like, too—what we talk about, what we do with our money, how we involve ourselves in the church's missionary enterprise. Heart monitors.

God's Promises

God's promises from Genesis to Revelation assure a successful conclusion to his plan of world evangelization. "I will make you into a great nation and I will bless you; I will make your name great, and you will be a blessing . . . and all peoples on earth will be blessed through you" (Gen. 12:2–3 NIV). That's the reason God blessed Abraham—to make him a conduit of God's blessings to the nations. And why does He prosper us? "May God be gracious to us and bless us and make his face shine upon us, that your ways may be known on earth, your salvation among all nations . . . God will bless us, and all the ends of the earth will fear him" (Ps. 67:1–2, 7 NIV).

Remarkable! Abraham's blessings and ours are for the same purpose: that God's salvation may reach all people. And it will happen. God promises both Abraham and us. Yet, in spite of this revelation of God's redemptive purposes, Jews, including Jesus' own disciples, expected Messiah to deliver them from Roman bondage and set up a Jewish state. In these two ancient promises of a coming Messiah note how mistaken they were. The Father promises the Son: "Ask of me, and I will make the nations your inheritance, the ends of the earth your possession" (Ps. 2:8 NIV). The Father promises the Son: "It is too small a thing for you to be my servant to restore the tribes of Jacob . . . I will also make you a light for the Gentiles, that you may bring my salvation to the ends of the earth" (Isa. 49:6 NIV).

Repeatedly the Old Testament prophesies the coming of Messiah, but he was not just for Israel. He was coming for all peoples. That's Old Testament. What does the New Testament predict about Christ's second coming? Jesus himself said: "And this gospel of the kingdom will be preached in the whole world as a testimony to all nations, and then the end will come" (Matt. 24:14 NIV). John draws the curtain on the final act of earth's drama: "After this I looked and there before me was a great multitude that no one could count, from every nation, tribe, people and language, standing before the throne and in front of the Lamb" (Rev. 7:9 NIV).

From Genesis to Revelation, the Bible is full of promises about God's plan of gathering his people from among all peoples. The Spirit has a global plan, and he is bringing it to pass in our day as never before. In fact, more people were born into God's family in the last quarter of the twentieth century than in all the centuries of church history combined until 1975!

God's promises assure that his salvation purpose will be accomplished. Surely this major theme of Bible promises demands that in my prayer life I reach beyond those glorious promises of personal peace, protection, and provision, constantly reaching out to embrace in prayer the world God loves.

Christ's Command

We often call Christ's command to preach the gospel throughout the world the "Great Commission." On how many different occasions after the Resurrection do you think Christ gave what might be called a "Great Commission"? I've put that question to dozens of pastors and church leaders in workshops designed to help churches evaluate their Great Commission involvement. Astonishingly, I've never yet received a correct answer!

1. On the night of the Resurrection, Christ appeared among the disciples in the upper room and said, "As the Father has sent me, I am sending

you" (John 20:21 NIV). With that same heart of love the Father had in sending me, Jesus said, "I'm sending you and with that same heart of love I want you to go."

2. Next we meet them up north in Galilee where he announced, "All authority is given me in heaven and earth, go therefore and disciple the nations" (Matt. 28:18–19).

3. Then we find them back in Jerusalem, again in the upper room where he explains to them about His intention of world evangelism, showing them from the Old Testament how "repentance and forgiveness of sins will be preached in his name to all nations, beginning at Jerusalem. You are witnesses of these things" (Luke 24:47–48 NIV).

4. From there, he led them out toward Mount Olivet where he was to be separated from them; they were still thinking about Kingdom restoration. He told them that wasn't their concern and they weren't ready for what was to be their concern, so they should wait in Jerusalem until the Holy Spirit would come on them. When that happened, he said, "You will receive power . . . and you will be my witnesses in Jerusalem, and in all Judea and Samaria, and to the ends of the earth" (Acts 1:8 NIV).

5. The most famous Great Commission of all is found in Mark 16:15, but the writer doesn't give enough context to know if it was on one of the other four occasions or on yet a fifth: "Go into all the world and preach the gospel to every creature" (NKJV). Four or five times he gave the command!

For a few weeks following his resurrection, Christ appeared among the disciples many times and talked of many things, but there was one theme he returned to on virtually every occasion: what he wanted them to do. We call it the Great Commission. Apparently this was the big thing in Jesus' mind. No wonder. God's character of love demands that world evangelism be central in his thinking, his activity demonstrates what his heart is like, and his promises assure us that it's going to happen. So naturally his commands require that we think the way he thinks and behave the way he behaves—Go! Go! Go! That's the mandate of the church.

So if evangelism and missions is point number D-12 in a believer's life—prayers mostly self-serving, talk mostly about earthly things, marginal personal involvement in missions, finances focused on living well in time rather than investing for eternity—perhaps they are not seeing things God's way. We turn now to the practical implications of this biblical foundation for world evangelism.

CHAPTER 13:

TWO LOCATIONS, TWO VOCATIONS

You will receive power when the Holy Spirit comes on you;
and you will be my witnesses in Jerusalem,
and in all Judea and Samaria, and to the ends of the earth.
(ACTS 1:8 NIV)

Questions for reflection:
1. Does our church make a clear distinction
between witnessing and evangelizing?
2. Does the leadership constantly articulate the goal for all members
to be faithful witnesses (as distinct from evangelism) in life and talk?
Are teaching and training provided to guide and empower
for effective witness? Is evidence of effectiveness in this approach
seen in consistent "body-life reproduction"?
3. Are leaders constantly on the lookout for those who might be
evangelistically gifted, who could provide training
and encouragement to make them more effective?
4. Is the church body as a whole knowledgeable and concerned
about the unreached of the world and is there a steady stream
of career missionaries moving out from the congregation?

Consider the geography of Acts 1:8, our theme verse for this unit. Note there are two locations: near and far, "across the street and across the seas," so to speak. Near (Jerusalem and Judea)—where they lived—and far (Samaria and the uttermost parts of the earth, where they were sent). More importantly, perhaps, note that for the two locations two different vocations are needed to fulfill Christ's commission—two locations, two vocations.

The first vocation is, "You will be my witnesses." They are the ones who lived with Jesus for three years, who saw him die and live again. Was the commission limited to them? They at least didn't think so, as the book of Acts demonstrates. It was for the church and for every member. But what is a witness? One who has first-hand experience and is willing to tell about it. First-hand experience. Remember, the courts rule out hearsay; you have to have a personal experience of the facts you witness to. But someone who has experienced some reality and won't talk about it is no witness either. So everyone who has a genuine, firsthand experience of the risen Jesus Christ is commissioned to talk about it. A faithful witness. It's her calling, his vocation.

Notice another thing about witnessing: it's show and tell. Some say they will just live the life, let their actions witness to the reality of life in Christ. But what is a non-talking witness? No witness at all. Suppose you're fifty pounds overweight and you discover a miracle pound reducer. One day you show up at your office or shop as slim as all your colleagues want to be. "How did you do it?" they ask. But all you do is smile and say, "Oh, I'm nothing special." You don't explain the secret and they're left out. The person who has truly experienced life transformation in Christ must talk about him or she's no witness.

The only worse thing than a non-talking Christ experiencer is a purported witness who yammers on about the wonders of Christianity and church but doesn't experience life in Christ. So show without tell is bad news, not good news. Actually, no news much at all. But to tell without showing is very bad news—a false witness, in fact. We call people like this "hypocrites."

So the calling of every member of your congregation is to be a witness, show *and* tell—across the street. That's their "Jerusalem," where they live. And Judea? Well, the surrounding area, perhaps the "same kind of people" in a larger geographical circle of nearby responsibility. And it's for every believer—no special gift is needed. Just be a faithful witness in behavior and talk. Of course, Holy Spirit empowerment is needed. So Jesus told them, "Stay put and stay quiet until the Spirit comes." Therefore, note that the first disciples waited in prayer. United prayer, at that. But no special gifting or specific assignment from God is needed to be a faithful witness across the street. It is the calling of every believer.

What about "across the seas," however? In our Acts 1:8 analogy, what is your Samaria? If the witness crosses cultural barriers into another ethnic group, we might call that our church's "Samaria." Samaritans lived near those early Christians but they were a different kind of people, a despised people, actually. The "Samaritans" or ethnically or culturally different people near us, if they don't already have the gospel, also are our responsibility. Few congregations survive when their neighborhood changes ethnically. Sad. That's their God-given "Samaria"!

I'm not too sure of the analogy for "Samaria," but the "uttermost parts"—that's clear enough. We're in the habit of calling it the 10/40 window, perhaps, but what we're really talking about is the spiritually dark one-third of the world, those peoples or tribes or cultural enclaves that live beyond the reach of present gospel witness. There's no witnessing church among them. How are they to be reached? Someone where the church is must be sent to where the church isn't or we will never fulfill Christ's mandate, the uttermost parts. And what is needed for that role? Are the necessary ingredients for the extension of the church into new territories the same as for local witness, just Spirit-empowered faithfulness? Or for uttermost-parts witnessing, is a special gifting necessary? Our text doesn't tell us, but the rest of the New Testament does.

What vocation is needed to do that job? Well, perhaps there's a clue in the definition of the task: someone must be sent. In Greek, the one who is sent is called an apostle (*apostolos*), a sent one. Who in the New Testament has that title, that vocation?[1] Several different kinds of people, actually. A simple messenger could bear that title. At the other end of the scale, Jesus himself is called "apostle," *the* apostle, the one sent from his homeland on the greatest missionary journey of all. And then there are the original leaders of the church with a commission to go implied by their title, the twelve apostles.[2] Most of them, however, didn't live up to the "sent one" part of the title, at least for a long time.

Then there were the pioneer missionary church planters, like Barnabas and Timothy—sent by the church to evangelize away from home and called by the name of their vocation, "apostle."[3] The *Didache of the Apostles,* the first post-apostolic document still extant, speaks of multitudes of apostles fanning out across the lands. So there is the apostolic calling or gift as distinct from the office held by the Twelve. In fact, in the list of Holy Spirit-given enablements in 1 Corinthians 12, the gift—or supernatural ability—to evangelize and start churches where there were none is called #1: First apostles, says Paul (1 Cor. 12:28).[4]

Unlike the command to witness, however, the apostolic commission does require a special gifting of the Spirit. We call it the gift of evangelism.

The Gift of Evangelism

To help identify the gift, consider which of the following have the gift of evangelism and which are just faithful witnesses:

- Billy Graham has preached to more people and won more to faith than anyone in history.

---

1. See John 13:16; 2 Corinthians 8:23; Philippians 2:25; Hebrews 3:1.
2. This is the most common use. See the first occurrence in Matthew 10:2.
3. See Acts 14:14.
4. The meaning of "apostle" seems to fit a list of gifts rather than "Apostle" with a capital "A" referring to the office, filled by one of the twelve designated players.

- Dennis shares his faith on the job so that everyone knows he's a Christian but none of them have come to Christ yet.
- Denise invites her friends to her home for coffee and talk, which she tries to turn to spiritual things. On special occasions the pastor's wife comes and shares the gospel. Several people have come to Christ.
- Jeb likes to wander around the local college campus looking for lonely students who want to talk. Several have prayed with him to receive Christ.
- Jill is on a team that calls on visitors who attend her church. Unlike some of the other teams, Jill sees someone trust Christ almost every week.

If the Spirit has given a person the gift of evangelism, we would expect to see results, right? So it would seem clear that Billy and Jill have the Spirit-given ability to win people to faith. Jeb and the pastor's wife probably do, too; but what of Dennis and Denise? If the gift of evangelism means the ability to consistently "close the deal," often leading people to acknowledge Christ as Lord and Savior, they don't seem to have the gift. They are faithful witnesses and God uses them as vital interdependent parts of an evangelistic team, the church; but they could hardly be said to have demonstrated an ability to consistently win people to faith in Christ. So there is a difference between the assignment to witness and the assignment to win people to faith and establish Christ's church in places it does not exist, "the uttermost parts."

There you have it—two locations, two vocations. Here and there, witnesses and apostles. Stay here and witness, go there and plant churches. Every believer called to witness, some called to evangelize beyond the borders of their own place and culture. Everyone called to share their faith, speak to others of spiritual things, as opportunity affords. As a way of life, in fact. Then there are those who seem gifted to "close" as business people put it, to bring people to a decision to accept Christ. We call it the gift of evangelism. Those who study such things tell us a healthy church in North America could expect about 10 percent of the members to be so gifted.

So what should the church do about it? Train everyone in evangelism, when Scripture says expressly that the Spirit gifts only some for that? "Some evangelists," it says. "Are all apostles?" Paul asks. Churches that try to make evangelists out of every member run the risk of so frustrating the 90 percent ungifted that they don't even become good witnesses, let alone effective evangelists. How about training all to be effective witnesses and count on "body-life reproduction" to bring people "across the street" into the fellowship of the family? And train those who are or have the potential of becoming gifted in evangelism to be more effective in that calling. Then, from among that gifted cohort, the Holy Spirit will guide the church in discovering and sending out the Barnabases and Pauls to pioneer the "uttermost parts," like the church at Antioch did.

But the need is so great, the gifted who hear the call so few, that we find ourselves woefully short of Christians who have responded to an apostolic calling. For example, how many sons and daughters of your local congregation are serving in the apostolic vocation? Of the more than one million full-time Christian workers in America, we send less than fifty thousand into cross-cultural missionary work. And only a fraction of those are apostolic, evangelizing and starting churches among the unevangelized. If God intends for us to send more in obedience to Christ's last command, what to do about the shortage of those who hear the call and obey it? How about desiring earnestly this particular greater gift (1 Cor. 12:31) as we considered in chapter 10? The "desiring" seems in 1 Corinthians 12–14 to be an individual thing, but it's in the context of church.

So the church as a whole is called to desire earnestly this gifting for some of its members. In Jerusalem they were to wait in prayer until the power fell. In Antioch they were in prayer together when the Spirit spoke and they sent out the first "uttermost parts" apostolic missionaries. So whether local witness or distant evangelism, it's a church thing. How much "desiring" and "asking" for apostolic ministry takes place in your life and the life of your church?

Witness or Evangelist?

Every Spirit-filled Christian will be a faithful witness. Not every Spirit-filled Christian, however, is a gifted evangelist (1 Cor. 12:29). When I agonized over not having the gift of evangelism, my definition of "evangelism" was too limited, as we have seen. Perhaps God heard my prayer, was giving me the gift, and I just wasn't smart enough to recognize it. When we got to Japan we found we could live in a community and love people in Jesus' name and many would come to faith. In a land where the average church has twenty-five members, even after decades of existence, we were baptizing twenty new converts a year. God had answered my prayer for the gift! Or had he? I rarely prayed with someone to receive Christ and we never gave a public invitation. Then how did they come?

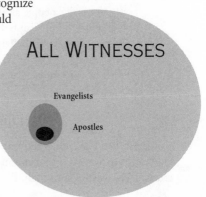

ALL WITNESSES

Evangelists

Apostles

Body-Life Reproduction: How the Church Brings to Birth

In Japan we discovered that the church as a body can bring to birth in God's family. If many members are living authentic Spirit-filled lives and are talking about that life, and if some are gifted at "closing the deal," people will come to faith. This body-life reproduction is the key to the explosive growth of the churches in China, for example, a growth unique in church history. It is clearly the secret to that same kind of growth around the world in the phenomenon of church-multiplying movements—every member "gossiping the gospel" and some gifted in drawing the net.

Those who study this sort of thing say that in the typical American community, a church should be growing at 5 percent a year. Not through baptizing its own children, important as that is; and not through transfer growth, baptized believers coming from other churches, as exciting as that may be. But 5 percent "conversion growth," baptizing people who come to faith. If a church is not baptizing new believers, something is wrong. Here are some possible reasons:

1. The church may be spiritually ill, incapable of reproducing, in need of revival (as we saw in chap. 11).
   - Members are not modeling an authentic Christian lifestyle that's attractive to unbelievers.
   - The passion for lost people has died out.
   - United prayer for the lost is weak.
2. Not many members may be "gossiping the gospel." Too few are faithful witnesses.
3. Too few members have the gift of evangelism.
4. In a few cases, the people to be evangelized may be especially unresponsive. For example, a missionary to Muslims in New York City would not likely get rapid growth. The problem with acknowledging this reason for non-growth, however, is that often we use unresponsive people as an excuse. Wherever I am, if people are not being saved, I'm tempted to proclaim it to be "hard soil." Assuming that we aren't rationalizing, unusual hardness in a given community can be a cause of little fruit.

How is it at your church? Are you pleased at the "birth rate"? Do you think God is pleased?

The Ends of the Earth

Every local church is responsible not only for its own community; it is God's will for every congregation also to participate fully in reaching "the ends of the earth," especially the spiritually dark one-third of the world where one out of three people on planet earth live out of reach of gospel witness. But not all churches take that responsibility seriously. In fact, very few do.

Tale of Two Churches

During the same month I spoke in two church missions conferences in the same state. There were many similarities. They were both noted widely for their missions interest; in fact, one was the anchor church for the eastern end of the state, the other for the west. Both were large, vibrant, growing churches. Both had very large budgets for missions, perhaps half their total giving. "East" supported 180 missionaries, but they had 1,800 members; "West" was half the size but supported, partially at least, about 75. There the similarities ended. "East" was only thirty years old, but those 180 missionaries were all their own sons and daughters! "West" was 150 years old, but only one of their own had ever gone to the mission field. And she was now retired and present in the conference. "West" paid for others' sons and daughters to go.

How is it at your church? Are you nearer "East" or "West" in recruiting and sending from among your own? "But the need at home is so great," we hear. True, and it's also true that our first responsibility is for those nearby. So it's not either/or, but both/and. That's why Jesus' command was Jerusalem and Judea, yes, but also Samaria and the ends of the earth. To get a feel for the relative needs of our world, consider my home—Columbia, South Carolina—and Calcutta where my son labored for ten years among the poor.

In America, one out of five people you do business with or meet at PTA will be a Bible-believing Christian; in Calcutta, one out of ten thousand. And how many Bibles are in Columbia, South Carolina? A million? Calcutta may have a few hundred and for many of the languages in that great city, none at all. In a population of three hundred thousand we have at least six hundred churches. In that city, among the five million slum dwellers, there are perhaps five small fellowships. We have three or four Christian radio stations, they, none; we have at least fifteen Christian bookstores, they none. No wonder we have perhaps a hundred thousand evangelical believers and they about one thousand.

I use Calcutta merely as an example of the spiritually dark places of the world where few people even have access to the gospel. If someone doesn't go in from the outside—if an apostolic missionary doesn't come—they cannot even hear the gospel. Yes, our first responsibility is for "Jerusalem," but God loves the world. Shouldn't we? And if our church is falling short in the "sending" responsibility, what should we do about it?

God's Scout

A large church contributed financial support toward seventy-five missionaries, including us. In fact, it was at that time the second largest missions donor church of any denomination in the nation. One day I walked down the long hallway in which the photographs of the missionaries were displayed, studying the biographies of each. To my astonishment, not one of their missionaries was from that church! They gave lots of money to support other people's sons and daughters. A young businessman moved to the city, joined the church, and noticed the same phenomenon. He decided to do something about it. Calling himself "God's scout," Frank volunteered to teach the college-and-career Sunday school class. Within five years eleven members of that church were on the mission field—all from that class! God hadn't called him to go as a missionary, but Frank participated in God's sending activity.

Perhaps God wants you to be his scout. If he did, how might you go about it? Think of the possibilities. Better yet, pray about them! Is there a boy or girl or young adult about whom you think, *That young person would make a great missionary, so spiritually alive, gifted and active in service to God?* If so, perhaps God would use you to help them find God's path. Here are some possible approaches:
- Pray for that person, especially that he will hear if God is calling.
- Talk with him about his future, his ambitions.
- Seek for an opportunity to suggest the possibility of full-time ministry, even of missionary vocation.
- Find a task in the church for him in which his gifts will be challenged, developed, and used.
- Encourage him often.
- Like Frank, teach a class in which you seek to inspire members with a clear, strong vision of God's purposes in the world and their responsibility to participate with him in achieving that purpose. Be God's scout!

"Here Am I, Send Me"

In the past, only young people who had not yet launched into some other vocation were considered potential candidates for missionary service. But no longer. Many missionaries today have joined the task force in midlife, leaving other vocations. Most Americans change careers several times anyway! Perhaps God would give you the high privilege of being his ambassador to a people who have had no chance to hear the gospel.

When I was eighteen, I began to ask God for the gift of apostleship. I wanted my life to count to the maximum for what God was up to in the world. Gradually I found the same ambition Paul spoke of burning in my spirit—to proclaim Christ where he had never been named (Rom. 15:20). I had been in education for several years, but still the ambition burned to go. Yet there were many obstacles. I didn't think I had the gift of evangelism, I had an illness which the doctors said was incurable, others didn't think we should go because "God is blessing you where you are" (a strange logic! Only those whom God is not using should go?), we had four children (several mission boards didn't like that!), and finally, after we boarded ship for Japan, my daughter was injured and we had to disembark. But we kept on obeying the command to "desire earnestly," we kept asking God to send us and use us. I'm so glad we did, for there is surely no joy quite like living among a people who have never heard the Good News and watching the Holy Spirit work in giving hope to the hopeless, healing broken lives, and forming a church where there was no witness before.

Perhaps God would give you that high privilege. At any rate, isn't the possibility worthy of a moment's reflection? If the passion burns, at least he might want to use you as a sender. Why not talk to him about it?

Two locations, two vocations. Everyone commissioned to give faithful witness by life and word, some commissioned to leave home and go to evangelize among those now out of reach of gospel witness. I perceive that to be the biblical paradigm for fulfilling the evangelistic purpose of the church, both near and far.

But there are other paradigms now prevailing in the American church. We turn now to those.

CHAPTER 14:

NEW PARADIGMS
OF MISSION

Questions for reflection:
1. Is short-term ministry carefully planned and
deliberately harnessed to maximize kingdom effectiveness?
2. Are there effective policies in place to make sure money sent overseas
is not causing collateral damage either for donors or recipients?
3. Is there any loss in the consciousness of leaders or congregation
that those who have not heard the gospel are lost?

Two new ways of approaching the "far" evangelistic mission of the church have become dominant in recent decades. They have become so pervasive among American churches that I have no illusions of changing them significantly. But since both seem to violate some of the biblical paradigm we have just suggested, I feel compelled to highlight some of the hazards as I see them. I will attempt to apply the principles studied in unit 1, bringing all aspects of ministry under the functional authority of Scripture. I do this in the hope that a rising generation may make enough course correction in these approaches to capture them for a new era of biblical mission advance in finishing the task Christ gave his church.

I was invited to address a large group of pastors from the Calvary Chapel network. The "father" of the Jesus People movement, Chuck Smith, is also the founder of the Calvary Chapel movement which at the time of my first visit numbered about a million strong across the nation. I was invited to talk to the pastors about missions. On the way from the airport to the conference center I asked about the movement's missions involvement. "Very strong," I was told. "We send tens of thousands of missionaries." That puzzled me, for the entire Protestant church of the United States sends fewer than fifty thousand of what I call "missionary." A week later I had begun to wonder about the significance of that conversation so, on the way back to the airport, I asked a more discriminating question, "How many career missionaries have Calvary Chapels sent?"

"We don't do numbers, of course, but I would estimate about two hundred." What I didn't know was that my speaking had been something of a setup. Some of the younger men wanted to introduce the novel idea of sending career missionaries. Calvary was the first major wave of the tsunami that has swept missions-interested churches in America: send all the people you can on short-term ministry. But as far as career missionaries are concerned, at two hundred, I figured they were sending about two-thousandth of 1 percent of their membership into career missionary service. The reason I was so startled was that up until then I had been preaching in churches that were sending 2 percent, 10 percent, up to 20 percent of their membership into apostolic missionary service!

Another thing I learned that week: they also spearheaded the other phenomenon in late-twentieth century North American missions: support the nationals. At the time they were supporting three thousand pastors in India, for example. I have returned for a number of their pastors' conferences by which some of the leaders hoped to move toward a more Pauline-type ministry, intentional targeting of the "spiritually dark one-third of the world," seeking to reach those who live out of reach of both national pastors and short-term witnesses. Many Calvary chapels have begun to send long-term missionaries to reach the yet out-of-reach peoples of the world.

In 2005, about thirty-five years after Calvary began this two-pronged approach to doing mission, Rick Warren launched what he believes will be a worldwide "new" paradigm for missions: short-term missions by all who will go, and doing it in a church-to-church (American congregation linked directly to an overseas congregation) relationship. The big difference is that while Calvary Chapel targeted only Calvary chapels churches, Rick Warren hopes to transform the entire evangelical world.

So if this is the new way to do missions, how do we capture the phenomena, or at least channel them into maximum impact for God's missionary purposes? In other words, how do we make sure mission is done under the functional authority of Scripture? Consider, then, the short-term missionary phenomenon and the "don't-send-people-send money" or "let-the-nationals-do-it" phenomenon.

Short-Term Missionaries

Everyone is called to go to "the uttermost parts of the earth," we're told. Don't worry about formal preparation. What Christ called for was witnesses, and everyone is called to that role. Actually, some would say, to prepare or train a witness undermines his authenticity, so don't pause for any kind of formal training. And don't worry about long-term commitment. Just go! If everyone goes—even for a few weeks—we'll get the job done quickly.

The new paradigm is so appealing not only because of the exciting potential, but because it fits beautifully the contemporary mind-set of the postmodern.

- Personal involvement creates ownership of the effort.
- You don't do it alone. You go with your friends and we all know relationships are the most important.
- Besides, there are no demands for long-term commitment since life is so iffy anyway.
- It's very democratic. No one is better than anyone else. Very egalitarian, with no super-saints or old-fashioned missionary-on-a-pedestal.

But there are some problems with the new paradigm. Biblical problems for starters. The Commander-in-Chief has not only designated all his troops as witnesses to the resurrected Christ; he's commissioned his church to disciple the nations. "Teaching them to observe all that I commanded," he proclaimed as the job description. Discipling takes more than a few weeks witness through an interpreter. Besides, we can't escape the model: "As the Father sent me." Jesus Christ did not come in a celestial bubble with all the accoutrements of heaven clustered about him, float over the earth for a few weeks talking Good News in Celestialese to be translated by a local, and then waft his way back home to heaven. He became one with us, lived among us, absorbed our culture, spoke our language. In fact, he emptied himself of all his heavenly prerogatives and became a servant among us (Phil. 2:6–8). Ultimately, he gave his life for us. Now, says Jesus, "As the Father sent me, so send I you."

Not everyone can do the Pauline thing, of course. That's why God designed a special role for special people. He didn't gift everyone with the ability to evangelize effectively and start churches where there are none. It takes more than short-term non-professionals to do that. That's why he put some people in the church as apostles. That's his plan and we bypass it only to short-circuit his purpose of building his church all over the world.

But it's not only Scripture, it's the reality of today's world. The dark third of it. One-third of the people on earth live today out of reach of gospel witness. They don't even have access to the Good News. Short-term witnesses aren't going to reach that dark third. First, the "sent one" must stay long enough among a people to understand them sufficiently to communicate clearly and winsomely the Good News and, second, long enough to win the trust of the people. Reaching the currently out-of-reach requires apostolic (called and sent by the Spirit and the church), incarnational (long term to live and communicate the gospel) missionaries.

For two reasons, then, we cannot discharge the church's Great Commission simply through sending short-term witnesses. To finish the task, the apostolic gifting and calling is essential. I call it the "incarnational" model. Not only was Christ fully incarnated as one of us to reach us; Paul followed that model and incarnated Christ for the people he would reach. And he had the special calling and gifting to leave the home base to evangelize and establish churches where there were none.

Some object that Paul himself was "short term" in most places. True, he didn't stay years in the same place very often, but he stayed among the same people, in the same culture throughout his recorded ministry. He already was one with the culture, and he spoke the language of the people to whom he witnessed. If, as some traditions have it, he ultimately reached Spain and/or England, one wonders how the church planting went through an interpreter! But where Acts reports on his ministry, he stayed long enough to establish a congregation with local leadership and he revisited, sent representatives and letters—stayed in constant touch with those whom he considered his very own children. He "became all things to all (varieties of) people" in order to save some (1 Cor. 9:22). That's incarnation.

God's revealed plan for pioneer church-starting evangelism is not an "everyman witness" for a few weeks or months, but a gifted "sent one" who becomes one with people, wins to faith, and establishes the church.

On the other hand, is there no role for the short-term witness? Since fewer are willing to become incarnational and the questions of preparation and gifting are bypassed, our task is to figure out how the short-termer can fit into the New Testament paradigm.

Are there places in which a drama team or athletic team or medical team, for example, can accompany the "apostle" and open doors, reinforce his ministry?

Another element in capturing this phenomenon for serious world evangelization is to dispel unrealistic expectations. The first unrealistic expectation we have already noted, the idea that we can fulfill the Great Commission mandate with short-term ministry. But there are other unrealistic expectations. For example, many go with the thought of testing their missionary call or competence. But that's impossible. It's sort of like trial marriage. You're testing something, but not marriage. So with the missionary vocation. The only way to test it is to do it—to make a commitment, to learn the language and culture, to become so one with the people that they feel your oneness with them. We must begin by erasing false expectations in the minds of those who go and the minds of those who send them.

It might also help to change our short-term objective from primarily ministry to primarily learning. The Saddleback model, of course, is specifically for the lay short-termer to teach the leaders of the receiving church. This seems more than a little arrogant to the typical church leader "overseas" with whom I am acquainted and holds the potential for great damage to relationships and to the cause of Christ. If the short-term team of nonprofessionals is welcomed as teachers of mature church leaders, it must be careful to be sure the welcome is not dependent on financial advantage. On the other hand, if the team goes, expecting to learn about another culture, about the glory of God's work in the world, about themselves and their prejudices and misconceptions, and they catch fire so it spreads when they come home, the experience can powerfully advance the cause of world evangelism. Even more, if the sending church proactively uses the experience as a recruiting method for identifying, inspiring, and sending career missionaries, the greatest potential of this highly expensive new approach will be reached. To gain these benefits, the sending church leaders must provide the following:

1. Thorough preparation. Spiritual preparation so those who go take a basin and towel to serve; cross-cultural preparation to keep the damaging faux pas to a minimum; and ministry preparation so the time is not wasted.

2. Experienced on-site supervision, preferably where God is at work in plainly visible ways. The receiving missionary or church leader must be enthusiastic about the assignment.

3. A careful reentry program to transform short-term service from an expensive religious tourism or disappointing ministry excursion into a life-transforming experience that will propel many people into career missionary service. This recruitment objective should be intentional on the part of sending leaders and field leaders as well.

The all-important questions about how to best prepare typical short-term missionaries, how best to deploy, how best to maximize their contribution on return to the church, and how to recruit incarnational missionaries from the short-term cohort lies outside the scope of this study. But it must not be neglected lest the phenomenon become a very expensive way of spiritualizing vacation junkets.[1]

Send Money, Not People

The second phenomenon, supporting workers from churches that are eager to receive financial assistance, is appealing for some of the same reasons as those that fuel the short-term phenomenon. It provides direct involvement of a sort, cutting out the middleman, the mission agency. Church-to-church is the mantra. Frequent trips back and forth enhance the personal relationship. Furthermore, it doesn't require long-term commit-

---

1. A great deal of assistance is available for maximizing the ministry of short-term missions. For example, Steve Hoke and Bill Taylor, *Send Me! Your Journey to the Nations* (WEA, 1999), distributed by Gabriel; David C. Forward, *The Essential Guide to the Short-Term Mission Trip* (Chicago: Moody, 1998); J. Mack Stiles and Leeann Stiles, *Mack and Leeann's Guide to Short-Term Missions* (Colorado Springs: InterVarsity Press); *Mission Maker Magazine* (STEMpress) standards of excellence have been developed and can be accessed at www.stemstandards.org.

ment. To send money rather than sons and daughters has a great appeal since we have so much money, and who wants to live a half world away from your grandchildren anyway?

The first problem, and a fatal one, is that in the dark one-third of the world, by definition there are not churches to partner with. If those now out of reach are to be reached, some churches somewhere are going to have to reach across borders without the luxury of a receiving brotherhood.

But there are other problems. Even for those the plan would seem best positioned to help, it can prove more damaging than helpful. Around the world this paradigm has created a spiritual welfare state, with poorer churches becoming dependent on American dollars. The need to trust God and sacrifice for him gives way to dollar searching. The church becomes spiritually anemic since God-dependency is the foundation of spiritual vitality. So great care must be given to accepting the invitation to send us your dollars, not your people.[2]

"Thank You For Not Coming" read the banner headline in a full page ad in *Christianity Today*. It was a promotional piece urging us to send money, not missionaries. The rationale is clear: "In most cases, sending just a portion of our surplus—fifty to one hundred dollars each month—will provide support for one full-time national worker. The typical cost to send an American missionary family overseas is more than fifty thousand dollars a year—the same cost to support fifty or more national workers. Think of what that money could do for the Kingdom of God!"[3]

More than 140 organizations are built on that premise, the money gatherers and senders. Perhaps that's one reason the missionary task force is in decline, baby boomers and busters unwilling to step forward as replacements for the hardy World War II veterans who stormed the frontiers for a half century. Chuck Bennett, of Partners International, one of the largest of the money-gathering agencies, reports they now support thirty-three hundred full-time workers in more than fifty countries.

"Let the nationals do it"—they have the language and culture and, most important, they cost so much less. True enough, but what about the dark one-third of the world where there are no "nationals," no witnessing church? If we're talking about "missions" as the original apostolic mandate of world evangelism, the fundamental premise of the "send money, not people" movement is misguided. At least a billion of the lost live among a people where there is no evangelizing church movement, often no witness at all. For these, by definition, someone must leave home to reach them. If a foreigner doesn't go in from the outside, they'll never hear the gospel. In fact,

---

2. The following is excerpted from the author's article in *Christianity Today* (March 1, 1999).
3. Bob Emery, president of Global Opportunities for Christ, in *Great Commission Opportunities Guide* (1998), 17.

because of the exploding population in the twentieth century, in spite of the unprecedented expansion of the church, there are exponentially more lost people today than ever before.

But, we're told, the burgeoning Third World missionary movement can handle the rest of the job since God seems to be bypassing the North American church. We exult in the move of the Spirit to mobilize a heretofore untapped resource, even if only a fraction of those thousands of Third World missionaries are going to the out-of-reach peoples. The problem is, though the newer mission-sending nations now account for half the worldwide missionary task force, the numbers from all sources combined are inadequate to finish the task. If present growth rates are sustained by the "new breed," it will still take at least a half century to complete the Great Commission. More likely, a full century.

It's not just that North American missionaries are still needed to complete the task, however; the North American church needs to send its own for the sake of itself, its own spiritual health. The sin of disobedience to the heavenly vision can't be atoned for with dollars, and the spiritual loss is highly visible in a self-centered, materialistically minded people. The original mandate has never been rescinded. The Pauline role of pioneering is still the primary mission of the church toward the world. Biblically, no church anywhere can claim exemption from the mandate until every person on earth has heard with understanding the way to life in Christ and a congregation has been established in every community.

Perhaps the solution is to send both our sons and daughters and our money. True, but we're going to have to rethink how we send money because sending money to support the ministry of others is very hazardous for the receiving church. Jerry Rankin, president of the International Mission Board, Southern Baptist Convention, puts it this way:

> It is a mistake to try to accelerate growth by an infusion of financial aid to build churches and support pastors. . . . One thing inevitably occurs when North Americans subsidize the work of churches and pastors on the mission field: potential growth is stalled because of a mind-set that it can't be done unless an overseas benefactor provides the funds. . . . Jealousy often develops among the pastors and churches who don't receive assistance toward those who develop a pipeline of support from the United States. . . . In the long-term, support breeds resentment, especially if the support is not sustained indefinitely, because it creates a patronizing dependency. . . . People are deprived of growing in faith, learning to depend on God and discovering that He is sufficient for all their needs.[4]

4. *The COMMISSION* (August 1997), 53.

The church or church leader in India or Africa who is successful in securing a financial pipeline to the USA quickly creates an ecclesiastical welfare state, weakening the soul of a church that should be, to use the old terminology, "self-governing" (which all want) and "self-supporting" (which ever fewer seem to value). Here are some of the results:

1. Local believers who know little or nothing of depending on God to supply through their own sacrificial giving, so that they learn to depend neither on God nor on themselves. The day of true indigenization is postponed for a people who don't need to give in sacrificial love and who never gain a sense of ownership.

2. Demoralization among leaders who can't get the "pipeline." The work can't be done without outside assistance, so why try?

3. Litigation over the properties of those who do get the American dollar. On my first trip through India, meeting with church leaders throughout the land, I was astounded to find few churches or ministries that weren't in the courts, at war over property.

4. A preoccupation with raising North American funds on the part of the leadership. On that first India trip I was overwhelmed by the many who "worked" me for a dollar connection, always courteous, sometimes subtle. Such a ministry orientation risks a weakening of faith and purity of motive, even integrity.

5. Creating an independent and unaccountable higher class of Christian workers who often espouse a lordly lifestyle unattainable by others, which also induces wrong motivation in those who don't yet have the connection. Should the donor seek to hold the recipient accountable for the use of funds to prevent such spiritual loss, he would be reverting to the old paternalistic pattern and would be roundly condemned for it.

6. Ingratitude. "Sure you gave us something, but look how much you have left." "It's not yours anyway, you owe it to us." Once we wanted to discover what was eating on some of the many African pastors studying with us at Columbia International University. Money was a chief bone of contention, though none could have been there without great generosity on the part of some sponsoring mission and the school. After several recounted how they were owed so much more, one Liberian pastor said, "Actually, you should not only fully support us now, you should support us for the first five or ten years after our return home since you have dis-fitted us for ministry in our homelands."

Perhaps the missiologist most knowledgeable about the hazards of North American financial support of ministry elsewhere is Glenn Schwartz, founding director of World Mission Associates. In an interview with *Missions Frontiers Bulletin* (January-February, 1997) he said: "We believe that churches in the non-Western world can do what God is calling them to do with the resources which he has put within their reach. . . . I don't think any-one would support that approach ('just support nationals') if they had gone out as a missionary to plant churches cross-culturally according to healthy principles of self-support and then had someone come along and entice away their best leaders with foreign money. That is what I call 'shepherd stealing.' The 'just support nationals' people are doing it shamelessly and on a very large scale" (p. 17).

The editor of *Missions Frontiers Bulletin,* Rick Wood, puts it even more strongly:

> Many churches in the US have bought into this scheme as a way of getting more "bang for their missions buck." But what they don't realize is that this "bargain basement" approach to missions is going to blow up in their faces—creating a dependency on the mission field to foreign funds that is deadly to the vibrant, repro-ducing church planting movements that we want to see within every people. Every church and every people has the God-given privilege and responsibility of supporting their own ministry and cross-cultural outreach. Foreign money robs these peoples of the incentive to give of their lives and resources to support the minis-tries of their own churches.
>
> Remember that your giving should always encourage "psycho-logical ownership" . . . never do for others what they can do for themselves. Avoid dependency like the plague that it is (p. 7).

Lest you think only North Americans like Schwartz and Wood come to such conclusions, many non-Western church leaders are quoted in the same issue. A sampling:

- Professor Zablon Nthamburi, presiding bishop, Methodist Church of Kenya: "The African Church will not grow into maturity if it continues to be fed by western partners. It will ever remain an infant who has not learned to walk on his or her own feet" (p. 18).
- Kingsley, a leader in the Friends Missionary Prayer Band, a leading Indian mission: "It's sad to say that foreign money has caused more harm than good in Indian missions. The result is culturally irrel-evant, pseudo-Christian leaders and organizations that have long forgotten their roots" (p. 23).
- Atul Aghamkar, an Indian specialist in urban ministries: "(Western money) continues to make the national church dependent on the West. It creates a sense of rivalry, greed and competition. It often robs the national church of its natural potential. When the easy money from the West is available, very few want to explore indig-enous ways of fund raising" (p. 23).

There are, then, great hazards in giving and receiving. We have not yet discovered how to use North American funds to assist non-North American ministry without negative spiritual fallout. For years I have resisted addressing the issue because I don't have a solution to offer. But, searching for the key to unlock this, the greatest puzzle in the current missions' enterprise, I've tried to discover biblical principles that should guide us. Let me share what I've discovered thus far. I'll use an illustration of how each principle might apply, but make no attempt in the scope of this chapter to solve the problems.

Controlling Objective: World Evangelism

It would seem axiomatic that the controlling objective of the pioneering mission team should be its purpose—evangelism. Paul was willing to become anything to anyone for his single-minded objective: to win the lost, to win as many as possible, as widely as possible. Everything he did—even to risk-taking and imprisonment—was measured in Great Commission terms.

So today. The test for any approach should not be which pattern most pleases one group or another, which pattern is in the ascendancy in the ever-changing missiological world, or some other criteria. The key question is, Which pattern in this situation gets the job done most effectively? Does this money investment promote or retard long-term church growth? The incredible story of the church in Korea is instructive. From the outset it was the showcase for the Nevius method—self-governing, self-supporting, and self-propagating. That may mean slow growth at first but look at the evangelistic and missionary impact today, with a third of the citizenry naming Christ as Lord and a missionary task force of thousands! There are other factors in the growth of the Korean church, of course, but the foundation of independent dependence on God is cited by many as the chief factor.

The first New Testament guideline, implicit in the very nature of the mission, is how well a proposed approach promotes the evangelistic objective.

Spiritual Integrity

Evangelization is the controlling objective of the missionary enterprise, but it is useless if it doesn't produce Christlike character in both the giver and the receiver.

Does the giving arrangement demonstrate generosity, humility, unity, and compassion on the part of the giver? All the attitudes the North American giver should have could be summed up in the expression, "incarnational giving." Does the church send money to fulfill its generous impulses or does the church also send its own sons and daughters as the Father sent the Son? Does the giver feel solidarity with and a responsibility for the brother in need, as Jesus did? Is the gift from the stance of a benefactor, or of a servant?

"I am among you as one who serves," said Jesus. I know an American missionary who, burdened by the corrupting power of the American dollar on giver and receiver, has chosen to live among the poor of Calcutta, along with his Indian colleague, on fifty dollars a month—for livelihood and for ministry. The balance of any gift income (unsolicited, by the way) is invested in a poverty-chained people. That isn't the only legitimate approach, of course, but I call that incarnational.

Does the giving arrangement produce in the receiving church a spirit of sacrificial giving, of responsible ownership of the ministry, including the cause of world evangelism, a greater reliance on God, and genuine gratitude? If these are not the results, the money is actually more a taking than a giving.

Church-centered Arrangements

The third principle governing giving and receiving is the New Testament pattern of church-centered giving and receiving, whether sending people or funds. People gave to their churches from which Paul received the offering (2 Cor. 8–9). When these funds were for the poor, not for the support of his own missionary team, he then delivered the offering to the church for distribution. The authority Christ invested in the church is lost when giving or receiving bypasses the church. The traditional independent mission or the contemporary money-gathering agency needs to exercise great care, especially when investing in something other than its own missionary team, not to bypass the supervisory authority of the church at both ends.

Giving

God's people are to give—compassionately, generously, sacrificially, and joyfully. This is a fundamental test of the quality of spiritual life. And the grace of giving is not for the wealthy alone, as the very poor (slaves?) of Philippi gave generously for the needs of the poor in Jerusalem (2 Cor. 8:2). If the giving of wealthy others undermines the need to give on the part of the poor, what a grave disservice! But for the wealthy there is a special obligation to give (1 Tim. 6:17–19), those who have for those who have not. Though this is a fundamental principle to govern giving, notice that it is not the first principle. I list it fourth because the other three are much more dominant in the commands and examples of Scripture. And yet many advocates of North American giving for non-North American causes seem to operate from this principle alone.

The primary focus in both the commands to give and the New Testament example was giving to the poor. The astounding offerings of property-tied people in the church of Jerusalem were to aid the poor (Acts 4:34–35), and the offerings Paul gathered from the "missionary churches" were also for the poor in Jerusalem, the home church. There is a reference to giving to support Paul's missionary team on the part of the "younger church" at Philippi (Phil. 4:10–19), and there is the incident of Paul asking for financial assistance for another missionary (1 Cor. 16:11). But I can find no instance, let alone any command, to give toward the ministry of another church.

One reason for this is evident. There were no church buildings or institutions like hospitals or schools, and local ministers were bivocational. If the early church is any model, it seems that paid ministry, buildings, and institutions emerged only as the church was able to afford them. From the beginning the little groups were self-supporting, self-governing, and self-propagating. Apparently the spiritual strength derived from this independent reliance on God was more important, in the mind of the apostle, than any kind of external subsidy to move things along more rapidly. And that New Testament pattern is fundamental to all the church-reproducing movements, as we have seen (chap. 6).

Scripture is clear, then, that those who have material resources are to share with those who lack them. In the New Testament this was providing the physical needs of the impoverished, what today might be called "relief" or "development" projects. But when we take the principle to mean assisting others in their spiritual ministry, we have no biblical command or precedent. If we justify the practice on the "giving" principle, we have yet to find the key to do so without spiritual damage to giver and receiver.

Some people who support the ministry of a poorer church, such as a pastor's or missionary's salary, are aware of this basic spiritual principle and do so on a sliding scale. For example, many indigenous church bodies will provide salary for the "apostle" in a church plant, but they diminish it by a percentage each year until the new work is self-supporting. The legendary Pastor Tsutada of Japan said, "If they haven't reached independence in five years, they don't have the gift." And such aspiring pastors became bivocational or entered the secular work force. All the burgeoning church multiplication movements around the world are led by lay pastors or bivocational pastors. That pattern is named as a key secret of their success, enabling rapid multiplication of churches. On the other hand, many thriving church movements have been retarded or even stopped in their rising orbit with the infusion of foreign funds.

Many mission agencies now provide American contacts or dollars to enable missionaries sent by poorer churches to join the diversity of a multinational missionary team. Many of these agencies are seeking to compensate for the potential spiritual damage this outside support and higher standard of living may inflict on the Third World home/sending church and pastor. Does that sending body still sense ownership? Are they still exercising faith and making sacrifices? Are they tempted to envy? Some agencies have had more success than others in developing policies to avert these damages.

Money is power, it is said, and power corrupts. These biblical principles should prove a helpful antidote to that corruption. Note the order of importance. If we begin and end, as many seem to do, with the single principle that the "haves" are to provide for the "have-nots," we shall inevitably be corrupted. At the least we will slow the progress of the gospel to the unreached. But we shouldn't be surprised. The church has been through this before.

The church at Jerusalem focused on its own needs so much that God had to bypass them for Antioch as the missionary-sending church. The Dark Ages were dark at least partially because the church was introverted. The Reformation wasn't mission-minded and never created sending structures, perhaps because of preoccupation with local political, ecclesiastic, and theological controversy. But most instructive, following the Edinburgh international missionary convention of 1910, the missions' juggernaut of the nineteenth century was sidetracked into focusing on ecumenical unity. The mainline historic churches began to concentrate their attention on interdenominational and cross-racial unification with financial assistance from North America, concentrating on meeting the temporal needs of humanity, and the evangelistic mission shriveled, in at least one major denomination to nothing at all.[5] If we shift the missions focus from reaching the unreached to demonstrating the unity of the body with financial aid, how do we differ from the ecumenical mission of the twentieth century?

So do we send money or people? Certainly we send people and keep on sending them to cross the frontiers until the task is completed. And we send money to assist the poor and disenfranchised in our worldwide family through relief and development. Beyond that New Testament pattern, I find no justification for supporting the ministry of other churches and great hazards in doing so. If we can find ways that will truly advance the cause of reaching those currently out of reach of gospel witness, the "dark half of the world," as some historic mission boards are seeking to do, we may be justified in assisting existing churches elsewhere. But sharing in a way that is spiritually empowering and Great-Commission-completing for both donor and recipient remains our greatest unsolved problem in the missions enterprise.

The Fear of Hell or the Glory of God?

"The ... core motivations for missions are changing. Once people preached and responded to the gospel out of fear of hell or because of the lostness of humanity. These motivations have waned in the postmodern

---

5. Of course, there were underlying doctrinal reasons for this shift as well. And many contemporary evangelicals are beginning to follow in that same direction. For example, the redefinition of who is lost and how salvation comes are doctrinal shifts plaguing the missionary enterprise. See the third paradigm below.

context. Motivation for missions is frequently defined by postmodern Christians as 'giving glory to God' or 'an overflowing of thankfulness.'"[6]

This quotation from *The Changing Face of World Missions* should not be construed as incipient universalism, for the author would repudiate such. Rather, he advocates going along with the contemporary change in motivation from "the fear of hell" to the "glory of God." My contention is that neither hell nor God's glory are, properly speaking, motivations. They are outcomes of the basic motivations of love for God and love for people. To make our appeal for involvement in missions to our love for God expressed in glorifying him is all to the good. But the deliberate downplay of the motive of other-love will prove fatal, I fear. Other-love in terms of "holistic" concern for health, education, and justice is OK, we're told by advocates, but other-love in terms of a rescue mission from a bad ending—well, that's so offensive to the postmodern that we mustn't even mention it, let alone emphasize it.

The way I read Scripture, however, is that God so loved people that he gave his one and only Son to—do what? Save them from perishing (hell), we read. I believe the increasing shift among evangelicals to de-emphasize hell could prove the demise of Pauline-style mission. And thus the death of multitudes who would, as a consequence, never hear the Good News of redemption.

If that should happen, of course, it would be déjà vu, for that is precisely what took place in the early part of the last century. As we have seen, the mainline denominations moved away from saving people from hell to saving them in the here and now. With every move in that direction, the missions enterprise shriveled. And no wonder. Why make such great sacrifice to reach the unreached if there is no eternal-destiny danger?

We may love others in many ways: seeking their health, promoting justice, advancing education. And we should. Furthermore, the missions movement always has. But above all, we should love them into eternal life, away from eternal death. May our churches never fail to love as God loves, to extend his provision of eternal salvation to the dark half of the world. God was motivated by people-love, so that must be our motivation as well, if we are to be God-like.

But we also are motivated by the first command, to love God. And one way to do that is to keep the spotlight on him, to glorify him. The move, however, to make "the glory of God" the primary "motive" so far has not increased missions passion in the churches. God's people seem to find other ways of glorifying God. At least if we gauge passion by the numbers of pioneer missionary evangelistic church starters we send, the talk of glorifying God has not increased the level of passion.

6. Michael Pocock, Gailyn Van Rheenen, and Douglas McConnell, *The Changing Face of World Missions* (Grand Rapids: Baker Academic, 2005), 161.

Love for God can be expressed in many ways: glorifying him by singing his praises, testifying of his accomplishments, living a godly life. But the proof of love, said Jesus, is that we obey his commandments. And the great commandment that he returned to again and again following his resurrection? Go and proclaim the Good News of redemption (Mark 16:15), go and preach repentance and remission of sin (Luke 24:47), go and disciple the nations (Matt. 28:19). Those who heard it, got it. And that's how they glorified God—proved their love, that is—as seen in the book of Acts.

Thus there are two issues surrounding "the glory of God": (1) why does the church not glorify God by obeying his last command? (2) dare we neglect God's own motive of people-love in terms of a rescue mission from hell?

I believe this third contemporary paradigm shift in approach to missions has the potential of far more damage to the cause than the other major paradigm shifts, problematical though they may be. Increasing numbers of those who consider themselves evangelical have come to believe people who have never heard the gospel may be acceptable to God through some other way. Not only the historic view of the way of salvation is increasingly questioned, but alternatives to the historic church view of hell are offered by more and more theologians. This paradigm shift has the potential of cutting the artery of missionary passion. Indeed, for many it has already done so.[7]

In this unit (unit 4) we are focusing on the mission of the church, world evangelism, and in this chapter (14) we have paused to consider three major paradigm shifts that impact that mission. We now return to the biblical pattern of doing mission. In considering the purposes of the church, we have given more attention to the evangelistic purpose because it seems to be the focal point of the New Testament church as viewed through the eyes of Luke and Paul in the book of Acts. And among all the facets of evangelism near and far, we have given more attention to the far and the plan God has for reaching "the far." But to do that requires more than finding, recruiting, sending, and going. The home base for those sent is of critical importance to their success. So we turn now to the two major elements in that support system: prayer and giving.

---

7. This most important topic and the defense of the biblical positions on the way of salvation and the reality of hell lie outside the scope of this study. I have made a brief defense of the biblical doctrine elsewhere (Ralph D. Winter and Steven C Hawthorne, *Perspectives on the World Christian Movement* [Pasadena: William Carey Library, revised 1999], chap. 26), but a thorough examination may be found in Ajith Fernando, *The Supremacy of Christ* (Wheaton: Crossway, 1995).

CHAPTER 15:

PRAYER SUPPORT

Devote yourselves to prayer, being watchful and thankful.
And pray for us, too, that God may open a door for our message. . . .
Pray that I may proclaim it clearly, as I should.
(COL. 4:2–4 NIV)

Question for reflection: Is prayer for global outreach informed,
vital, pervasive throughout the body, throughout the year?

J ust as a military operation requires far more support troops than front-
line combatants, so the missionaries in "far evangelism" require a strong
home base or they will soon become casualties. Although there are other
elements in a strong support system, the two main supports are prayer and
finance. Let us consider each.[1] First, the most important: prayer.

A magnificent southern thunderstorm was entertaining me one evening.
As I watched the display of cosmic fireworks from my side porch, suddenly
there was a mighty explosion right in our own backyard, an extravaganza of
sight and sound. Lightning had struck the transformer and in a moment we
lost all light and power. For days. Interesting, because giant towers trooped
through the fields just a half mile away, bearing unlimited supplies of light
and power. How like many Christians—the power flows all around them,
but they aren't connected.

The Source of Power

The power connect is an attitude: yield and trust. Until we have an obedient and believing mind-set or heart orientation, the deal is off because
the Holy Spirit doesn't force his way on us. But if we meet that simple
condition—the same faith response that connected us to him in the first
place—we are poised to let the power flow. Yet the power flow is more than

---

1. Much of the material in this chapter is derived from chapters 40 and 41 of my *Life in the Spirit*
(Nashville: Broadman & Holman, 2000).

an attitude; it's an activity. It's through prayer, the human conduit of divine energy, that Holy Spirit power and light flow. When it comes to world evangelism, since the Spirit acts in response to the believing prayer of an obedient people, prayer is the most important part of the missionary enterprise. As E. M. Bounds said, "Much prayer, much power, little prayer, little power, no prayer, no power."

The "How" of Prayer Warfare in the Spirit

Paul gives straightforward instruction on prayer for missions in his letter to the Colossians: "I want you to know how much I am struggling for you and for those at Laodicea, and for all who have not met me personally" (2:1 NIV). "Continue earnestly in prayer, being vigilant in it with thanksgiving; meanwhile praying also for us, that God would open to us a door for the word, to speak the mystery of Christ, for which I am also in chains, that I may make it manifest, as I ought to speak" (4:2–4 NKJV). "Epaphras . . . always laboring fervently for you in prayers, that you may stand perfect and complete in all the will of God" (4:12 NKJV).

If we pray for our missionaries at all, it may be a routine mentioning to God of some brief request we've read or been given. But the kind of prayer Paul describes is so different—"struggling," "earnestly," "always laboring fervently." It sounds like a spiritual battle in prayer against unseen enemies that fight to hold captive those we aim to release. And notice that our prayer isn't to be occasional but continuing, regular—daily, at least. Furthermore, our fervent labor in prayer is not only to be the regular, set times for prayer, but in between times. The term *vigilant* is a military term, meaning "on battle alert." We are to be sensitive to the Spirit's intimations of special need for special prayer. To summarize what prayer was meant to be, in Paul's parallel passage in Ephesians (6:18) he instructs us to pray "in the Spirit." Spirit-guided, Spirit-energized prayer is the secret to world evangelism. And when our prayers fall short, the Spirit, who knows the mind of the Father, goes to him for us with strong pleading (Rom. 8:26–27). That is the ultimate guarantee in this spiritual warfare.

I was under arrest in central Africa, detained at the border town "airport" because my papers weren't in order. When we had landed at the dusty outpost, the officials admitted the other handful of passengers, but said the pilot would have to take me with him. He refused, saying he was going on to Uganda and if he took me there I'd be in big trouble. I would stay there at the airport, the officials seemed to have decided, until someone flew me out of the country. But what was the chance of that? The future looked bleak, especially if they transferred me to the local jail.

As I sat in that small room with my guard, without food or drink, I thought, *Today is Thanksgiving Day at home!* I told the guard what we did on that day in the hope that when next he went for his own food he'd remember me. No such luck! What would the outcome be?

Thousands of miles away in a New Jersey nursing home, a ninety-year-old lady I had never met was strangely moved to pray earnestly for me at that very time. She was "on battle alert," she was "in the Spirit!" The British pilot who had put me down in that tiny outpost was concerned about me, changed his plans, and late in the day returned from Uganda to whisk me away, not on the wings of a Cessna so much as on wings of prayer.

Most of us are quite self-centered in our prayers, using prayer to capture some of God's power, if possible, to propel our personal interests. How sad, for all along the Spirit intended to use the channel of prayer for funneling blessing to others, especially to a world in darkness. Spirit-filled Christians are world Christians on their knees. As we companion with the Spirit throughout each day, we begin to see the world with his eyes, and he catches us up into himself until our hearts beat with his.

One more thing about how we are to pray. When Paul says, "with thanksgiving," he doesn't mean merely saying thank you when God answers, important as that is, but rather thanking God for the answer even as we ask. In other words, faith-filled prayer. That's the powerful kind. In fact, that's the only kind that prevails in heaven.

The "What" of Prayer Warfare in the Spirit

Paul gives instruction not only on how we're to pray, but also on what we're to pray about.

Pray for the Missionary's Ministry

Paul told the Colossians to pray that doors of opportunity would open up and that the missionary team would have the ability to make the mysterious gospel understandable. That's Spirit-energized ministry, because without the Spirit's intervention, heart doors will remain closed and the gospel will sound like gibberish to those who hear.

But your missionary needs not only the gifts to accomplish ministry; he or she must have the fruit of the Spirit or nothing of eternal significance will be done.

Pray for the Missionary's Spiritual Life

You can see this in Paul's instruction to believers in that same passage: "Walk in wisdom toward those who are outside, redeeming the time. Let your speech always be with grace, seasoned with salt, that you may know how you ought to answer each one" (Col. 4:5–6 NKJV). Why, we could hardly do better than pray those very words for our missionary!

Furthermore, Paul tells the Ephesians in a similar passage (Eph. 6:19–20) to plead with God that he might have courage. Paul, the warrior who faced down lions in the arena, asked prayer for courage? Indeed! He wrote of "conflicts on the outside, fears within" (2 Cor. 7:5 NIV). The most intrepid missionary needs prayer for faith, for courage, for all the fruit of the Spirit, because, though he may have the most glorious Good News, if his life doesn't demonstrate the beauty and strength of Christ, his proclamation will be bad news, not Good News.

These, then, are the themes of missionary prayer warfare: the ministry and the life. Another way to put it, pray daily for the gifts of the Spirit and the fruit of the Spirit in the life of your missionary.

There's one more thing, however. We need to make it our business to find out the specific needs of the missionary.

On returning from service overseas, I had just completed my report on Japan and stood at the door of the meeting place to greet the people when I felt a tug on my jacket. Looking around I saw a tiny retired school teacher who said, "Robertson, I know you're busy, but please don't leave until I have a chance to talk with you for a minute."

"Why, Miss Ethelyn," I responded, "I'm not busy; let's talk right now." She was one I knew who prayed for me continually and fervently, one who was combat-ready and fighting my spiritual wars with me. She had first claim on my attention! We went over to a nearby stone wall. No sooner had we sat than she began to pepper me with questions about my work. I soon realized she knew more about my work than my fellow missionaries. When she began to ask about the conference I had left in Japan just forty-eight hours earlier, I said, "Miss Ethelyn, how do you know all this stuff?"

"Why, Robertson," she remonstrated, "you're my missionary! I've been praying for you for twelve years. I ought to know something, shouldn't I?"

Are there missionaries about whom you could say, "He's my missionary, she's my responsibility for daily prayer warfare"? If you don't have such a prayer partnership already, perhaps it's time to link up with someone out on the frontiers, someone who faces daily hot spiritual combat. Not only do you provide "cover" for your missionary; you become a full partner in the war. What a high privilege!

If you're not already a co-combatant, how could you get linked up? Many ways, but primarily through your church. When missionaries visit the church, invite them home for dinner. And don't spend the time replaying the Super Bowl! Pull their story out of them, learn what their prayer needs are. Then pray! Most missionaries send out regular reports with prayer requests. Ask the missionaries you choose to put you on their mailing or e-mail list. If you don't have a missionary you could call "my missionary," why not make a telephone call to the church office or write a letter right now? Get started! Because the most important part of the missionary enterprise is prayer.

The leadership of the church should take the responsibility to set up the link between missionary and prayer partner and, indeed, to mobilize the entire body for in-the-Spirit prayer, personal as well as united. But there's more to great commission prayer than holding the lifeline for the individual missionary.

Strategic Prayer Warfare

We are commissioned not only to pray for individual missionaries but for the cause at large. Jesus commanded us, for example, to pray—and keep on praying, is the force of the verb—for laborers for the harvest. Because, he said, the unreaped harvest is so great and the laborers are far too few (Matt. 9:37–38). I imagine that is the prayer the church at Antioch was praying when God told them to send out their senior pastor and his associate, Barnabas and Paul (Acts 13). And they weren't just offering an occasional "missionary moment" prayer. It says they were fasting and praying, and it takes more than thirty minutes of united prayer to be a fast!

For some years I conducted Great Commission workshops with local church leaders, eight hours of evaluation and planning. Only churches that considered themselves strong in missions would invite me for such a grueling exercise, of course. I discovered a startling thing: the average amount of time devoted to united prayer by some group (large or small) was three minutes a week. And these were the premier missions-minded churches. Even that token prayer was almost exclusively for their own sons and daughters in missions. I found almost none praying as Christ clearly commanded—for laborers for the harvest. Of course, that kind of prayer could be hazardous. Begin to pray that way and God might call the senior pastor, as in Antioch. He might call one of the sons gathered at the family altar if such prayer were made on a regular basis with faith and fervor.

Another strategic prayer is suggested by the Father's invitation to the Son: "Ask of me and I will give you the nations for your inheritance, the uttermost parts of the earth as your possession" (Ps. 2:8). We must join the Son in asking the Father for all the nations as an inheritance for the Son. I've long prayed that prayer for Japan and the Bengali. And not just because I have a daughter who has labored in Japan for almost two decades and a son who labored for ten years among the Bengali slum dwellers of Calcutta. I pray that kind of focused prayer because I long for these nations to become part of the Lord Jesus' inheritance. I plead with the Father, "You've answered the prayers of the Son and are giving him China and Korea in unprecedented harvests. Why not just across the water, the people of Japan, and to the south, the largest unreached people group of all: the Bengali?"

I claim the Father's promise and do what has been called "adopt a people" for focused prayer until the gift is given. Years after I began that prayer, God began to answer among the Bengali of Bangladesh in which there is unprecedented turning to Christ in one of the most hard-core Muslim nations of the world. Now for the Bengali of India! If you don't know an unreached people group for your family or Sunday School class to adopt for prayer warfare, check out *Operation World* by Patrick Johnstone, a prayer manual that identifies the spiritual needs of every nation on earth.

I don't understand about spiritual warfare in prayer like Daniel did. He read in Scripture what God's will was for the nations, as we have done, and then, unlike us, he went to his knees for days, for weeks, pleading for the fulfillment of the promise. We read that God heard him and sent the heavenly emissary to answer that prayer, but that Gabriel was detained in mighty combat with celestial evil forces. And Daniel, not knowing that, nevertheless participated in that war through fasting and prayer until victory came (Dan. 8 and 9). I don't understand how all that works, but I know for sure there is powerful resistance by the evil powers of spiritual darkness to gospel advance and that we are called to participate in the battle through prayer.

So the most important part of the missionary enterprise is prayer, individual and corporate, persistent, fervent, untiring. There must be prayer for the individual missionary representative of the church, but there must also be strategic warfare for laborers for the harvest and for the unreached peoples of the world.[2]

Looking back on the journey we've traversed together, remember that the Holy Spirit has given, is giving, or will give you some wonderful gift, an ability to do an important job for him (1 Cor. 12). He then wraps that gift in the package of you and gives you as his gift to the church (Eph. 4). After thinking about gifts of the Spirit (unit 3), we turned to the special gift of evangelism (unit 4), including evangelism-at-a-distance or missionary evangelism. "Apostles" are so important in God's program of reaching the whole world because they are the Spirit's point men (or women), his only strategy for completing the church and saving humankind. We've seen how all believers must witness, some must evangelize, some of the evangelists must go to those out of reach of present gospel witness. And we've seen

---

2. To learn of the spiritual condition of each nation and thus identify some unreached people for prayer adoption, there is no better source than Patrick Johnstone and Jason Mandryk, *Operation World: When We Pray God Works* (Waycross, Ga.: Gabriel; WEC International, International Research Office, 2001).

how the "going" will be effective to the extent that prayer is offered for its success.

But there's one more thing, and it's for everyone—another lifeline of support for the cause of world evangelism. It doesn't sound as spiritual as prayer, but Scripture actually says more about it than it does about prayer. We turn now to the second major support for missions—finances.

CHAPTER 16:

FINANCIAL SUPPORT

*We want you to know about the grace that God has given
the Macedonian churches. Out of the most severe trial,
their overflowing joy and their extreme poverty,
welled up in rich generosity. . . .
See that you also excel in this grace of giving.*
(2 COR. 8:1–2, 7 NIV)

Questions for reflection: How much emphasis is given
to help people progress in their level of investment in ministry?
Is tithing expected, honest managership encouraged,
and sacrificial love giving celebrated?

One of the greatest blockades on the road to victory for King Jesus is something very practical, quite earthy, really—money. And the lack of it for the missionary enterprise is a major roadblock to world evangelism. We seem to have plenty for our own needs and for the needs of our local churches, but when it comes to sending out American missionaries, it dries up. In fact, only four cents of each dollar given by evangelicals in the USA is used for world missions. Ninety-six percent of giving is spent at home, on ourselves. Many people are fully prepared and ready to go, but the money isn't there. What's the problem?

Part of the problem of funding the enterprise may spring from mis-guided priorities. There often seems to be funding enough for building church edifices and even for sending more than a million short-termers annually at a cost of several billion dollars. And many churches give to support the ministries of poorer churches overseas. Actually, the wealth of American churches is unprecedented in church history. But put in the con-text of the need and the proportion Christian people keep for themselves, giving is far from sacrificial. Even far from generous when compared with what the church in other places and at other times has done. So the basic problem may be one of spiritual maturity.

Measuring Maturity

We may be startled to discover that Jesus measures spiritual maturity by how we relate to material things. In fact, he taught far more about our relationships to possessions than he did about prayer. Apparently he considered our check stubs an accurate measure of the level of our spiritual maturity.

Isn't it amazing—plain old down-and-dirty money is God's way of tying together the fruit of the Spirit and the gifts of the Spirit! At least the gift of pioneer evangelism. Notice how he links spiritual maturity with our relationship to possessions in the Gospel of Luke. To calibrate the levels of maturity, let's assign names we can readily identify: kindergarten, elementary, secondary, higher, and graduate.

Infancy: Nongiving

Jesus actually begins before kindergarten, but we can hardly call infancy a level of giving. The infant is basically a self-centered nongiver. Every church has its quota of infants who are there to get, not give. A platoon of the faithful is needed to quell the squabbles, to entertain, to clean up the string of messes. Jesus told us about this stage of nongiving: "The ground of a certain rich man produced a good crop. He thought to himself, 'What shall I do? I have no place to store my crops. . . . This is what I'll do. I will tear down my barns and build bigger ones, and there I will store all my grain and my goods. And I'll say to myself, "You have plenty of good things laid up for many years. Take life easy; eat, drink and be merry"'" (Luke 12:16–19 NIV).

How did God respond to this reasonable plan? "Fool! Dead man! Tonight your soul will be required of you." Actually, the self-centered getter is already dead, spiritually. One of the first signs of genuine spiritual life is the desire to give.

Kindergarten: Impulse Giving

Luke introduces a kindergartner to us, one who began to get his kicks, not out of getting and saving and spending, but out of giving. The wealthy little big-time chiseler wanted to see Jesus but couldn't get at him for the thronging people. So Zacchaeus—imported brocade robe tucked up under his sash—climbed a tree to get a view of the famed itinerant preacher. As the procession passed, Jesus stopped and invited himself to a meal with the despised head honcho of the local Roman tax unit. Was it there on the spot or later over dinner that the conversion took place? That there was a radical conversion we know because of the announcement the host then made: "I give half my goods to the poor; and if I have taken anything from anyone by false accusation, I restore fourfold" (Luke 19:8 NKJV).

Quite a surge of generosity for an ex-getter! On impulse he risked bankrupting himself. Most genuine Christians in most churches give at the impulse level. That's why it's easier to raise funds for starving orphans in Rwanda than to raise funds for a Bible school library in neighboring Kenya. If you watch religious television, you may feel there is a new crisis every week. But you are probably mistaken. The industry standard for fund-raising is twelve to fifteen crises a year. The promotion people know that most Christians, most of the time, give on impulse. This is kindergarten level.

Elementary: Legalistic Giving

When a Christian moves from sporadic, negotiable, impulse giving to giving as a way of life, he often becomes a tither. "Will a man rob God? But you have robbed me."

"How do we rob you?"

"In tithes and offerings" (Mal. 3:8 NKJV). The kindergarten Christian hears that and says, "That's Old Testament legalism." Jesus, too, had problems with the legalists of his day, the Pharisees. In fact, among the terrible woes he pronounced on them was one dealing with their tithing. They were so careful to obey the law of tithing that they even measured the harvest of tiny herbal seeds to give God his tenth. At the same time they were not nearly so devoted to the heavy concerns of God: justice and the love of God. "Woe to you Pharisees, because you give God a tenth of your mint, rue and all other kinds of garden herbs, but you neglect justice and the love of God" (Luke 11:42 NIV).

Surprisingly, Jesus did not tell them to stop the foolish tithing. "What you should do," he remonstrated, "is concentrate on the big ones, justice and the love of God. And don't stop the tithing."

The tithe is affirmed by Jesus. Better to give legalistically, apparently, than not to give illegalistically! Tithing is the elementary, basic, primary level of giving, but the majority of faithful church members do not reach that level.

I was asked to speak on giving at a large, influential church. Often pastors like the visiting preacher to do the money talk. He's a moving target! In that church there was every sign of dynamic vitality, including a budget of more than three million dollars. In the 1980s, yet! A third of that was for missions, a sure sign of clear biblical priorities. After the message, the church business manager called me aside to share a bit of inside information. "We did a demographic study of our congregation," he said, "and discovered that if every member quit his or her job, went on unemployment, and began to tithe, we could double our budget!" Most pastors find that hard to believe, but statistics consistently testify that most church members don't tithe, remaining at the kindergarten level of impulse giving.

Tithing graduates the Christian from impulse giving at the kindergarten level to giving as a way of life—the basic, elementary level of giving.

Secondary: Honest Managership

One of the clearest passages on managership has been distorted by centuries of strange interpretations of the story Christ told about the cheating manager (Luke 16). The story is straightforward. An owner discovered that his manager was a cheat and when he announced that he was going to fire him, the shrewd fellow used his boss's assets to win friends for himself by officially canceling large portions of their debts. Jesus was making a single point: even worldlings are smart enough to use available resources to prepare for their future, so why are the "people of the light"—who should know better—so stupid? "I say to you, use your worldly wealth to win friends for yourselves, so that when money is a thing of the past you may be received into an eternal home" (Luke 16:9 NEB).

Then Jesus explained about temporal wealth and eternal wealth. The temporal is very little at best, sort of a test, the eternal is great wealth (16:10); the temporal is fake, sort of play money, the eternal is the real thing (16:11); and—the central concept—what you have now is not your own. You are just a manager of some of God's property (16:12). It's impossible to live for both, to work for temporal and eternal payoffs with equal fervor. You cannot serve both God and money (16:13). The audience was having a love affair with money so they scoffed at Jesus' teaching (16:14). With that he told those cheating managers, those who used God's property for their own benefit, what the final payoff would be—hell (16:19–31).

This teaching of Christ rocked my life. As a young adult I continued my childhood pattern of tithing. God got his 10 percent first. Always. I didn't feel self-righteous about it anymore than I did about paying taxes. But when it became clear to me that I was not an owner at all, just the manager of the property of another, I stood convicted as an embezzler. I was avidly getting, saving, and spending 90 percent of God's property on myself without a qualm of conscience. I shrank from embracing managership as a way of life, fearing I would be fenced off from the good life. But when I finally gave up and accepted God's view of my possessions, the very opposite of what I feared took place. It was like the cage door swung open and I was free. My intensity about making money was gone, my grief over losses and ecstasy over gains, my apprehension about the future—they all took wings. I was at ease because the corporation of my life belonged to the Infinite One and he guaranteed my life (12:31). That's what happens when we get honest about who the owner is!

The manager looks at the King's business differently than the tither. The tither looks at his paycheck, calculates the 10 percent and asks, "Where should I invest this money?" The manager, on the other hand, looks at the needs of the business and asks, "How can I rearrange my resources to meet this great need?"

> The angels from their realm on high
> Look down on us with wondering eye
> That where we are but passing guests,
> We build such strong and solid nests;
> And where we hope to live for aye,
> We scarce take thought one stone to lay.

Jesus says, "That's dumb, really dumb. You ought to be using what little I have put under your control temporarily to build your eternal estate, not squander my possessions to build your own petty kingdom here on earth. At least be an honest manager."

Higher: Love Giving

Next we find ourselves in church with Jesus doing something your pastor has never done. If he did, that would no doubt be his last Sunday as your pastor! Jesus watched the offering plate, so to speak, and noted how much each person put in. There he discovered a very beautiful woman. Thin, with hunger-pinched features, no doubt, and shabby in appearance, but how beautiful she was! Out of a heart of love she gave everything she had. "Jesus saw the rich putting their gifts into the temple treasury. He also saw a poor widow put in two very small copper coins. 'I tell you the truth,' he said, 'this poor widow has put in more than all the others. All these people gave their gifts out of their wealth; but she out of her poverty put in all she had to live on'" (Luke 21:1–4 NIV).

As God follows the ushers down the church aisle today, how does he measure love? How calibrate the intensity of it, measure the depth of it? Jesus answers: love is measured by the sacrifice it makes.

Bob, a student at Columbia International University, asked for help with a difficult passage he had found in Luke 18. "Let me guess," I responded, "you've got problems with the story of the wealthy young aristocrat, right?"

"Yes," he responded. "Why did Jesus tell him to sell what he had and give it away?"

"Well," I said, "the way to life for that young man was blocked by things, his sin of covetousness. For the woman at the well it wasn't money, it was men, so Christ brought that up. Nicodemus, on the other hand, so self-righteous, needed to hear about a second birth. Jesus identified the key issue, the roadblock for each." I was quite pleased with my explanation.

"I see," said my young friend. "If his possessions were the sticking point for him, would you say there are any in America today with a similar problem?"

I wondered where Bob was headed with his line of questioning. "Yes," I chuckled a little nervously. "Just about everyone, I suppose."

"Why then," he asked, "in all my life have I never heard a sermon on the subject?"

"That's a very good question, Bob." Instantly I knew how good it was! "Because," I continued, "Christ gave exactly the same teaching, not to some wealthy aristocrat, but to anyone who wanted to be his disciple: 'Sell what you have and give alms; provide for yourselves money bags which do not grow old, a treasure in the heavens that does not fail, where no thief approaches nor moth destroys'" (Luke 12:33 NKJV).

Does anyone actually do this? Some years ago I wanted to personally thank two of our graduates for their many generous gifts. When we'd have a special need, a gift of a thousand or two thousand dollars would come from this couple. I wondered how they could do this because they were school teachers in a poor district of Appalachia. One day I was in the area and called to see if a visit would be convenient. They were delighted, had something they wanted to tell me. They met me at the highway and escorted me on foot through the muddy ruts that snaked around the hillside. There, nestled in the little mountain cove was the reason they could give so generously. A small log cabin housed all their earthly possessions. Or so I thought.

The husband was so excited. He said, "Robertson, isn't the Lord good?"

"Yes," I responded, "He is. And how has he been good to you?"

"You won't believe how good he's been to me. This week has been fantastic!"

"Tell me about it," I said.

"No," he said, "you have to sit down." So we crossed the rough-hewn planks of the porch into a small living room. When I was settled in, he told his story. "You didn't know it, but north of Atlanta, we've had a farm in the family for many years and it's begun to be a headache for us because the city of Atlanta has grown out all around our farm."

I said to myself, *Some problem. I wouldn't mind having that kind of problem!* He continued, "This week we were able to sign that property over to Wycliffe Bible Translators! Isn't that fantastic!"

"Yes!" I responded enthusiastically.

He continued. "That's not all. We had another small acreage out in the clay country that was not worth much and we couldn't sell it. Tried for years. Now at last—this week—we were able to sell it to a government agent who will buy it over ten years and give us $1,500 a year. So we've decided to take early retirement, go to the mission field, take care of MKs, and live on what we get from the sale of this property! What do you think about that?"

"I think you're crazy," I responded. "What are you going to do when that money runs out?"

"Oh, we'll be in heaven by then!"

Now, you probably agree that he's a little crazy. But there is one thing we don't even have to ask: whom did he love and how much did he love him? Love is proved by the sacrifice it makes.

Love giving graduates a person from the secondary level of honest managership to the higher level of sacrificial love giving. Mother Teresa was being interviewed on television and I swelled with pride, along with the young woman who was interviewing her, as Mother Teresa told us how wonderful Americans are. She said, "I don't know if there has ever been a nation that has been so giving. You are such generous people." The interviewer was visibly pleased.

Teresa continued, "Of course, you give out of your muchness." She chuckled and said, "Muchness is a word, isn't it?" Teresa paused, then continued, "You don't really give 'til it hurts." The young woman's eyes grew large as she looked at Mother Teresa with astonishment, "Must it hurt?"

The angel of Calcutta responded, "Love, to be genuine, must hurt." She understood that love is proved by the sacrifice it makes.

Graduate: Faith Giving

Paul speaks of the gift of faith (Rom. 12:3–8; 1 Cor. 12:9). It seems there are those George Muellers of the world who trust God for miracle provision—finances far above that which could be provided even by sacrificial giving. George Mueller cared for thousands of orphans on God's daily miracle provision. In fact, his faith stretched beyond caring for the orphans as he was able to give millions to foreign missionary work around the world. That's faith giving! I call this the "graduate level" of giving because this gift of faith is not given to all equally.

But there's another sense in which faith must validate any level of giving for God to be pleased. "Without faith it is impossible to please Him" (Heb. 11:6 NKJV). The Pharisees were not the only ones who had problems with Jesus' radical teaching about managership and sacrificial living. The disciples did too. Jesus' teaching cut across the grain of everything they believed about money and things. So he told them, "If then God so clothes the grass, which today is in the field and tomorrow is thrown into the oven, how much more will He clothe you, O you of little faith?" (Luke 12:28 NKJV).

Indeed, faith must validate every level of giving, whether the legalistic minimum, honest managership, or sacrificial love giving. For example, the impoverished widow living on Social Security must have faith to give ten percent. Furthermore, when she does so, it is certainly sacrificial love. So love, too, must validate every level of giving. My relationship to my possessions is, according to Jesus Christ, a clear indication of my faith and love, my level of spiritual maturity.

Those levels, then, are not always clear-cut. But they are clear enough for me to evaluate my own life. I know the painful—then liberating—move I made from tithing to managership. And I know very well, as I see the abject poverty of the world, that I don't live a sacrificial lifestyle. Spurts of sacrifice, maybe, but far from Jesus' model of giving. How about you? Honesty about our finances may be the most difficult honesty of all. As you review your giving for the past year, checking your records if you aren't sure, at what level of giving have you been? Are you pleased with that level? Is God pleased? What kind of lover does that show you to be? What kind of truster?

God's standard for giving is one that he himself models. He created me, so he is owner. I stole his property—took possession of myself. But in love he purchased me at terrible cost, just as if he had no claim on me, making me twice his. If I will only respond with love in obedient giving, he guarantees my livelihood (Luke 12:31); rewards me lavishly in this life as if I were giving what is my own property; and in heaven he rewards me all over again! (Luke 18:28–30). That's God's level of giving, love giving.

In response to such love, are you ready to move up one step? If you've never been a faithful tither, isn't it time to promise him that 10 percent? Trust him! He'll take care of you. Perhaps you've been a tither for years but you did pretty much what you pleased with the other 90 percent. Isn't it time to stop that foolishness and become an honest manager of God's property? Whatever level of maturity you've achieved in your walk with God, don't you want to step up? If I'm unwilling to move up from my present level of maturity, it may be because I don't trust God to meet my needs, a lack of faith. Or love. If because of your love for Jesus, you're ready to take that leap of faith to the next level, tell him so. Now.

Perhaps you say, "That's too costly. I'm not up to it." Maybe it would help to remember our theme verse for this chapter where Paul teaches that the willingness and ability to give is a grace, a gift from God. Paul viewed every disciple as living in the flow of the grace of God, into a life and then through that life. This is not just in terms of spiritual blessing. The grace of physical financial resources are provided as an act of God's grace and then flow through the Christians to others (2 Cor. 8:7). I may not be able to graduate to a new level of giving, but God is quite able to grace me up a step. Trust him!

We've listened to Jesus teaching about giving at this point in our study because lack of giving is a major obstacle to world evangelism, the main theme of these chapters. So money is a key factor in both the missionary enterprise and simultaneously in the life of participants. Anyone can evaluate your spiritual maturity if you'll let them see your check stubs, Jesus seems to say. In this way, giving ties together the fruit of the Spirit with the greatest of all gifts of the Spirit—evangelism. And because the key to our response about money is love—the chief of the fruits the Spirit gives—this very earthy part of our lives becomes of critical importance to personal spiritual health and world evangelism.

I've emphasized the role of the individual in missions finance, but the church has a critical role. It should teach and encourage all members toward biblical giving, nurturing spiritual maturity. It should also manage what has been given with biblical priorities in control of the budgeting process.

As a final exercise for evaluating your congregation's involvement in missions, by each percentage in the article reprinted below, enter an estimate for your congregation.

What Is Your GCQ?[1]

For thirty years I've crisscrossed the country, evaluating the GCQ of churches. Of course, the churches I visit have a pretty good GC Quotient—otherwise they wouldn't invite me in for an evaluation! After a while, a person begins to get a feel for what a true "Great Commission" church is. Of late the data have come together in sort of a formula, the 5-10-50-100 formula, to be exact.

In using this formula to evaluate the Great Commission Quotient of your own church, however, caution is needed. In the first place, this formula is found nowhere in Scripture. But the case studies we look at will be churches that have demonstrated fidelity to certain principles of Scripture that have led them to achieve remarkable success in some aspect of world missions. Since the formula isn't biblical revelation, these churches don't provide a mandate; but they do provide two things—inspiration and a measurable goal.

The inspiration is in seeing a church achieve a certain standard—5, 10, 50, or 100. That means we might do it too! And the goal they have achieved provides a benchmark for me to use in my own church. No longer can I comfortably "think fuzzy." I'll have to look hard and put a number of some kind on the performance of my church.

Another caution is to note that each of the churches we'll look at achieved in a different area—none in all four. And in the area in which they did achieve, they are gold medalists. That is, not everyone can be a Carl Lewis. But the Carl Lewises of the world set a standard for all the other athletes to evaluate their own performance and to strive toward. So my church may, in the will of God, never reach 5, 10, 50, or 100—let alone all of them. But it's exciting to know what has been done and healthy to honestly face where my church is in the Great Commission race.

---

1. Reprint from *Trinity World Forum* (Deerfield: Trinity Evangelical Divinity School, Winter 1997). Some of the stories appeared earlier in the text.

Five

Some years ago church growth analysts came up with the conclusion that, in most communities in America, a church ought to have a 5 percent conversion growth rate each year. Not transfer, not children of the church, but baptisms of new believers. A little reflection will show how unlikely such a formula is. Five percent might be rather slow growth for a church of ten people and would be truly remarkable for a church of ten thousand. At least it can't go on at 5 percent indefinitely or the whole world would become one congregation! The Yoido Full Gospel Church in Seoul may seem to be headed in that direction, but even David Yonggi Cho has some limits!

Nevertheless, the point is clear. If a church has members who live authentic Christianity, most of whom faithfully witness, and a few who have the gift of evangelism—that is, who are good at "closing"—that church will see substantial growth in new converts. So the first evaluation is this: how many baptisms of new believers did your church have last year?_____ What percent of the membership is that?_____ Does that satisfy you? Does it satisfy God? Does that qualify your church as a Great Commission church, fully obedient to Christ's last command? Perhaps it's time to set a faith goal—the number of converts you're asking God to give in the next year, in the next five years. Of course, faith without works is dead, so it must also be time to set plans in motion to achieve that goal.

Ten

The church at Jerusalem is a wonderful model to follow. That first year, at least, they beat the 5 percent formula by a fair margin: five thousand baptisms in a few weeks following start-up! And they were models also of prayer, of Spirit-anointing, of race relations, of care for the poor, of godly and wise leadership. But one thing they weren't good at—obeying Christ's last command to go into all the world. God had to send persecution to get them moving and even then they didn't go very far. But Antioch—that's another story. They were so in tune with the Spirit that when he spoke to them in a prayer meeting they immediately sent off their senior pastor and his top associate in the first recorded proactive missions thrust. Twenty percent of their pastoral staff!

I've been in a few churches like that. The first time I visited Calvary Church in Lancaster, Pennsylvania, I asked the pastor how many missionaries they supported. "One hundred eighty," he said. And how many are from this church? "All of them." With eighteen hundred members it wasn't hard to figure out—10 percent, a tithe of the membership. But the most Antioch church I've seen is the Faith Bible Church of Sterling, Virginia. I could see immediately they were into evangelism. With only 270 local members in that young church, they had 600 in attendance, many of them seekers from the international community of the Washington area. I could tell they weren't merely reaching their own "Jerusalem," however. They had a vision for the world. But I wasn't prepared for the answer when I asked how many missionaries they'd sent out. "Seventy," they told me. That's 20 percent, not of the pastoral staff, like Antioch, but of the membership! Incredible! Just like the Moravians who launched the modern missionary movement.

But that's a little much, I suppose. There's no danger of it happening, but if every church followed their example it would take some pretty heroic sacrifice on the part of members-at-home to support such a task force. So I suggest half that—10 percent—as a gold-medal performance standard. How is it at your church? 1 percent? _____ 2 percent?_____ 5 percent?_____ 0 percent?_____ Is it time to set a faith goal and step up 1 percentage point?

Fifty

I've seen many gold medalists in this category, but only once have I seen a seventy-five. When I meet a missionary in some distant part of the world and inquire about their roots, often I hear "Norfolk." Then I know they found Christ or heard the missionary call at the Norfolk Tabernacle Church. There's a church that obeys the Great Commission! A constant stream of U.S. Navy personnel find Christ in the Tab and fan out across the world to serve him. But, following my first visit many years ago, I was unprepared to discover in their annual report how they supported those missionaries. Seventy-five percent of income was invested away from the home church! Meeting for decades in a wholly inadequate set of buildings, they refused to cut back on their investment in reaching the rest of the world.

That's the only church I've seen that gave 75 percent, but many churches reach the 50 percent level and that seems to me appropriate—half for "us" and half for "them." How is it at your place? _____ percent of total gift income is invested in missions. Would God be calling you to a 10 percent increase? Perhaps it's time to reorder your priorities and take a leap of faith.

One Hundred

Right up front let me admit I've never seen a church that met this standard. But I still believe it's biblical, and I've been to one church that comes close. The most important part of the missionary enterprise is prayer, we would all concede, and I remain convinced that 100 percent of true disciples ought to be involved in praying for the world and for those sent to reach that world—individual and family prayer, which the church may not be able to measure, but also group prayer which we can easily measure.

In Martinez, Georgia, a group of pastors from many denominations gathered to think about missions in the local church. I told them of my experience in serving as consultant in dozens of churches to help them evaluate their missions program. I told them the average time spent in some form of group prayer for missions, including prayer for their own missionaries, totaled three minutes a week. Then I asked how it was in their churches. Pastors from one denomination agreed it was about one minute a week. A leading pastor from another denomination that prides itself on a strong missions program suggested that the dozens of churches he ministered in probably averaged five minutes a week. A missionary, fresh from visiting many churches of his denomination—perhaps the fastest-growing church both domestic and overseas—said those churches probably averaged thirty seconds. And yet another admitted that in his churches the score was zero.

But the representative from a nearby church, Augusta First Presbyterian Church, didn't speak. Since he was reluctant, I told them the story. When their pastor came twenty years earlier, there was no prayer for missions and precious little prayer for anything else. In fact, not one elder could or would pray in public. That historic church did give token financial support for one missionary, but no one knew her—she wasn't from among them.

Little by little the pastor led his people to become a praying people so that by the time of that meeting in Martinez prayer pervaded the atmosphere. And each Sunday night for an hour before the evening service—which was a packed house—hundreds gathered in "prayer bands" to pray for the world and for their dozens of representatives in Asia, Europe, Africa, South America. You'll not be surprised to learn that such a praying church is filled with newborn believers, that in the last missions conference I attended, thirty new volunteers stepped forward for career missionary service, including many professionals, and that the budget that year once again was more than 50 percent for missions. No one would claim that 100 percent of the members pray for missions and God only knows what that percent is. But they're headed in the right direction!

There you have it: 5-10-50-100. That could be a formula for frustration, even guilt. But it need not be. It could be a wake-up call or a beacon of hope. If God is calling to some faith action that will raise the Great Commission Quotient of your church even one point, listen carefully and act boldly! To participate more fully in completing his plan for world evangelization—what could be a greater joy?

Conclusion to Unit 4

We've completed our study of the role of each believer and each church in God's great plan of redemption. But that's not going to happen—indeed, none of the principles studied thus far will get anywhere—without the firm foundation of the absolute lordship of Jesus Christ in the life of the believer and of the church. We turn now to that capstone doctrine.

Unit 5:

THE LORDSHIP
OF CHRIST

GAUGING SERVANT LEADERSHIP

You call me . . . "Lord," and rightly so, for that is what I am.
(JOHN 13:13 NEB)

"Do you remember me?" That's a terrible question to ask an itinerant preacher, but you don't say so, you stall for time.

"Are you from Birmingham?" I asked the bubbly teen who greeted me before the youth conference began. I'd noted a large bus from Birmingham in the parking lot.

"Oh, yes." And with that she let me off the hook. "Do you remember at the end of last year's conference when you and I sat over there on that stone wall and talked?"

"Indeed I do, Debbie," I said as the memories flooded back. "How have things gone?" I asked, but I already knew the answer. Her youth leader had just told me of how a couple of the girls had returned from the conference, started an early morning prayer meeting in their high school, and how a mighty movement of God erupted, shaking the entire school.

The year before, after the closing meeting, she wanted to talk. "I didn't go down," she said forlornly. She meant she had not responded to the public invitation. "That's all right," I said, "not everyone is supposed to 'go down.'"

"I know. But I'm so tired of going down. I go down to surrender, to reconsecrate, I go down to dedicate and everything is so great. For a week or two, a month or two. And then, boom, it's back to the old me again. What's wrong with me?"

"I don't know, Debbie. But let me ask you something. Who's in the driver's seat of your life?"

"Oh, Jesus is!" She paused, then added, "Most of the time."

"Oh, no," I said, "you can't do that. You can't turn the wheel over to him and then at the first intersection reach out and grab the wheel."

"Well," she said, "I guess I do sometimes."

"But you can't do that!"

Deb bristled. "But I do!"

"But you can't, really. Maybe this is what you're saying." On a sheet of paper I wrote out two words: N-O and L-O-R-D.

"What does 'Lord' mean?" I asked.

"Jesus," she said.

"No, I mean what does the word 'Lord' mean?"

"Savior?"

"Well, Jesus is both Savior and Lord, but what does the word 'Lord' mean?"

"I give up. What does it mean?"

"Well, how about king? What does 'king' mean?"

"That's easy. He's the big boss."

"Do you say 'no' to the king?"

"It would be risky," Deb said.

"'Lord,'" I said, "means King of all kings, Lord of all lords. You can't say 'no' to him. It would be very risky. You can say 'no' or you can say 'Lord' but you can't say 'no, Lord.' If he's Lord of your life you are saying, 'yes, Lord.'" I tore the sheet of paper in two and held out the "no" and the "Lord," and asked her which it would be. She dropped her head and was silent, her long hair covering her face. I wondered what was going on behind that veil. At last she threw back her head and reached out toward the 'Lord' half of the paper. I pulled it away. "How long do you want him to be Lord?" I asked.

"Oh, forever," she said and made her choice. New life surged and changed her world. Was she new-born at that time or did she just become a true disciple? We don't have to make a judgment, of course, because acknowledging Christ as Lord is the only way into life and is also the only way to advance in that life.

In these studies we've considered the church's twofold responsibility: to win to faith (unit 4) and to disciple the believer (units 2 and 3). To engage in each of these requires a personal relationship with the Lord. Leading people to acknowledge (enter into life) and live under the lordship of Christ (grow as true disciples) is what church is all about.

Yet even churches that are good at one or both of those fundamental tasks—leading individuals to accept Christ as Lord and discipling them to live under his authority—seem to have missed the way in making him true Lord of the church as a body. In this unit we will probe the implications of what it means for Christ to be Lord of his church.

I keep asking that the God of our Lord Jesus Christ, the glorious Father, may give you the Spirit of wisdom and revelation, so that you may know him better. I pray also that the eyes of your heart may be enlightened in order that you may know the hope to which he has called you, the riches of his glorious inheritance in the saints, and his incomparably great power for us who believe. That power is like the working of his mighty strength, which he exerted in Christ when he raised him from the dead and seated him at his right hand in the heavenly realms, far above all rule and authority, power and dominion, and every title that can be given, not only in the present age but also in the one to come. And God placed all things under his feet and appointed him to be head over everything for the church, which is his body, the fullness of him who fills everything in every way. (Eph. 1:17–23 NIV)

CHAPTER 17:

LEADERSHIP

Question for reflection: **Are safeguards in place to keep leaders from slipping into lordly attitudes or behavior?**

It is true that Christ alone is absolute Lord of his church, but the amazing thing is that the Lord God Almighty has chosen to mediate his lordship through human beings. Consider:

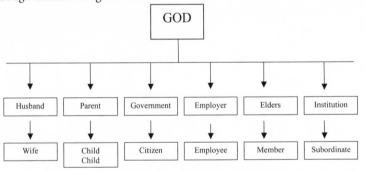

- "Wives, be in subjection unto your own husbands, as unto the Lord" (Eph. 5:22 ASV).
- "Children, obey your parents in the Lord" (Eph. 6:1 ASV).
- "Let every soul be in subjection to the higher powers: for ... the powers that be are ordained of God ... for he is a minister of God to thee" (Rom. 13:1, 4 ASV).
- "Servants, be obedient unto them that according to the flesh are your masters ... as unto Christ" (Eph. 6:5 ASV).
- "Obey them that have the rule over you, and submit to them: for they watch in behalf of your souls, as they that shall give account" (Heb. 13:17 ASV).
- "Be subject for the Lord's sake to every human institution" (1 Pet. 2:13 RSV).[1]

---

1. See also Matthew 23:5–12; Luke 6:46, 22:24–27; John 13:12–17; Ephesians 4:1–6; Philippians 2:3–8; 1 Peter 5:1–11.

We are uncomfortable with words like these. And the depth of our discomfort may be a measure of the depth of the crisis in authority which marks the twentieth and twenty-first centuries in the Western world. A driving value of the past one hundred years has been that personal autonomy is a given right and anything that infringes on that is illegitimate. Of course, this spirit did not originate in the Western world of the twentieth century. From the days of Eve and Adam, humans have followed the example of Lucifer and sought to usurp the throne. As a minimum, each seeks to rule her or his own life.

If a measure of personal autonomy is achieved, men, especially, but increasingly women as well, seek to use that power to control others. Both of these efforts reflect basic rebellion against the lordship of Christ. The rejection of human authority and the abuse of that authority ultimately stem from a quarrel with the Almighty, since he has chosen to mediate his authority—under strict limitations, to be sure—through subauthorities. Our acceptance of his lordship in our lives, then, is tested and proved by our acceptance of the mediated authority on the one hand, and, for the subauthority, by its subjection to the ultimate Authority.

If we don't follow the guidebook, the Bible, we reap the harvest of this abuse and rebellion. The damage and destruction because of rebellious use of personal power applies to all spheres of mediated authority, but in this unit we examine only relationships within the congregation, where Christ is named absolute Lord of the church. We seem to have developed an infinite variety of ways to subvert that authority, to our own great loss.

Followership

Church health and, consequently, church member spiritual health begins with acknowledging Christ as absolute Lord. Unconditional allegiance of the human heart to the one true King is proved at the point of willing acceptance of the congregation's leaders. Obedience to human authority, of course, is not absolute, since human leaders sin and err. So ultimate allegiance is only to the Lord of the church. But willingness to accept human leadership is often the testing ground of one's allegiance to the Lord who instituted that authority. And there is a further significance in faithful "followership." No one qualifies to become a leader until he or she has learned to follow (John 13:14–17; Luke 22:24–30).

A congregation of autonomous members, all setting their own agendas and pursuing their own goals, is a sure recipe for failure of all the purposes God intends for his church.

Having identified the basic foundation for congregational health in all members' relationship to the Lord of the church, and having indicated the vital role of interpersonal relationships, with non-leaders willing to follow appointed leaders, we must move on to address the key issue—leadership in the congregation.

Leadership

Leadership is the key to successfully achieving any of the purposes of the church we have studied. But what is leadership? There are probably as many definitions of the term as there are books on the subject. And there are quite a few of those! "Amazon lists 1,902 books with the term 'Leader' in the title and 4,626 with 'Leadership' in the title. When one expands the search to leadership as the subject or category of the book, 10,244 entries are available."[2] This astonishing fact means two things for our study:

1. We won't try to synthesize the various views of what leadership is about, but rather go with a simple definition: A leader is one whom people follow.
2. We will not explore the entire field of leadership, but focus rather on the single aspect of leadership that is critical for the success of any congregation: What are biblical principles to assure that Christ is the final and functional authority among God's people?

In this chapter, we will consider the fundamental principles of godly leadership. Then we will reflect on the models of leadership God has provided—first the ungodly, then the godly. Following these foundational considerations, we will examine the impact of leadership on the unity and purity of the congregation. All of these considerations will focus on the question of how a congregation may truly live under the lordship of Jesus Christ.

Servant Leadership

The term "servant leadership" has gained wide currency, but I wonder about its usefulness. The reason for my doubt is not in the term itself, but in the elasticity of its interpretation. In a denominational convention of thousands, I was the keynoter, speaking on servant leadership. The person who had invited me also spoke and took violent exception to the idea of leadership. Though he once wrote a booklet on leadership, he now told the congregation that leadership is nowhere taught in Scripture; only servanthood. What is the problem with that? This lifetime friend of mine is as authoritarian a leader as you can imagine.

This is not an isolated experience. So what does the term "servant" mean? Many of those who speak most vigorously of "servant leadership" are domineering autocrats in their own ministry. How can this be? Perhaps they are thinking of themselves as servants, but servants of the Lord, not

---

2. Don N. Howell Jr., *Servants of the Servant, a Biblical Theology of Leadership* (Eugene, Ore.: WIPF and Stock Publishers, 2003), 1.

so much servants of his people. But that won't do. To truly serve the Lord is evidenced in one's attitude and relationship to those for whom one is responsible (2 Cor. 4:5). The problem is that there is a built-in drive in each of us to control outcomes. To do that we must control the people within our influence. On the way to achieve commendable goals, therefore, we usurp the role of the Lord of the church.

This tendency is not confined to a particular form of church government or to a particular culture, though some forms of government and some cultures may promote human lordship. Of the three basic forms of government—episcopal, representative, and congregational—the episcopal would seem most likely to produce lordly behavior on the part of its bishops. But in many Presbyterian churches (representative form) the "ruling elders" do not rule; rather, the "teaching elder" is in full control. Again, if a Baptist (congregational form) pastor survives the first two years in a new tenure, he can easily become pope-like to his congregation. For example, the pastor of a large Baptist church in California called to ask my advice. Should he leave his church which was in crisis? What kind of crisis? Well, he had just called the police to evict the four deacons he had fired and who refused to leave the premises. His view was that the pastor was the single elder in charge and the deacons served under him at his pleasure. So, form of government may be no safeguard against lordly behavior. The human heart is effective at discovering how to get its way within any structured governance.

Culture also has an impact. In a feudalistic, authoritarian culture like Japan, it seems very difficult for the pastor not to assume lordly behavior. The people expect it, and hardly know how to function without it. Of course, biblical leadership will be exercised in ways different from churches in a more democratic society, but keeping Christ as true Lord of his church may be more difficult in such a society.

During our first term of service in Japan, in establishing a new congregation we sought to implement the principal of Christ's lordship. We trained new believers in leadership, including teaching and preaching as the ability developed. I did not do all the baptizing, marrying, burying, presiding, or preaching. I wanted to follow the New Testament pattern of a plural eldership in the church. But it was totally counter-cultural. The first Japanese pastor to whom the work was entrusted took as his first objective getting rid of those threatening non-professional church leaders. He himself had to be present for every meeting of members, even the women's meetings. Each member must be tied to his authority and dependent on him for all vital spiritual services. He closed all the daughter churches, insisting that those in outlying districts fold their lives into the mother church. He could not control those four or five congregations-at-a-distance. Although he lost most of those outlying members, he was a strong leader and the church thrived.

Depending on the strength of the leader, that is what may well happen anywhere.

I learned my lesson. On the second term we started a church more in line with Japanese patterns of relating. Years later, I learned that the pastor of the first church also learned his lesson and grieved for what he had done to the flock. Surely there is a biblical way of leading that is both culturally appropriate and biblically sound.

But the same violations of the lordship principle can take place in a strongly democratic society. For example, in the seventies the booming charismatic movement was divided over "shepherding." Strong natural leaders felt that loose doctrinal understandings must be tightened, and that the frequent unbiblical behavioral patterns needed correcting, so they became "shepherds." For example, the shepherd (read "pastor") of the flock decided who should marry whom and directed job changes. Virtually all of life was controlled by the shepherd in an effort to advance true discipleship. Then one of the leaders of the movement had an encounter with the One who desired to be Lord of the flock. *Christianity Today* reported: "Bob Mumford, fifty-nine, was one of five prominent leaders of the discipleship, or shepherding, movement. He left it in 1984 and recently made a public apology for the damaged lives that have resulted from abuse of the shepherding concept."[3]

Long ago, A. W. Tozer warned us of what was happening in our evangelical churches:

> The present position of Christ in the gospel churches (read: evangelical) may be likened to that of a king in a limited, constitutional monarchy. The king . . . is in such a country no more than a traditional rallying point, a pleasant symbol of unity and loyalty much like a flag or a national anthem. He is lauded, feted and supported, but his real authority is small. Nominally he is head over all, but in every crisis someone else makes the decisions. On formal occasions he appears in his royal attire to deliver the tame, colorless speech put into his mouth by the real rulers of the country. The whole thing may be no more than good-natured make-believe, but it is rooted in antiquity, it is a lot of fun and no one wants to give it up.
>
> Among the gospel churches Christ is now in fact little more than a beloved symbol. "All Hail the Power of Jesus' Name" is the church's national anthem and the cross is her official flag, but in the week-by-week services of the church and the day-by-day conduct of her members someone else, not Christ, makes the decisions. . . . Those in actual authority decide the moral standards of

3. March 19, 1990, p. 39.

the church, as well as all objectives and all methods employed to achieve them. Because of long and meticulous organization it is now possible for the youngest pastor just out of seminary to have more actual authority in a church than Jesus Christ has.[4]

The problem, however, isn't restricted to professional clergy. Tozer speaks of pastors, but actually a church may be ruled by someone else—the wealthy person who is indispensable to the operation, the family that has "owned" the church from its inception, the best educated, even the loud and domineering chairman of the board or wife of the pastor. But most often it is the senior pastor who begins to assume lordly attitudes. And if he is gifted and strong of personality, he may well be successful, so long as the measurement of success is derived from extrabiblical sources.

In my experience, most leaders do not move up the escalator to usurpation of God's prerogatives as far as Tozer laments, but no leader and no church is immune. Why is that? Perhaps it has to do with the source of our fallenness. Immediately following Peter's classic description of godly leadership (1 Pet. 5:1–6) he gives a warning: "Be self-controlled and alert. Your enemy the devil prowls around like a roaring lion looking for someone to devour. Resist him, standing firm" (vv. 8–9 NIV).

Satanic Influence

Whether or not Isaiah quoted only the spirit of the king of Babylon when he referred to Lucifer or whether he had in mind the evil power behind that king, he certainly captured the spirit of Satan when he said:

I will ascend into heaven,
I will exalt my throne above the stars of God; . . .
I will be like the Most High.
Isaiah 14:13–14 NKJV

Without doubt Satan, like humans, was created in the moral image of God. But he was not satisfied with that. He aspired to God's divine authority, his incommunicable attributes—his sovereignty, his power, his knowledge, his glory. And thus he became God's adversary. As enemy, then, he seduced God's creatures who had been created in God's moral likeness for intimate companionship with himself, and all humankind fell. Forsaking God's likeness in moral nature (holiness, love, justice, goodness, truth), humans reached for God's likeness in authority, power, wisdom. "You shall be as God," promised the deceiver. They were already as God in character, but in aspiring to be like God in his infinities they lost the likeness God had graciously given. In his rescue operation God is seeking to restore the original model. We are destined to become perfect (in moral attributes) as the Father is perfect. He does more. The "incommunicable" attributes also

---

4. *The Alliance Witness* (May 15, 1963), 3.

he distributes to humans—but, lest they grasp at God's prerogatives, he distributes them among his people. "Gifts of the Spirit" we call them (unit 3), by which he gives his wisdom and power to his church.

In these ways the Spirit makes headway in personal godlikeness for every believer and dynamic ministry through those believers gathered in congregations as he forms these new re-creations into sub-families of his own. But Satan is on the prowl, seeking to subvert God's purposes, keeping humans like himself in his fallenness, deceiving them with illusions of grandeur, to be like God in his sovereignty. And what better way than to seduce the leaders of God's people?

Prowling like a lion, said the first senior pastor, Peter. I always considered the lion to be very bold and all-powerful, but on reflection he may be something of a coward. He does not often attack the strong, only the weak, the ill, the young, the small. So it is with Satan. There are signs to recognize in a leader when the enemy is gaining ground in a church, devil-like characteristics that may begin small but gradually lead on to more and more usurpation of God's role as ultimate Lord of the church.

- If the pastor is not functionally accountable to anyone but himself in the day-to-day management of the "corporation," watch out. The enemy is on the prowl.
- An early indication is for the leader to become less and less approachable. The "little people" do not find a warm welcome, especially when they don't agree with what the leader has said or done.
- Then there is more and more isolation—isolation from criticism, isolation from a close personal relationship with ordinary members, as the "yes men" are gathered around in protective formation.
- This leads soon to infallibility; the "pope" cannot be controverted. A telltale sign is when the pulpit often resounds with phrases such as "God told me." If God told him, there is nowhere to turn; that settles the matter. Infallible direction, vision, and even building plans are all baptized under God's name and beyond challenge.
- Finally such a leader reaches the pinnacle—immutability, incapable of change. He has taken on the prerogatives of deity.

The stages of his ascent to the throne are, then, less and less accountable, then less and less accessible, then less and less pliable, and finally less and less fallible.

In reality, of course, those heights are impossible to attain. When a leader tries to project an image of infallible wisdom, fully adequate strength, and unfailing success, it is actually a false image. No leader should feel embarrassed when the truth of his humanity becomes known. A Christ-dominated leader will be mature enough and transparent enough not to attempt to cover his own ignorance, weakness, and failure.

This fact of life needs balance, however. It doesn't mean he should go with the contemporary in "honestly" making himself "vulnerable" by flaunting his "humanity," or, as some seem to do, celebrating his sinfulness. If he is truly spiritual, the lordship of Christ in his life will be a constant reminder to the people that it is possible to maintain an attitude of irrevocable and unfailing commitment to Christ as Lord, never failing through consciously rejecting the known will of God. This is true servanthood, bowing to the Lord of life in every aspect of life. Thus there is an appropriate "open heart" of vulnerability and transparency of leaders while consistently modeling the life of spiritual maturity, a balance of grace with truth (2 Cor. 6:11–13).

Not only must leaders be examples of living with Christ as Lord; they must constantly train those for whom they are responsible in this basic relationship. If they are not able to disciple the people in this, all else is to no avail. No matter how powerful the preaching, no matter how lucid the teaching, and no matter what other great gifts they may have, leadership cannot accomplish God's purposes for the congregation if the members do not relate to Christ as Lord of all life. When the pastor becomes a minilord or demigod, the members of the congregation no longer have one master. "Messianism" can be detected when affection, allegiance, or obedience to the Lord seems to be shifting to a human being. And what results from this devil-like usurpation of Christ's role as Lord of the congregation?

Results from "Lordship" Failure

No matter how great the leader in natural and spiritual gifts, he is only one person, not the whole body. Therefore, if the leader is a very gifted person, the work will grow and achieve a measure of success. It cannot be as strong and effective as it should be because many members are not freely functioning as the Spirit intended. The vision and gifts of others will not be used as he designs in giving gifts to each member for the profit of all (1 Cor. 12:11). Since the leader does not have all knowledge and all wisdom, God's highest and best for the congregation may never be known.

On the other hand, if a person's Spirit-directed role is not permitted or is neglected, there is a tendency to assume a spectator role. This can create a cheering section—or a jeering section. But in either case, individual members will not grow as they should because they are not functioning as God intended. Furthermore, others will not grow as they should because they will not benefit from the ministry God intended to give through the nonfunctioning members.

Again, if the dominant leader is not a person of great leadership ability, the other strong leaders in the congregation will tend to drop out. Man-dependency, if not man-worship, tends to develop. One final result of human lordship is the potential division or loss of membership when the pastor leaves or dies; the central authority figure is no longer there, but loyalty to him lingers on.

Why Congregations Fail in Lordship Principles

Responsibility for failure may lie with leaders or with followers. Or with both. There may be personal reasons in the leaders: unbelief (a lack of confidence in the Holy Spirit in other people), pride, fear, desire for recognition, insecurity. But equally culpable are followers who may be lazy. People are often unwilling to assume responsibility. This is not merely a passive failure, but is actually active rejection of the will of God and reflects unbelief. Again, many times there are non-Christians in the church, or members who behave like non-Christians, and this often leads to the exaltation of a man.

As noted earlier, the form of church government or the leadership style in the local culture can foster human lordship. Again, though they cannot of themselves create ungodly behavior, lordly acts, words, titles, and costumes can promote human lordship. Whatever the reasons, historically, virtually all churches and human organizations seem to move in the direction of centralization of authority.

Those are the problems of faulty leadership. We turn now to solutions for this endemic problem of the church, to reflect on the ultimate model of godly leadership—Jesus Christ himself.

CHAPTER 18:

LEADERSHIP: POSITIVE ROLE MODEL

Questions for reflection: Do all church leaders—lay or professional—
authentically model God's own qualities of leadership?
Do the people enthusiastically follow the leaders?

We have considered the failure of the lordship principle in the congregation, especially in its leadership. It seems strange that God who graciously shared his very nature with us, creating us in his moral image and
who by his Spirit works to restore that likeness, should also share as well his
incommunicable attributes—his authority, his wisdom, his power. The difference is, he distributes those qualities among his people rather than vesting
them in any one individual. We call that distribution the gifts of the Spirit
(unit 3).

What wisdom! There is no limit to his intention for us to advance
in holiness. The Spirit's goal is to make us just like him, all of us. But he
never intended any single person to arrogate to himself those incommunicable attributes. So he distributed them. He gave gifts to each as he willed
(1 Cor. 12–14, especially 12:11, 29–30). His purpose was that through us
corporately, together, the congregation, we could do his (supernatural) work
in this world.

How sad, then, that we, while pursuing holiness, also reach in unrigh-
teous pride for his incommunicable attributes, especially his lordship. Perhaps that is why God says several times in slightly different ways, "I resist the
proud but give grace to the humble" (see 1 Pet. 5:5). And following Satan's
rebellion we are in danger of falling, of losing it all—both the powers we
sought and the holiness we neglected. So what should we do about it?

Solutions to Failure in the Lordship Principle

The first part of the solution is for the leader to demonstrate personally
an example of yieldedness to God, obedience to him alone, brokenness over

and hatred of sin, openness with the brethren, and unaffected acceptance of the servant role.

It is just as important for the leaders to hold before the people constantly the lordship principle. This must not be preached just as a doctrine, but discipleship training in this relationship with the head of the church must characterize the life of the congregation.

Each member must also be discipled in her or his role as a member of the body, recognizing one's own gift and esteeming the gifts of others. "Don't cherish exaggerated ideas of yourself or your importance, but try to have a sane estimate of your capabilities by the light of the faith that God has given" (Rom. 12:3 Phillips). "As each one has received a gift, employ it for one another . . . in order that in everything God may be glorified through Jesus Christ. To him belong glory and dominion" (1 Pet. 4:10–11 RSV).

An essential element of demonstrating that Christ is indeed Lord in a congregation is a heart attitude of humility and love. We must submit in love and humility to the authority above us. We are to be subject to one another (Eph. 5:21), in honor preferring one another (Rom. 12:10), giving honor to whom honor is due (Rom. 13:7). On the other hand, those who lead must do so in love and humility. The brother or sister's welfare—not one's own—is master of the spiritual leader (1 Cor. 10:23–11:1; 9:19–23; Rom. 14). Paul said his freedom of choice was freedom to make himself the servant of all. In humility, the leader must count others better than himself (Phil. 2:3), in honor preferring the other (Rom. 12:10), not lording it over the flock (1 Pet. 5:3).

We have noted how organizational structure may adversely affect the lordship principle. One way to ameliorate such a negative impact is to follow the biblical pattern of a plurality of elders. Whatever the structure, if the New Testament model is to be followed, the authority and responsibilities of leadership will be dispersed among several, not reserved for a single leader. Another practical measure for promoting the lordship of Christ is to promote interpersonal ties with many people rather than maintaining exclusive relationship in spiritual authority with the pastor alone. It may be hard on one's emotions or ego to find people dependent on other members of the congregation or holding them in high esteem as spiritual leaders. So it may be difficult to permit it, let alone plan for it. But by the same token it is essential. This means a division of labor so that all who are gifted as teachers have ample opportunity to teach, all whom God would gift in counseling would have ample opportunity for a pastoral ministry, and so on throughout all the spiritual ministry of the church.

We have noted the general malaise of the church and some ways to cure it, but we must return to the initial truth that God does indeed exercise his authority on earth through human leadership. This delegated authority, whether in the home, society, or church, is not absolute, to be sure, but it is real—authority not merely to give benevolent advice or to enforce obedience to the Ten Commandments. It is an authority to make rules and to supervise conduct for the benefit of all members of the group. All human authority is limited by human finitude and warped by human sinfulness, but God has chosen to accomplish his purposes in the world through people in authority. When it comes to church, what that authority should look like may come as a surprise.

The Model: Christ Himself

Perhaps it comes as no surprise to discover that our human impulses lead us to usurp Christ's role as the functioning Lord of the congregation. But it may surprise us to discover that the role model for making him Lord is the Lord Christ himself! Without seeking to be exhaustive, let us note some of the major characteristics of God's authoritative leadership. We take our cue from one whom some have called the first prelate, the prince and lord, the pope of the church—Peter, whom we shall discover did not arrogate to himself those lordly titles. In his first letter, Peter spells out the pattern of godly or godlike leadership: "To the elders among you, I appeal as a fellow elder. ... Be shepherds of God's flock that is under your care, serving as overseers—not because you must, but because you are willing, as God wants you to be, not greedy for money, but eager to serve; not lording it over those entrusted to you, but being examples to the flock. ... Young men, in the same way be submissive to those who are older. ... Clothe yourselves with humility toward one another, because 'God opposes the proud but gives grace to the humble.' Humble yourselves, therefore, under God's mighty hand" (1 Pet. 5:1–6 NIV).

Eleven Characteristics of Godly Leaders from 1 Peter

Shared Authority

"The elders who are among you I exhort, I who am a fellow elder"
(1 Pet. 5:1 NKJV).

It may come as a surprise, but should not, that the first elder should consider himself a "fellow elder," for that is the nature of God himself. The Trinity is a beautiful model for what God seems to have intended in human leadership. Although God the Father is preeminent in the relationships of the Trinity, the Godhead is a shared authority. Not only does the Trinity share in authority with one another; God has chosen even to share his responsibility and authority with people, as we have seen, even to exercise his authority through human beings.[1]

The model is made most clear in family relations. Though the husband is designated head of the home, it is the husband and wife jointly who are to receive the honor and obedience of the children. Parenthood is a participatory leadership. In the same way, there is a plurality of leadership in the church. In the New Testament, as we have seen, when the office of elder is used of a local church, it is consistently plural, never singular. For example, Titus is told to appoint elders (plural) in every place (Titus 1:5).

In my first ministry assignment in which I was the responsible leader, headmaster of Ben Lippen High School, I did the natural thing. As an inexperienced twenty-five-year-old, I just did what came naturally and that was to make the decisions and rally the troops. But things weren't going well. In that crucible I learned about the plurality of leadership. I learned to trust the Holy Spirit in the responsible body of believers more than I trusted him in my own, independent judgment. Whether board of trustees or the faculty body, I learned there was far more wisdom and effectiveness in decision making by the body of leaders than on my own. I learned the hard way about what is called, in academia, collegiality, and the ministry thrived. It was a lesson that has lasted a lifetime.

For years in church planting in Japan, and somewhat counter-culturally, the new believers eagerly participated in discovering and executing God's will together. Then when I went to what is now Columbia International University, I discovered a legacy of forty years of top-down leadership and introduced the idea of team or shared leadership. The ministry that had been on hold for two decades prospered in unprecedented ways. But even if visible prosperity had not followed so dramatically, I was committed to shared leadership as modeled by God himself.

Leadership that becomes solitary rather than participatory, drawing all authority to itself, is actually Satanlike rather then Godlike. It is marked, as we have seen, by unaccountability, inaccessibility, pretensions of infallibility, and stubborn immutability. Godlike leadership, on the contrary, is shared. In shared leadership there is often an order of preeminence in role as in the Godhead and in the family, but this does not in any way detract from the trinitarian model of shared authority and responsibility for leadership.

Loving

Peter testifies that he is a witness of the sufferings of Christ (v. 1) and John gives the same testimony: "We have seen and testify that the Father has sent the Son as Savior of the world. . . . And we have known and

---

1. In George Cladis, *Leading the Team-Based Church* (Jossey, 1999), the first third of the book is devoted to examining how the Trinity models several key principles of healthy teams.

believed the love that God has for us. God is love, and he who abides in love abides in God, and God in him. . . . As He is, so are we in this world" (1 John 4:14–17 NKJV).

God is love by nature, the very Trinity itself bound together by living bonds of love. Then, in the overflow of that love we are redeemed and bound together to him (v. 15). But even more; we are bound by those same love bonds to one another. If not, says John, we are none of his at all (vv. 20–21). In the world, strong leadership can be exerted successfully through bonds of fear such as the fear of consequences if one does not obey. A measure of success can be achieved through admiration or based on the acceptance of a leader for a sense of identity with his success or in confidence that he will accomplish something good for his followers. God also is one to be feared and admired. But his bonds are bonds of love.

When love is the bond that binds leaders together and leaders and people together, openness, trust, and loyalty all help in making the bond even more firm. Other bonds in the relationship may work to some degree, but love is the ultimate bond that holds together and gives strength to achieve the goals of the group. As a by-product, this bond not only provides strength; it also provides meaning and joy in the relationships as well.

Purposeful

"The glory that will be revealed" (1 Pet. 5:1 NKJV).

When God's purposes are brought about in and through his church, what honor it brings him! But let's not be more spiritual than the Bible, thinking God's glory is the only legitimate goal. It is the ultimate goal, of course, but there are many contributing goals or outcomes. For example, Peter says that he looks forward to our participation in that glory. He also says that we will receive the crown of glory that does not pass away (v. 4). Though God's glory is our ultimate goal, there are many intermediate or contributing goals that have been the themes of our study of biblical principles for ministry.

God's leadership, then, is marked by the dynamic of a great unity of purpose in the Trinity. In the same way, godlike leadership is goal-oriented. God is active and his activity has an end, a goal, a destination. Some human relationships are not voluntary, as with children in the home. But the church is a voluntary organization. It is the unity of purpose, our shared objectives that challenge us to participation and that hold the body together.

Because of this a leader who follows God's model must have a clear vision of what the group should be and do. This is what the guidebook, the Bible, is given for, to define and refine that vision. That is what this study is all about. To communicate a common purpose, goal, or vision is the responsibility of the leaders. Then they must continually evaluate the achievement of those purposes, that vision, and lead in planning for it. Very little motivation and endurance will be stirred up by simply reproducing certain services or events week after week. The meetings of the church are never the end, the goal.

Of course, as we have seen, this purpose-discerning and purpose-achieving is not a solo flight by the leader. It is also the responsibility of the leadership to identify those who can participate in discerning the vision and achieving the goals and to organize and direct them toward that achievement. All that is to no avail, however, if their efforts do not prove productive. God's purposes being achieved is the measure of the effectiveness of human leadership.

Everyone was astonished—not the least I—when, on the initial application for accreditation by the Association of Theological Schools, Columbia Biblical Seminary was approved without notations. This, when the senior theological schools of America, applying for reaffirmation that year, were given multiple notations, requirements for change and improvement. How did such a remarkable thing take place? One reason was the unity of purpose the official representatives found on campus. They testified they had never seen a seminary where the entire faculty—not to mention other staff and students—knew the purposes of the institution and were enthusiastically committed to them. I hope God was just as pleased. God's leadership is purposeful.

Shepherding

"Shepherd the flock of God which is among you" (v. 2 NKJV).

God himself as the chief shepherd (v. 4) is our model as undershepherds. The shepherd role (literally, "pastor") hints at what the leader should be—guide, caregiver, counselor, friend.

As soon as I arrived for a missions weekend, the pastor asked me to go after his board of elders. A former missionary, gung ho for missions, he wanted to invest heavily in the missionary enterprise, but the board balked. They had a different priority, the building program. Would I please set them straight? I said, "J. D., did God call you to be a shepherd or a sheep dog?" The pastor grew silent. The next day he came to me in jubilation. "The board has just adopted my proposed missions budget!"

"How did that happen?" I asked in astonishment.

"Well, we had a special called meeting and I apologized. I told them I was in the wrong. I had been like a sheep dog yapping and snapping and seeking to drive them my way. They were the elders and I would go along with their plans. With that, there was a motion to adopt my proposal!" The leader may not be called "pastor," but that is his role.

Strong

"Serving as overseers" (v. 2 NKJV).

God rules with authority. His leadership is positive, not passive. He takes the initiative. And he is the one who appoints the leaders of his people. In any human organization a strong, positive leadership is essential to success in achieving the purposes of the organization. Weak, passive leadership will not do. Chaos or some other force or personality will fill a leadership vacuum. An organization that has no leadership or a leadership that will not assume the responsibility and exercise the authority inherent in that position is doomed to mediocrity and failure.

In the New Testament, "presbyter" or, literally, "elder" was the title of an office used interchangeably with "bishop" or, literally, "overseer." Another title is "pastor" or, literally, "shepherd." Technically speaking, the office is that of presbyter, and this person functions as a shepherd or overseer. This responsibility is assigned by God (for example, 1 Pet. 5:2–3) and is a responsibility to supervise, give direction, provide, protect, discipline, and teach. A real problem exists in the American church in which young people, unproven, are given eldership. Care should be taken on the part of the young pastor to compensate for this non-biblical aberration through shared leadership and accountability. Timothy was not young by our standards, but rather in his late thirties or forties, when told not to allow people to despise his youth. So the young person cast in a role of leadership should strive to earn the respect of one who deserves that role. Godlike leadership should be positive and with authority.

Free of Compulsion

"Not by constraint, but willingly" (v. 2 KJV).

Jesus was under no compulsion to come to earth, but he did so freely. He gave not only life itself but gifts beyond measure free of charge. That's why we call them "graces" (*charis,* often translated "gift"). And so the leader is called to give unstintingly of life. Leadership is painful, like crucifixion. Jesus told us on at least four different occasions that we are to take up our cross and that such action is a continual action—daily, he says. We are to give and give of time and energy and emotional resources, not because we're compelled to, nor for the money, says Peter. Willingly. That's the way our model lived. And that is the way he died.

Eager

"Serving . . . eagerly" (v. 2 NKJV).

This is similar to the "freely" characteristic, but adding the positive. Not only should the service not be coerced; it should be with enthusiasm, not reluctance. Jesus endured the cross for the joy set before him. He took up the towel and basin in the upper room because of his great love for the disciples. Great love is the seed from which eager serving is the fruit.

Non-Coercive

"Shepherd the flock of God which is among you, serving as overseers not . . . as being lords over those entrusted to you" (vv. 2–3 NKJV).

Although God's authority is absolute, he doesn't use this authority in a coercive way. God goes to great lengths to teach, to persuade, to motivate, yes, to woo. He forces no person to accept his lordship. There is coming a day when all people will bow before his sovereign authority, but the model of authority which he presents to us is one of restraint, of persuasion. Jesus never manipulated or forced anyone to be a disciple. He created our capacities for thinking, feeling, and choosing. He influences but doesn't short-circuit or override our capacity for response, even to reject his love and rule.

Peter instructs us to lead God's people in the same way. A domineering relationship is strictly prohibited (v. 3). To dominate is the great temptation of human leaders. But it is the way of defeat in achieving the purposes of the congregation and also, ultimately, damaging to those relationships which would make success possible. The role of the godlike leader is to communicate, like the Word in flesh, the ultimate communicator, to persuade, confront, comfort, motivate, and instruct—but not to drive, demand, or coerce.

Modeling

"Nor as being lords . . . but being examples to the flock" (v. 3 NKJV).

God himself models what he intends for his people to be and do. In fact, revelation is, above all else, the disclosure of God himself. Both the written revelation and the living revelation in the person of Jesus Christ are the models for our individual behavior and for church doctrine and life.

In the same way, the responsibility of the leader in Christian ministry is to set the example. The idea of making oneself an adequate model is not an instantaneous decision or experience but a continuing activity.

The main emphasis in both 1 Timothy and Titus on qualifications for spiritual leadership is the model role, not the ministry role. To Timothy, of the sixteen qualifications for an overseer (1 Tim. 3:1–7) only one is ministry qualification; fifteen are character or what Paul would call the fruit of the Spirit. In a different, though overlapping, list to Titus (1:6–9), once again only one of the sixteen is giftedness. The leader must be an example of what a person should be and how the work of God should be done. Paul repeatedly told people to follow him, to imitate him. "As he followed

Christ," to be sure, but sometimes he did not even add that qualification! Would people be safe, would the church be healthy, if all were like me? What a startling reminder of the serious nature of the modeling responsibility of leadership!

Leading an exemplary life, by itself, does not make one a leader, of course. Followers have the identical calling. Though godliness alone does not qualify a person for leadership, a breakdown in godliness disqualifies one for leadership. His role model, then, is primarily that of a Christlike character. But it also includes providing a model in how God's work is to be done. He must model the spiritual gifts that qualify him for leadership. In both realms the godlike leader will serve as a reliable model of what God himself is like. Not a perfect replica at this point in our salvation, but an authentic reflection, safe to follow.

Humble

"Serving . . . Likewise you younger people, submit yourselves to your elders. Yes, all of you be submissive to one another, and be clothed with humility, for 'God resists the proud, but gives grace to the humble.' Therefore humble yourselves under the mighty hand of God, that He may exalt you in due time" (1 Pet. 5:2, 5–6 NKJV).

Finally we have reached a characteristic of biblical leadership that could hardly derive from God's own character? Wrong! The astonishing thing is that this is one of the chief characteristics of God as revealed in Jesus Christ. Remember, humility is not denying the gifting and responsibility to lead. The humble person lives out those God-graced realities but does not use that position to aggrandize himself or to gain power over others.

The mode of leadership on the godly model is to serve. Jesus himself is the model: "I am among you as one who serves" (Luke 22:27 NIV). And with that he took the apron and basin of the slave, telling us that we were to follow his model (John 13:1–17). Notice that in Peter's instruction manual for the leader we have been considering, he calls on us to take the initiative, to humble ourselves. He doesn't tell us to pray for humility or to feel humble or to say humble things. No, the leader is to act in humility. He is joyfully to accept orders from those to whom he is responsible, to serve others, to fit into their arrangements, to confess his sin, to share his leadership role with others, to do the servant thing. Maybe "servant leadership" isn't such a useless term after all! Just be sure to fill it with Peter's meaning. Though we have derived ten characteristics of what a leader should be like from Peter's exhortation, humility occupies fully 38 percent of his entire discourse on godly leadership!

It's strange that the word for servanthood, "minister," should have come to refer to one who is many times the opposite, one who is exalted and served by others, whether a minister of state or a minister of the church. Perhaps that is evidence of where we have gone astray. The leader who follows God's model will be among God's people as one who serves.

Faith-Filled

"Casting all your care upon Him, for He cares for you" (1 Pet. 5:7 NKJV).

To become, even in partial measure, all that Peter says the godly (read godlike) leader should look like, only God himself can accomplish. And our access code is faith. Only as we lean on him will it ever happen, and we can do so with confidence because "he cares." Faith is the key, but it must be expressed in prayer. So the prayer of faith, as we saw in unit 3, is the indispensable means of accessing the resources God provides for leaders. So the leader must above all be a person of prayer—faith-filled prayer.

How beautiful that our model above all others models dependency on his Father and a life of prayer. If Jesus Christ needed to pray incessantly, how much more does the leader who would be like him!

Notice how beautiful is God's model for leadership in the church or in other Christian ministry—shared, loving, purposeful, shepherding, strong, free of compulsion, eager, non-coercive, modeling, humble, and faith-filled. Just like Jesus.

The church where the leadership fails to do it Christ's way will find two essential characteristics sabotaged: unity and purity. We turn now to consider how the lordship of Christ in a congregation promotes the unity and purity of the body.

CHAPTER 19:

UNITY
OF THE CONGREGATION

Question for reflection: Is unity seen not only in the absence of conflict,
but by caring relationships that provide a safe haven
for everyone and a sense of family solidarity?

Unity and Purity

God designed the church on the pattern of his own character. But today
that pattern is twisted and distorted, sometimes beyond recognition.
What is the character of God? "Hear, O Israel: The LORD our God is one
LORD" (Deut. 6:4 KJV). God is one, and he intended his church to be one:
"Keep the unity of the Spirit in the bond of peace. There is one body, and
one Spirit . . . one faith . . . one God and Father of all, who is above all, and
through all, and in you all" (Eph. 4:3–6 KJV). "Holy, holy, holy, Lord God
Almighty" (Rev. 4:8 KJV). What is the character of God? He is holy, and he
intended his church to be pure and undefiled in faith and in life. "Put away
from among yourselves that wicked person" (1 Cor. 5:13 KJV).

How important is it for the congregation to be united and pure? The
answer is apparent in another question: How important are these characteristics of God? How important is it that God be holy, separated from all
defilement? How important is the righteousness of God to his nature? Again,
how important is the unity of the Trinity? What if each member of our triune
God had his own agenda, went his own way? Our universe would implode!
And how important is love as a characteristic of God? Perfect love, the bond
that unites Father, Son, and Spirit! And so with his body, the church. The
congregation was designed to be both holy and united in love. When it is
unholy or disunited, it denies the character of God.

To the extent the congregation loses this basic character of God, it loses
its power. When either the unity or the purity is lost, the body of Christ no
longer has a right to expect its ministry to be fruitful. A fighting, bickering,
divided church projects an image of God that can be expected to turn people

away. It is when people see the love that disciples have for one another that they believe (John 13:35). When the church compromises and becomes hypocritical either in doctrine or in life, the power is drained off.

But this is not all. A disunited congregation or a compromising church not only denies the character of God and loses its testimony to the world, but it cannot fulfill God's purpose for its own members. For each member to grow into the likeness of Christ, the relations among the members ought to be right. For example, consider the worship experience of the church. Paul connects unity with the capacity to worship (Rom. 15:5–7). Can a disunited body bring true worship to the triune God?

God designed the congregation to be a true family; the eternal blood ties of Calvary are even stronger than human blood ties. It is in the context of this koinonia or loving mingling of life that God does his work of building Christians into the likeness of Christ (Eph. 4:11–16). This is no superficial Sunday-club relationship. God intended an intimate sharing of life on the pattern of the character of God, the Trinity, as we considered in chapter 7 on member care. Furthermore, to have such family solidarity, there must be discipline. Fellowship without purity of faith and life is flawed at its core. Unity and purity are interdependent elements of a single relationship. Just as in the family so it is in the church that where either love or discipline is missing, the children will be greatly handicapped. "Love without criticism brings stagnation, criticism without love brings destruction."[1]

And yet, as it is difficult for theologians to balance the justice and mercy of God, and as it is difficult for parents to balance firm discipline and loving acceptance, so it is very difficult for the church to maintain unity and purity at the same time. It is much easier to go to a consistent extreme than to stay at the center of biblical tension. Whether in the local congregation or in the church at large, the church of Jesus Christ seems incapable of living out both godlike oneness and godlike purity simultaneously. The result is that the reflection of God's image is distorted, the evangelistic thrust of the church is blunted, and Christians are stunted in spiritual growth.

On a larger scale, the church universal, there is a great polarization between the professional unifiers on the one hand and the professional purifiers on the other. It seems that a person must work at uniting all churches no matter how delinquent in doctrine or life or that he must give himself wholly to separating all the wheat from the tares. Now!

Do not misunderstand. Separation is good. This is the very meaning of the word "holy" or "sanctify." But there is an unholy separation that begins in the neglect of the complementary characteristic of love, descends quickly into an unlawful judgmental role, and ends in the terrible sin of schism.

1. John W. Gardner, "Uncritical Lovers, Unloving Critics," *Journal of Educational Research*, 5.5, 1969.

Unity is good. It is the ultimate character of God and is his revealed will for the church. But there is an unholy unity that begins by failing in faithfulness, quickly descends to unbiblical compromise, and ends in the terrible sin of impurity—defilement of faith or life.

Is there no solution to this great dilemma? Can we have success in one characteristic only at the expense of the other? I believe God intended that we be successful in both at once. Furthermore, I believe he has given clear and rather simple instructions for achieving success in both.

It is significant that the New Testament emphasis on both unity and purity has to do with the local congregation. In contrast, most of the emphasis throughout the twentieth century, whether on unity or on purity, was on larger interchurch or interdenominational relationships—the ecumenical movement or the separatist movement. But it is at the level of the local congregation that both unity and purity are most important. There the presence or absence of unity or purity is most visible to the world. And that is where the battle for unity or purity will be won or lost. The local congregation is also where unity and purity are most difficult to achieve and maintain.

Consider, then, first the unity of the congregation. Discussion of purity will follow in the next chapter.

"Now I plead with you . . . that you all speak the same thing, and that there be no divisions among you, but that you be perfectly joined together in the same mind and in the same judgment" (1 Cor. 1:10 NKJV). "Endeavoring to keep the unity of the Spirit in the bond of peace" (Eph. 4:3 NKJV). "Fulfill my joy by being like-minded, having the same love, being of one accord, of one mind" (Phil. 2:2 NKJV).

Not only did unity in God's family bring joy to Paul; surely that is what brings joy to the Father. And to the extent people live under the lordship of Christ, to that extent there will be unity. Consider first some of the enemies of unity, how wholeness in the body can be fractured, then reflect on how healing and wholeness may be promoted.

Enemies of Unity

Satan is the great enemy of unity. He is the great divider and, indeed, one of his names is "the Destroyer." God's purpose is to give wholeness and life; Satan's is to bring division and death. Division in the church is Satan's strategy to gain the upper hand, says Paul (2 Cor. 2:5–11). Above all, he determines to divide God's children from God, but he is also determined to divide husband and wife, parents and children, friends and neighbors. Indeed, he works to divide a person against herself or himself. Just as he plots to destroy humans and God through division in every other area, he seeks to destroy the church by dividing it. It is significant that more than half the works of the flesh (Gal. 5:19–21) are attitudes and actions of schism and "those who practice such things will not inherit the kingdom of God" (NKJV)! And so today to divide the body, Satan works in many ways. At the very beginning there was paradise, unbroken unity with God and one another (Gen. 1–2). Once Satan's lie became the basis for choice, oneness evaporated. As a matter of fact, one definition of sin could be "anything that damages oneness." In order to oppose the works of the devil, it may be helpful to identify some of the enemies of unity.

Doctrinal Differences

Some division is necessary because of false teaching. Paul teaches this in the letter to the Galatians, and this is the main burden of Jude. We'll return to this theme in chapter 20.

Even more division in the church takes place, however, because of squabbling over nonessentials as in the church at Corinth. Paul exhorted believers to stop disputing about words (1 Tim. 6:4–8). This would be doctrinal differences that make no difference.

Doctrinal difference, whether major or minor, is sometimes used as a screen for sin, an independent spirit, or congenital belligerence and bull-headedness. The schism and division is sinful in either case, but the root problem is not as socially acceptable or spiritually justifiable as "doctrinal differences," so the doctrinal screen is often used. Sometimes, through rationalization, this is quite sincere; but nevertheless, that division is of the enemy, Satan.

The problem with church conflict, as distinct from political, academic, or business conflict, is that often it is not the obvious power struggle like those. Usually, each side tries to take the high ground. "This is God's will," or "this is biblical," is the stance. "You can't expect me to back down—that would compromise the truth. We're on God's side, don't ask us to betray him!" That's why purported doctrinal issues are often as divisive as actual doctrinal difference; or marginal doctrinal issues are raised to critical importance.

Leadership Failure

Division often comes when the leader falls into sin. But it also may come when the leader fails to lead. He may be insensitive to what is taking place among the people, appear to play favorites, give the impression of a domineering approach, fail to fulfill some essential function in the church, or fail to seek and allow someone else to fulfill the function in which they themselves lack strength. All the characteristics of godlike leadership that we considered in chapter 18, if neglected or absent, could sow seeds leading to disunity in the body.

Group Failure

The Corinthian believers divided into cliques, some following Paul, some following Apollos, and some too "spiritual" to follow either. Furthermore, the group as a whole condoned sin. Hypocrisy resulted, as we find in Paul's first letter to the church at Corinth. On the other hand, sin ultimately was judged, but in a proud and unloving way, according to his second letter to the Corinthians. These were failures of the entire group. Sometimes kinship ties or a clique composed of those who were founders of the church prevent others from becoming truly part of the family.

Racial and class prejudice are great dividers. There are few churches left in America that officially discriminate against any race or class, but the unspoken group attitude of many—if not most, on both sides of the social or racial divide—certainly would cause disunity if any of an "out" group sought or gained entrance. Even when they might be allowed admittance, should they seek change or a voice in the leadership it would not be tolerated. This is not merely a cultural phenomenon; it is a sin that grieves the Spirit. "There is neither Jew nor Greek, there is neither slave nor free, there is neither male nor female; for you are all one in Christ Jesus" (Gal. 3:28 NKJV). To the church in Colossae Paul added some more categories: circumcised, uncircumcised, barbarian, Scythian (Col. 3:11). Paul in these passages identified racial (Greek nor Jew), religious (circumcision nor uncircumcision), social (barbarian, Scythian), sexual (male nor female), and economic (slave nor free) barriers to unity. I believe if Paul were writing today he would add: "There is neither black nor white, there is neither Brahmin nor Dalit, for we are all one in Christ."

On the other hand, I've not been able to find a teaching or principle of Scripture that justifies the currently popular "affirmative action" approach, mandating aggressive pursuit of diversity for its own sake. In the 1970s Donald McGavran promoted what he called the "homogeneous unit" principle, an evangelistic strategy that advocated planting a culturally specific church in each language and culture. He taught that people prefer to come to faith with those who are like themselves. He advocated this, not as a doctrinal truth, but as a strategy for evangelism. He held vigorously to the unity of the body and that no one should be discriminated against for cultural difference, but that to bring people to faith we should not make advanced sanctification (barrier-free thinking in this case) a prerequisite to becoming a Christian in the first place.

The homogeneous unit principle is axiomatic, of course, in real life; and as a basis for evangelism, especially pioneer evangelism among the unreached, seems to me quite justifiable biblically. And perhaps it is not only legitimate in pioneer situations where the evangelist reaches one tribe, one culture at a time. For example, when it is insisted that every African-American be compelled to share a common worship experience with a traditional white congregation, or visa versa, it seems the burden of proof rests with those who so insist. The most common result of such culturally induced "unity" is division, either warfare within the church or, more often, some people leaving for a more compatible worship environment. Having said that, however, I must emphasize that excluding or in any way diminishing full social and emotional incorporation in the congregation on the basis of race or culture is sinful schism.

Though a forced combining of disparate people may not be justifiable, some report that many non-Christians in the U.S. and some other places are very alert to monoethnic groups and will be repelled by them. While at times this may be a surface political correctness, it is true that many will avoid enrolling their children in sports teams or dance classes of only one ethnicity. Perhaps a new evangelism strategy, modeled by congregations like MOSAIC in Los Angeles, will be to show a visible multicolored "stained glass" demonstration of the uniting powerful love of Christ. Whether this will prove a broadly successful evangelistic strategy in American culture in the twenty-first century remains to be seen. But it should not be demanded in every nation and culture as the only biblical pattern of evangelism.

Group failure, then, often causes division.

Personal Failure

Personal failure is the most common cause of division in the church. There can be personality clashes or temperamental differences as in the church in Philippi. There can be personal animosity developing from envy, selfishness, pride, or even from misunderstanding. When this morally cancerous attitude is spoken in criticism or gossip, it can easily become group failure and schism results.

Someone has said that when Satan fell, he fell into the choir loft. The implication is that music is often the focal point of division in a church. The same might be said of those in charge of the finances of the church. Why should the areas of music and money so often prove the scene of church fights? Perhaps because in these areas a worldly person can succeed whereas in a ministry such as teaching or evangelism, success would not be so common through efforts unaided by the Spirit. Again, there may be those who serve in the areas of music or finance who are motivated by something other than the welfare of the church. At any rate, these two areas are often the scene of conflict and division, so the leadership does well to be on alert.

Structural Failure

Division in the congregation can happen because of failure in some program. Again, the form of government may enhance or militate against unity. But another factor, least suspected, may be size and geography.

The potential for superficial unity increases and the potential for deep family solidarity decreases with the increase in the size of the church and the distance between the residence of members and/or from the central meeting place. If the church is a large congregation or the flock is widely scattered, true biblical solidarity will prove impossible unless compensating structures are provided within the larger congregation. Two approaches to compensate have proved popular. The plan to assign each member of the congregation to a small accountability group, geographically based, has been observed more in theory than in practice, perhaps, but the cell group concept has sometimes proved successful. The other approach is to separate off new congregations as a policy, rather than simply growing larger. I do not advocate one approach over the other, but I do advocate that some compensating approach is necessary if members of a megachurch are to have the unity in family solidarity, the caring and responsible relationships necessary to experience God's purposes for the church (see unit 2).

Culturally Induced Problems

Individualism, the dominant mood of the Western world, is a great enemy of true unity. On the other hand, Eastern feudalism is no friend of biblical unity in the congregation, either, though it can provide a much greater solidarity in a subgroup such as that within a family group or clan. By the same token, that very unity militates against true unity in the larger family, the congregation as a whole. The leadership of a congregation that doesn't address constantly from Scripture the issue of individualism (in the West) or feudalism (in the East), or take proactive action in creating structures and programs to correct these errors, will doom the congregation to failure in the core biblical doctrine of family solidarity.

We have mentioned racism and classism as culturally induced prejudices that have an impact on interpersonal relationships within the congregation. But there are other cultural factors that can cause division such as nationalism, especially prevalent in the missions context. Again, from time to time generation gaps appear, causing disunity. The tidal wave of population shift from rural to urban means large numbers of people are uprooted and transplanted to places where there is cultural clash. Furthermore, when the rural person or family is transplanted to an isolated cage in a high-rise apartment, the isolation creates an almost insuperable barrier to evangelism. A faceless society is no friend of solidarity in God's family.

Happy the congregation where the leaders are culturally sensitive when preaching and planning.

Change

When the leadership decides that change is necessary, that there is some better way to accomplish some particular objective, success in making that change without causing division depends on many factors apart from the merit of the objective. If these other factors in the management of change are not fully observed, division and failure to reach those objectives is predictable.

The timing of the initiation of any change and of the various stages in that change is of great importance. Are the people ready for the change, has the education and preparation been adequate? Are all those affected by the change incorporated in the decision, structure permitting, or at least in the communication network?

Not only is timing important, but the rate of change has a great deal to do with success in making the change. If the rate of change is more rapid than can be sustained by the group without division or, on the other hand, more slow than can be tolerated by the group without division, the rate of change must be modified. This is an extremely difficult factor to manage. Ordinarily, one cannot hope to manage the rate of change with perfect success in terms of approval of all members of the fellowship. The most that can be expected is that the pace will be within the tolerance of all members so that division does not result.

I was trapped between a board that seemed determined to remain, as I joked, in the nineteenth century, and a segment of the faculty which was equally determined to leap into the twenty-first century. They were a quarter-century premature! A young faculty member came to persuade me to make changes more rapidly, especially since a third of the board had just resigned over the issue of freedom to wear beards and he had concluded we were ready to move ahead on all fronts. I told him that I was in the cockpit and could see more of the instrument panel than he, and if we made all the changes as rapidly as he wanted we would pull the wings off. He backed off, and the craft stayed intact and soared through the turbulent years of the seventies. But we suffered loss of both board and faculty in the process. The timing and the rate of change have much to do with reaching the desired destination.

The method chosen to make a change and the person who initiates or who carries through some aspect of the change are major factors in potential for making the change without causing fragmentation of the body. Our school pioneered the concept of distance learning, and the man responsible was an unparalleled visionary. But he was not an unparalleled change agent. He so disrupted the unity of the body that the vision was a quarter century in coming to fruition. In that case, the visionary was the wrong person for leading change.

Here's another example. An institution was in financial crisis and the only way to regain stability was to cut the largest expense—staff salaries. But the method chosen was to send "pink slips" through the mail—no preparation, no personal conversation. One-fourth of the faculty and staff lost their jobs. But so did the president who chose that method! Change is often desirable and sometimes essential, but the method of making the change and the person leading the change must be carefully chosen.

A new pastor or leader is sometimes—but not often—called because the people want change. He may work for change with a clear conscience so long as the group stays with him. But if there is resistance and potential division, he has only one of two options: (1) he may stop pressing for change and wait for the right timing when it can be accomplished without division, or (2) he can leave. He does not have the option of splitting a church that was unified until he began to make changes.[2]

Furthermore, if he comes with a hidden agenda to change the doctrine or denominational connection, for example, an objective he does not communicate before accepting the call, he is acting as a thief and deserves the condemnation he will surely receive. If he has a strong personality and works craftily, he may pull it off, but only with division and loss to the congregation and the cause of Christ.

At the end of a graduate course on biblical principles of ministry, the final exam was oral. The student would come to my office fifteen minutes before the exam and be given a case study to review. I managed—in this imaginary church description—to describe the violation of every principle studied in the course. The exam consisted of one question: what would you do if called to pastor this church? The experience was educational for me. Every person who had come through seminary without pastoral experience described with remarkable clarity the changes needed to bring every malfunction into alignment with the principles we had studied. But, without exception, those with pastoral experience responded, "I would not change anything; not for at least six months."

Would that Sam could have learned that lesson. He came to me for counsel because the church to which he had recently been called was in free fall. It would be hard to imagine a church in such turmoil, division, and loss in so short a time. He told me all the changes he had tried to make and they seemed unexceptionable. But the timing, the method, and his own hard-driving personality with overtones of infallibility made division and loss inevitable. On inquiry, I learned from him that he came to his present

---

2. Of course, a leader may not be the cause of change-induced disunity. For example, there may have been a surface unity with hunger for change fermenting under the surface by a segment of the people. With a new leader this hidden voice comes to the surface and it appears the leader caused the disunity. The reality is that disunity was exposed or became more visible because there was a sense of potential for change.

charge after a similar brief tenure in five other churches. He told me of the error and evil in each of the former churches, elements that made his own ouster inevitable. Such was his evaluation. Change toward desirable goals can be doomed if it is not well timed, if the person implementing the change is not wise in methodology, and if he is not trusted by those he leads.

As C. V. Mathew, an Indian educator, puts it, "It may take months or years to build a ministry, but only a moment to destroy it." Paul declared, "Him shall God destroy" (1 Cor. 3:17 KJV). I don't know exactly what that would look like, but Paul says destroying God's church is very serious business.

Friends of Unity

Just as we could not, in the scope of this study, fully explore all the causes of disunity, so we cannot give a full exposition of the cure, that which promotes unity. In truth, every biblical principle of ministry we have examined in this study (units 1 through 5) promotes unity in the body. Especially is that true of this unit on the lordship of Christ. If Christ is actually functioning as Lord of the congregation, unity is more likely; if he is not Lord, division is inevitable. Unless it is the unity of the grave! Let us, however, name a few of the factors essential to unity.

Regeneration

In both letters to the Corinthians Paul makes it clear that a major cause of disunity is the presence of unregenerate people in the fellowship (1 Cor. 2:6–16; 2 Cor. 3:14–18). An essential for unity of spirit is the presence of the Spirit in each participant.

Faith in the Book

The first approach to change is to use all the principles of making the Bible the functional authority, studied in unit 1. For example, "What is the basic idea?" Is the proposed change understood by all? Second, is it biblical? Is it required by Scripture? If so, then the task of the leadership is to teach and persuade. Is it merely permitted by Scripture? If so, the integrity of the leadership may be tested as to how the church corporately finds God's will in matters not revealed in Scripture.

Making the Scripture the true functional authority is the only sure basis for unity in the congregation. If some members are not committed to the authority of the Bible, schism is almost inevitable. This faith is biblical faith—commitment to obey. And that can't be merely passive obedience; it includes proactively searching Scripture on the part of the whole body whenever an issue that divides arises. A pronouncement by the leader won't suffice. Faith in Scripture means not only determination to obey, no matter if it means painful change; it means openness and ruthless honesty. The believers in Berea were commended because they "received the word with all readiness," and because they "searched the Scriptures daily" to find out whether the teaching of the esteemed visitor were true (Acts 17:11 NKJV).

On the solid rock of biblical truth alone can a church find true unity. It may be important for practical reasons to unite on some teaching that the church through the ages has not always agreed on. But such peripheries should not become part of the foundation of faith demanded of the members or it may well become divisive. As Augustine said, "In essentials, unity; in non-essentials, liberty; in all things, charity." Deciding among those three categories may not be easy but should always be attempted when divisive issues arise.

If, for prudential reasons, the foundational demands become narrower than the clear mandates of Scripture, be prepared to accept that the fellowship becomes narrower. For example, if a church will accept no one into membership who has experienced divorce for any reason—a requirement for membership narrower than scriptural demands—the fellowship of those who chose that basis of fellowship will be fewer.

Prayer

The principles of chapter 11 must be fully operative and that includes reliance on the Holy Spirit of unity to guide into all truth in answer to the united prayer of faith by an obedient people.

Only a praying people will ever be truly united. Often it is only on its knees that the church will find unity. Since it is Satan himself who attacks the church through fostering division, there is spiritual warfare and that can be waged only in prayer. We invested heavily in considering the prayer factor in chapter 11, so here we simply mention it because to leave it out would be to omit one of the essentials of unity.

Humility

This fruit of the Spirit may not come easily for one who is in leadership, especially successful leaders. Power holders (or aspirers) usually emphasize the virtue of unity! So for the church to experience unity at the deepest level, leaders must give special care to produce an abundant crop of this fruit.

This characteristic is required for unity, especially on the part of the leadership, as we have seen. Why should the leader be humble? Because he is finite and fallen. We are finite so we know ultimate truth only partially (1 Cor. 13:12). That's because God's ways and his thoughts are infinitely above us (Isa. 55:9). Humility is the only legitimate garb for a finite person. Furthermore, we are fallen. What we do know is distorted (2 Cor. 3:14–18).

And though our minds are in the process of being straightened out, being brought more and more into alignment with Christ's mind (Rom. 12:2), still we are fallen; reality is still obscured by sinful understandings and predispositions.

When the leader's demeanor is one of humility—willingness to accept correction, to admit failure, to change—unity is much more possible in the body. "Therefore if there is any ... fellowship of the Spirit, if any affection and mercy, fulfill my joy by being like-minded, having the same love, being of one accord, of one mind" (Phil. 2:1–2 NKJV).

And how does that happen? "Let nothing be done through selfish ambition or conceit, but in lowliness of mind let each esteem others better than himself" (v. 3 NKJV).

Even when they obviously are not? Yes. "Let each of you look out not only for his own interests, but also for the interests of others" (v. 4 NKJV).

Why? "Let this mind be in you which was also in Christ Jesus" (v. 5 NKJV).

If the Lord of creation is humble, how can I not be? And that is a prerequisite for unity in the congregation. Here's how it works:

I ... beseech you to walk worthy of the calling with which you were called, with all lowliness and gentleness, with longsuffering, bearing with one another in love, endeavoring to keep the unity of the Spirit in the bond of peace. There is one body and one Spirit, just as you were called in one hope of your calling; one Lord, one faith, one baptism; one God and Father of all, who is above all, and through all, and in you all.

But to each one of us grace was given according to the measure of Christ's gift. . . . And He Himself gave some to be . . . pastors and teachers, for the equipping of the saints for the work of ministry, for the edifying of the body of Christ, till we all come to the unity of the faith and of the knowledge of the Son of God, to a perfect man, to the measure of the stature of the fullness of Christ . . . speaking the truth in love, may grow up in all things into Him who is the head—Christ—from whom the whole body, joined and knit together by what every joint supplies, according to the effective working by which every part does its share, causes growth of the body for the edifying of itself in love (Eph. 4:1–16 NKJV).

Such is the magnificent vision of Paul on what God designs the church to be and how he intends to accomplish it!

Practical Measures

There are practical measures that seem to promote unity. For example, Mike Ballast, longtime missionary to the Philippines, tells of one method for uniting a congregation of diverse background. Perhaps his experience points to an intermediate step before full social integration can take place. The church was heterogeneous, with wealthy, middle class, and squatters as members. Their unity was based not so much on "fellowship" as on ministry. They didn't come together to drink coffee, but they did unite for ministry. For example, a mixed committee—millionaire diamond exporter, middle-class professionals, and poor squatters—was formed to reach the poor of the community with a health clinic. It's dangerous to evaluate as an outsider, but that seems to me a halfway house toward true biblical unity. But it may be a pointer. Unite in ministry as a first step toward deeper and comprehensive unity.

Another practical measure is to always involve as participants in the process of change as many of the group as the structure will allow. At least there should be no surprises. Still another practical measure is to promote change in stages.

Did you notice how each principle for Christian ministry we have considered in units 1 through 5 is essential to building up to completion a united fellowship of God's family? Unity is God's design, but to achieve a biblical unity, we must do a difficult thing—pursue purity. We turn now to reflect on the purity of the church.

CHAPTER 20

PURITY
OF THE CONGREGATION

Questions for reflection: **Is there an accountability structure
that includes all members? Is biblical church discipline practiced?
Is anyone allowed to continue in the fellowship who is guilty
of unrepented moral dereliction or teaching heresy?**

In an age when tolerance is the chief virtue and intolerance the chief evil, it
comes as no surprise that the church practicing biblical church discipline
may be sued in secular courts. So the fundamental issue may be ideologi-
cal. When is tolerance biblical, when is intolerance demanded? Karl Barth
declared: "Tolerance is, no doubt, a virtue without which none of us can
live, but we must, nevertheless, at least understand that it is, strictly speaking, destructive of fellowship, for it is a gesture by which the divine distur-
bance is rejected. The One in whom we are veritably united is himself the
great intolerance. He willeth to rule, to be victorious, to be—everything. He
it is who disturbs every family gathering, every scheme for the reunion of
Christendom, every human cooperation. And he disturbs, because he is the
Peace that is above every estrangement and cleavage and faction."[1]

God is holy and he intends us to be holy. And not just "us" individuals—
holiness, "without which no one will see the Lord" (Heb. 12:14 NKJV)—but
holiness as a congregation. As a result, the Bible is very clear in teaching
that there should be church discipline and that the ultimate discipline is
the breaking of fellowship, or separation. Certain people should be separated from the church.

I take it that those who speak of a doctrine of "separation" base the
doctrine on this New Testament principle of church discipline. When one
does not have power to put out the person who should be put out, the only
way to separate is to leave oneself.

How does one identify a congregation that is guilty of unholy unity, the

---

1. Karl Barth, *The Epistle to the Romans,* E. C. Hoskyns, trans. (Oxford University Press, USA, 1968).

sin of unbiblical compromise? The New Testament clearly outlines a pattern for church discipline—who is to be disciplined, why they are to be disciplined, and how they are to be disciplined. If for any reason such a person or persons are not disciplined, the congregation is sinning against the revealed will of God.

How does one identify a congregation that is guilty of unholy separation, the sin of schism? Since God has told us who should be disciplined, why they should be disciplined, and how they should be disciplined, if that discipline or separation is of the wrong person, of the right person for the wrong reason, or of the right person for the right reason but in the wrong way, the Christian or congregation is guilty of the sin of schism.

Who Should Be Disciplined?

The New Testament teaches that a person must be disciplined if he is guilty of unrepented, overt, moral delinquency (for example, 1 Cor. 5:1, 11) or if he is guilty of teaching heresy (Gal. 1:6–9; 2 John 7–11). It is important to notice that the discipline is not for one who fails in some sin of the spirit or who sins and repents, but for one who sins deliberately and continues in it. Discipline in matters of faith is not for one who has doubts. Jude 22 says clearly that we should show mercy on those who have doubts and save them. But when one teaches heresy, he must be disciplined.

When a congregation does not discipline in either of these cases, it has an unholy unity and is guilty of the sin of impurity, standing under the judgment of God. On the other hand, when a congregation or individuals discipline for reasons other than moral dereliction or the teaching of heresy, they are guilty of an unholy separation, the sin of schism, and they come under the judgment of God.

In the light of this biblical teaching, it does not take much discernment to see that a great deal of ecumenical promotion is uniting the wrong people and a great deal of separatist agitation is dividing the wrong people.

The only point on which Bible-committed Christians can legitimately differ on this clear teaching is the question of what constitutes heresy. Without going into a detailed defense of the position, I suggest that biblical example would seem to limit a definition of disciplinable heresy to a denial of one of the great fundamentals of the faith, those doctrines confessed by the church at large in all ages. Disciplinary action for teaching deviant doctrines of a lesser kind is schismatic. The exception to this would be for teaching against some lesser doctrine, practice, or position of the congregation on which members have publically united. In other words, the basis of the fellowship may be narrower than Scripture by common agreement and then it is not necessarily schismatic to insist on adherence to those standards.

But even then, the discipline should not be such as to imply the person is a heretic, no longer of the faith.

Why Should One Discipline?

The primary purpose of discipline in Scripture is to save or restore the person who has sinned (1 Cor. 5:5; 1 Tim. 1:19–20; 2 Thess. 3:13–15). Discipline is designed as a means of grace, not of destruction; as an evidence of love, not of hate or of fear. A secondary legitimate motive is that discipline may serve as a warning to others. It has a deterrent value (1 Tim. 5:20).

We may derive a third legitimate motive from biblical principles in general. Church discipline can be useful in protecting the reputation of Christ and of the church. It is also useful in protecting other believers from defilement. However, it is quite significant that when the New Testament deals with the problem of church discipline, it does not use protection as a motive. First John 1:19–20; 1 Corinthians 5:6–8; and 2 John 11 may include this concept, but this is obviously not the central thrust of the teaching of the passages. Jude, who uses stronger words to denounce heretical teaching than any other biblical author, does not end with an injunction to begin disciplinary procedure or to separate from such people but instead exhorts the Christians who were faithful to keep on being faithful (Jude 20–21). He then concludes the passage with these words: "And on some have mercy, who are in doubt; and some save, snatching them out of the fire; and on some have mercy with fear, hating even the garment spotted by the flesh" (vv. 22–23 ASV). Following this, Jude again turns to the faithful ones, assuring them that God is able to guard them from stumbling and to keep them until that day when they will stand in the presence of his glory without blemish in exceeding joy (v. 24).

One could reasonably expect the protection of the reputation of Christ and the protection of the church to have been the primary motives given for church discipline. But the Bible seems to take a rather nonchalant attitude at this point. Why? Perhaps because the name of Christ and the church of Christ are strong and quite able to care for themselves. Or is it because if these were the primary motives rather than that of love for the sinner, discipline could quickly degenerate into inquisition? Christ also seemed to be less than careful: "He that is not against us is for us" (Luke 9:50 KJV). Paul also rejoiced that the gospel is preached whether in pretense or in truth (Phil. 1:18). He condemned the heretic, but he didn't give protection as the reason for church discipline.

Note that one motive is excluded as a motive for discipline or separation. Church discipline is not to be punitive or retributive. God clearly reserves this motivation to himself: "'Vengeance is Mine, I will repay,' says the Lord" (Rom. 12:19 NKJV). This is different from God's pattern for relations with governmental authority and in the home where punitive intention may be legitimate. In the church, only God can be the ultimate judge: "Who art thou that judgest the servant of another?" (Rom. 14:4 ASV). We are all in the fellowship of mercy receivers.

From this brief outline of biblical teaching on motivation for disciplining an errant brother or sister, when Christians discipline or separate from motives of legalism, vindictiveness, fear, or pride rather than with the basic motivation of saving the brother, they are guilty of the sin of schism.

How Is Church Discipline to Be Administered?

Before any thought of discipline, of course, there must be prayer and self-examination (Gal. 6:1; Matt. 7:1–5). If a person has not given himself to prayer for the brother or sister and if he has not carefully examined his own life, he is disqualified because he does not have the love and humility necessary to be God's agent in discipline.

The Bible doesn't outline a comprehensive pattern for administering church discipline. By combining all teaching concerning the subject, however, it's possible to discern several distinct levels of severity of discipline.

Personal Counsel

The first stage of discipline is personal counsel (Matt. 18:15–18; Gal. 6:1–2; Rom. 15:1). This stage may be divided into two levels in which there is one-on-one personal counsel and another level in which several people counsel the one who has sinned. Titus 3:10–11 and 1 Timothy 5:19 seem to imply adherence to this pattern given in Matthew 18:15–18.

This level of personal rebuke, exhortation, admonition, and correction should receive the greatest concentration. It ties in with the other biblical purposes of teaching and fellowship. It should be noted that personal intervention is not limited to moral failure or heretical teaching. Any trapping sin calls for caring involvement (Gal. 6:1–10). This first stage of discipline is greatly neglected in our churches, much to the loss of the congregation. When this initial level of loving counsel is part of the congregation's ethos, more severe levels are preempted and trust-based love grows.

Is the passage in Matthew an absolute requirement? That is, though the passage does not prohibit going to the second or third level of discipline before following through on the first, is that the implication of Jesus' teaching? Many treat it so. But are there complementary teachings in Scripture? "Whoever corrects a mocker invites insult; whoever rebukes a wicked man incurs abuse. Do not rebuke a mocker or he will hate you; rebuke a wise man and he will love you" (Prov. 9:7–8 NIV).

This passage leads back to the basic purpose of discipline—restoration of the offender. If the situation is such that the restoration purpose is not likely to be accomplished, but rather the relationship is likely to further deteriorate, Proverbs seems to indicate that we need to exercise caution. For example, there may be circumstances in which the person who has done wrong may be violent or for some other reason the person who has been wronged may be afraid. Should a young person, sexually abused by a youth leader, be required to rebuke the person in private before taking any other action? When the offender is in a position of authority or power, as, for example in the school situation, when a professor has offended a student, is the requirement inviolable to first confront that teacher personally? Solomon would seem not to require the student to go alone in private to straighten out the matter. So there would seem to be exceptions to the principle, "Go alone to the offending party before going to anyone else."

There are other teachings that add a complementary dimension. Matthew 13:24–30, 36–43 records the parable of the wheat and the tares. There is the possibility of premature discipline, causing damage unnecessarily by rooting out what is causing offense. In fact, the statement is rather extreme. The disciples are to leave intact "all that cause to stumble and do iniquity" for God to remove at the judgment. Note that these two varieties of wrong are the specific reasons for church discipline as taught elsewhere! Rather than taking this parable as the abrogation of all biblical teaching on church discipline, as some have done, I take it as a caution that church discipline should be exercised with great care lest we punish the wrong person or do so from the wrong motives or in the wrong way.

So there are two principles: (1) the congregation is responsible for the behavior of its members and (2) there are times when action should be withheld. To put these two teachings together without doing violence to either, additional biblical principles are needed, such as refusing judgment when one is not responsible or when one does not have an adequate basis for judgment. All actions should be governed by a biblical love that "gives the benefit of the doubt" if motives are being deduced from words or actions (1 Cor. 13:7). Judging motives is hazardous at best, and ultimately only God truly qualifies to do so.

Are there biblical examples of bypassing the personal confrontation? Christ did not personally confront Herod but rather said, "Tell that fox" (Luke 13:32 NKJV). Paul's example with the church at Corinth illustrates a church leader who passed judgment without seeing the offender (1 Cor. 5:1–5). He had simply heard about the offense. Apparently the man who sinned had not been rebuked because the people were proud of their liberty, but Paul nevertheless demanded discipline. Again, Peter did not seem to confront Ananias with his sin and persuade him to confess and forsake it. He bypassed these first stages and concluded with the ultimate discipline (Acts 5).

To use another analogy, there are times when one is not to "give that which is holy to dogs" (Matt. 7:6), or to "cast pearls before swine" (Matt. 7:6). In other words, give spiritual truth only to those who can use it to benefit.

My own conclusion about this difficult question is that the personal confrontation with a person who has sinned is the general pattern to be followed, but that this pattern should be modified in these three situations: (1) when one's responsibility to act is not clear, (2) when judgment or evaluation is not certain, and (3) when the person has demonstrated that he will not listen and that the situation can therefore be expected to deteriorate rather than improve if he or she were confronted. Note, however, that this evaluation should not be used as an excuse to evade responsibility to confront.

Though there may be exceptions, under extraordinary circumstances, then, the first stage of discipline is personal one-to-one counsel.

Suspension of Rights and Privileges (1 Tim. 5:20; Titus 3:10–11)

Note that this second stage of church discipline, unlike the first, is the responsibility of the congregation as a whole. Christ said that should the offender not hear the plea of the one offended or of those others who together confront her or him, the matter becomes one for the church as a whole to decide.

Paul spoke of those in the Corinthian church who were partaking unworthily of Communion and who suffered for it. One should examine oneself before partaking of Communion (1 Cor. 11:28). In other words, one who is guilty of unconfessed sin should take the initiative and bar himself from the Lord's table. If, however, the sin is of a disciplinable level and the person does not voluntarily refrain, one measure of minor church discipline would be to bar that person from Communion.

Requirements are made for those who hold particular office in the church. When these requirements are not met, the person is not eligible to hold office. The absolute way in which the requirements are made would seem to indicate that a person already holding office who no longer meets the requirements would no longer be eligible to continue in that office (1 Tim. 3; Titus 1).

Withdrawal of Fellowship

This is seen in several of the passages already noted. The sinning member is no longer treated as part of the family; fellowship as a brother or sister is withdrawn. Perhaps this is what Paul had in mind when he said to turn the brother over to Satan (1 Cor. 5:5). "If anyone does not obey our word [about working for a living], note that person and do not keep company with him, that he may be ashamed. Yet do not count him as an enemy, but admonish him as a brother" (2 Thess. 3:14–15 NKJV).

Excommunication

The Matthew passage speaks of relating to offenders as to non-Christians. Apparently they are no longer recognized as members of the church (Matt. 18:15–18; see also 1 Tim. 5:20; 2 Thess. 3:6, 14–15; 1 Cor. 2:5–11; Titus 3:9–11). There is to be no association with such a person, not even to share a meal (1 Cor. 5:11; Eph. 5:7). To strike from the membership role would have little effect in contemporary America because there's always another church down the street. But if the family solidarity is all it was intended by God, this severest of all levels of church discipline may well prove to be the salvation of the erring one. At least that was to be its intent, and at Corinth it worked!

Note that in all levels of discipline but the first, it is *church* discipline. Before appointing oneself as disciplinarian, one must be very sure he is the one responsible for disciplinary activity at whatever stage. It is dangerous, schismatic in fact, to assume responsibility for administering discipline outside the responsible relationships of the congregation.

From this brief outline of the biblical pattern for the exercise of discipline, it is plain that a person who goes to others, to the church, or to the general public without first attempting to restore the person on an individual and private basis has violated the biblical pattern and is guilty of the sin of schism. Furthermore, those who separate a brother through means other than official church action are guilty of the sin of schism. There are many ways to break fellowship, to separate a brother, to separate from him, to hurt, discipline, or punish him. It can be done through critical talk, through political activity in the church, through pressures from the pulpit or the pen, and in other ways. But these ways are not biblical, and those who use them are guilty of the sin of schism. God does not view lightly the sin of schism: "Now the works of the flesh are manifest ... enmities, strife, jealousies, wraths, factions, divisions, parties, envyings ... of which I forewarn you, even as I did forewarn you, that they who practise such things shall not inherit the kingdom of God" (Gal. 5:19–21 ASV).

With this brief overview of the biblical doctrine of discipline, it becomes quite possible to identify the sin of impurity and the sin of schism. If a church leaves undisciplined a person who is guilty of moral dereliction or the teaching of heresy, it may preserve or create unity among Christians. But such unity is unholy and not the unity of the character of God. It is a mixture of pure and impure, and lacks the cement of truth. Sooner or later it will come apart. Purity is essential to true, lasting unity.

On the other hand, to discipline in any way—through word or action—one who is not biblically guilty; to discipline one who is guilty without the primary motivation of restoring him; to discipline without first seeking to restore the brother on a personal, private level; or to discipline him in ways other than official, responsible action of the congregation may give the appearance of purifying the church, but it will be an unholy separation, not partaking of the character of God. Such an action cannot be called a means of pursuing purity, because it is impure at the core—failing to reflect the loving character of God. True biblical purity of doctrine includes purity of life, which above all else is solidarity in love with the rest of God's family.

Throughout most of the twentieth century the purifiers who were weak on love and the unifiers who were weak on faithfulness wreaked havoc with the image of God seen by the lost world. Furthermore, those who follow in their train are guilty of something else as well. They are in danger of creating a climate that makes growth to spiritual maturity exceedingly difficult. Amid this strong polarization, is biblical balance possible?

Imbalance does not come from an overemphasis. It is impossible to have too much love or too much faithfulness. However, it is quite possible to have unfaithfulness masquerading as love. When God's people compromise through sentimentality or self-love or for some other reason are unwilling to exercise church discipline, they are unfaithful though they speak much of love. Again, it is quite possible to have unlove masquerading as faithfulness. When God's people create schism by disciplining the wrong person, or with the wrong motive, speak much of faithfulness, they are unfaithful to the very first commandment, to love others as they love themselves.

I do not ask the ecumenist to be less loving. I urge him to be more faithful. I do not ask the separatist to be less faithful. I urge him to be more loving. "Depart from evil and do good; seek peace and pursue it" (Ps. 34:14 NKJV). This is God's balance. God's Holy Spirit will give us the ability to speak the truth in love (Eph. 4:15).

Righteousness and peace, usually estranged, embraced at Calvary. May they embrace again in our congregations, lest the King return and find us compromised and polluted or dismembered, grotesque and impotent. And yet, since there was no way for righteousness and peace to meet except on the cross, no doubt they will meet in our day only where there are those willing to be crucified. When God's people fill up that which is lacking in the suffering of Christ (Col. 1:24) through choosing the way of personal sacrifice, God's own character will shine through again as it did at Calvary. The way of the cross is to exercise discipline faithfully, and with love that chooses to act for the welfare of another even at personal sacrifice. And the cross is always painful. The innocent always pay for the sins of the guilty.

CONCLUSION

There you have it—the "five smooth stones" for your David, whether church or other ministry, to slay Goliath and all his brothers!

- The *Bible* only and the whole Bible our only final authority for life and ministry
- The *Church*, central to all God's plans for redeeming a world
- The *Holy Spirit*, his energizing power indispensable to all life and ministry
- The *Plan of Redemption*, the calling of every disciple to full participation
- The *Lord Jesus Christ*, sovereign in every believer and in his church

The Bible. To get anywhere with God's purposes through his church, the leaders and congregation must take seriously the responsibility to bring every aspect of the ministry under the functional authority of Scripture, every new idea, every old tradition, every activity, every plan. Otherwise it will fail to be what God intends. It won't be easy. Diligent, objective, thorough Bible research combined with determined full compliance and eternal vigilance are the essentials.

The Congregation. Don't forget that a congregation weak in even one of the purposes of the church is crippled by so much, falls short of full obedience.

Remember, too, that for a parachurch ministry, concentrating on some specific purpose of the church, to be biblically authentic, must flow into and/or out of the local congregation.

Worship

Making disciples

Ministry of Compassion   CHRIST   Evangelism Near and Far

Member care

Foundation: Prophets & Apostles

The Holy Spirit. His energizing power in a congregation is seen primarily in the supernatural abilities he gives each member. The church is responsible to make sure every member fully uses his or her gifting—discovering, developing, deploying and, when a purpose of the church is weak, united in desiring earnestly the gift needed to lead the church in fulfilling that purpose. But the Spirit does so much more—guiding, providing. All this activity of the Spirit, however, is released only as we connect with him in prayer. A praying congregation is a growing, victorious congregation, fulfilling all the God-designed purposes.

A prayerless church or other ministry is limited to what can be achieved by purely human wisdom and power.

The Plan of Redemption, every member's calling. Beyond the varied callings and enablings of the Spirit is the first and paramount calling of all—to complete what Christ began, to fulfill Christ's last mandate, to participate fully in redeeming a lost humanity. Near-evangelism for all as witnesses and far-evangelism, specialists sent by the church to enable it to reach its goal. That goal? Every person on earth hearing with understanding the way to life and a congregation of God's people established in every place. Until that task is complete, the primary assignment of the church remains unfulfilled. And for that every member must accept the Spirit's call.

The Lordship of Christ. For any of this to happen, of course, Jesus Christ alone must be absolute Lord of his church. First he must be Lord of each member, but for him to actually function as Lord of the congregation or ministry, the leaders must embody the leadership model of God himself. To the extent he is Lord in their lives and ministry, to that extent will the church be united and pure, bringing about the fulfillment of all the purposes God has for the congregation.

Thank you for journeying with me through my life of searching for the key to success in ministry. Perhaps for you, too, it will be found in the wedding of theology and ministry in some combination that pleases God.

CROSS-CULTURAL
COMMUNICATION

When speaking of cross-cultural communication, we may think of a culture foreign to our own, but in truth all communication of spiritual truth is cross-cultural. The more distant the fundamental cultural elements of a given culture are to our own, the more aware we are of the unbiblical elements, perhaps, but the closer to our culture, the more subtle and difficult the distance is to discern. The necessity to try is essential, however. In this book, we're using hermeneutical principles to discern accurately the single message any Bible author intended and what response the Holy Spirit expects of us. We're seeking to wed theology with ministry to bring all ministry under the functional authority of Scripture. But to communicate God's truth, we also need to study the recipient of our communication carefully. That study has been called "cultural anthropology."

It's beyond the scope of this study to adduce principles for doing cultural anthropology under the functional authority of Scripture, but we should at least illustrate the approach. Since cross-cultural communication is most clearly seen in "foreign missionary" endeavor, we'll use that as our paradigm. In my inaugural address as general director of the Evangelical Missiological Society in 1995, I spoke on the theme of the society for that year: "The Social Sciences and Missions." First I described something of my own pilgrimage and then outlined some of the benefits and some of the hazards of relating one of these "bridesmaids," anthropology, to the bride, the church of Jesus Christ and its mission.[1]

My Personal Pilgrimage

When getting my education in the forties, anthropology was not part of the missionary's preparation, so I decided to do something most

---

1. "A Use and Misuse of the Social Sciences: Interpreting the Biblical Text," *Missiology and the Social Sciences* (Pasadena: William Carey Library, 1996), 165–84. The chapter in this book is a digest of the original.

evangelical missionaries of the time considered suspect. I gave myself a crash course in cultural anthropology. But the textbooks I studied and the university courses I took were not helping with what Donald McGavran was later to call "church growth anthropology." Yet that is what I was passionately interested in as a church planter, even though I didn't know the terminology. Years later, when I returned to the presidency of Columbia Bible College (now part of Columbia International University), McGavran advised me: "You must find and employ church growth anthropologists. Not traditional historic anthropologists and not just cultural anthropologists," he said, "not just applied cultural anthropologists and not just applied cultural missionary anthropologists. You must get church growth anthropologists!"

Before McGavran burst on the missions scene, however, I was sensing that anthropology must be focused on getting the task done, so I began the serious study of the Japanese value system. I wanted to know what Japanese valued, not what I valued. For preevangelism I wanted to connect with some motivational point for which our faith offered help. I was astounded to discover that many things important to me were of little or no importance to Japanese: eternal life, propositional truth, individual freedom, forgiveness of sin, a personal God, history. These were things I had been trying to "market." At the same time I found things important to the Japanese that were not priorities for most Westerners. But I also discovered things to which Scripture speaks: approval and sense of belonging, security, relationships, feelings, honor of parents, here-and-now "salvation," obligation, loyalty, beauty, love of nature, and the value of suffering.[2]

These studies prepared me for the dawn of McGavran and the church growth movement in the sixties. Great controversy raged as many evangelicals opposed the movement. This drove me to examine Scripture. Well, actually, to examine McGavran. Since he was quintessentially a pragmatist, he did not favor us with a statement of his presuppositions, let alone an analysis of any biblical basis for them. So first I had to analyze what he was saying and distill the presuppositions and then examine them in the light of Scripture. Though he did not engage in such activity, he agreed that my analysis was accurate, proving his agreement by asking me to report my findings as a lectureship in his school. I found that most of McGavran's basic ideas, including his use of anthropology, were either demanded by scriptural teaching or permitted by it.[3] I was trying to bring the insights of anthropology under the functional authority of Scripture. Anthropology was a legitimate tool of missiology, if pursued rigorously under the authority of God-revealed truth about human nature and relationships. But many

2. See my article, "Japanese Values and Christian Mission," *The Japan Christian Quarterly* (Fall 1967).
3. *Measuring the Church Growth Movement* (Chicago: Moody, 1973, 1974).

evangelical missionaries at the time did not agree that it was legitimate at all, and few used the tool.

Imagine my surprise, then, in the early seventies, when Donald McGavran said to me, "Robertson, the major battle in missions during the rest of this century will be with anthropology." As was often the case, the old gentleman was uncanny in sensing the future before it arrived. But he put me on to something important. Though anthropological insights were rapidly gaining acceptance in the world of missions, not all of them were examined in the light of Scripture. The end result was a flood of unbiblical and even anti-biblical ideas and practice. Not all of this is attributable to anthropology, of course, since our whole society has moved into a relativistic, postmodern approach to life.[4] But the social sciences, either as the first-born of postmodern thinking or as a parent of it, bypassed what Scripture had to say about human nature and society. So it was, that, beginning in the seventies, I wrote on themes relating to doing social science under the authority of Scripture.[5] I who had so vigorously advocated the use of these tools was now defending against their misuse.

Sensing that the basic problem was hermeneutics, I began to address it in that context, especially in the eighties. Traditionally, hermeneutics had dealt with correct exegesis, getting at the meaning intended by the author.[6] Very little attention had been given to principles for making valid application, determining what God intended as a response to his revelation. The bypass of scriptural authority by evangelical scholars was not taking place so much in the interpretation of the meaning, but in the application of that meaning, identifying the significance of the teaching for us today. Thus I sought to develop a "hermeneutics" of application so that we could use our cultural tools authentically.[7]

Though my hermeneutics text has been widely used and quoted, I was too late. Under the impact of postmodern thinking, many of our evangelical theologians have moved into the camp of partial relativism or, as some have called it, "relative relativism." In this way, theological colleagues, using cultural tools for understanding and applying Scripture, have exposed the

---

4. See chap. 2.
5. "The Behavioral Sciences Under the Authority of Scripture," *Journal of the Evangelical Theological Society* (March 1977); "Limits of Cultural Interpretation," *JETS* (June 1980); "Problems of Normativeness in Scripture: Cultural Versus Permanent," *Hermeneutics, Inerrancy, and the Bible* (Grand Rapids: Zondervan Publishing Co., 1984), 219–40.
6. Note that I use the term "hermeneutics" in its normal meaning, "the science of interpretation," not as it is used by Paul Hiebert, *Anthropological Insights for Missionaries* (Grand Rapids: Baker, 1985), 19), who apparently follows the lead of Nida (Eugene A. Nida and William D. Reyburn, *Meaning across Cultures* [Orbis, 1981]), who gives a new definition: "Hermeneutics . . . may be described as pointing out parallels between the biblical message and present-day events and determining the extent of relevance and the appropriate response for the believer" (p. 30). Ascribing the task of applying the meaning of Scripture to the current context (often called "the significance of the text") to the interpretive role is not a matter of mere semantics. It paves the way for allowing the current context to determine, not merely the significance, but increasingly, the meaning of the text.
7. *Understanding and Applying the Bible* (Chicago: Moody, 1984, 1992).

flank of our missiology forces by stripping away the defense of a Scripture held to be normative for contemporary obedience. In response to this, I and colleague Brad Mullen researched all recent literature on hermeneutics by evangelical scholars and were dismayed to discover pervasive postmodern assumptions. In the resulting article in the *Journal of Evangelical Theology* (JETS), "The Impact of Postmodern Thinking on Evangelical Hermeneutics," we argued that an understanding of the culture of the author of Scripture and of the recipient is helpful in identifying the meaning intended by the author and the response intended by the Holy Spirit. But if such understanding is used to alter the meaning or set aside the authority for contemporary obedience, we have forfeited the authority of Scripture.[8]

Imagine my surprise, after writing that paper, to sit under a lectureship on Hinduism in Calcutta and discover the close affinity between Western postmodern thinking and the ancient Eastern world of myth and illusion, subjectivity and relativity. I sensed immediately a basic reason for the remarkable advance of New Age thinking in the West. And now I sense the increasingly hazardous task of missiology in using the tools of Western social science in a postmodern age to understand and impact the thinking, feeling, and behavior of Eastern peoples.

This, in brief, has been my pilgrimage. From that background we come to examine an approach to bringing all cross-cultural communication under the functional authority of Scripture, especially when we use the tools provided by the social sciences. First, then, let us outline a few of the benefits of using the tools of anthropology and then note some of the perils.

Benefits of Anthropology for Cross-Cultural Communication

To Sensitize to Cultural Factors for More Effective Communication

The study of cross-cultural communication in the preparation of missionaries has become an accepted norm so that comment or illustration is hardly necessary. Nevertheless, ethnocentric thinking and behavior is so ingrained and so unconscious that those who would reach a culture different from their own need the constant prodding of cultural sensitizers. The husband who holds the door for his wife may be commendable in American society, but if he does so in some societies it may irreparably damage the reputation of his wife. He may carefully guard himself from questionable behavior toward the opposite sex only to discover that a far greater offense

---

8. The implications of postmodern thinking for ministry were explored in chapter 2 of this study.

is impatience. Cultural anthropology can be a missionary's best friend in teaching to communicate cross-culturally!

To Identify Values for Preevangelism

Hirota was soundly converted and grew like an amaryllis. About six months after his conversion he came to me. "Sensei, you always talk about heaven and I've said to myself, 'Who wants that? One life is enough!' But now that I've gotten acquainted with Jesus I really want to go there to be with him forever."

I had been trying to entice with visions of heaven a people whose idea of paradise is cessation of existence, to get off the wheel of reincarnation altogether. I was using bad bait. Cultural anthropology is a great tool to discover the values and non-values of a people so that the would-be communicator can start with good news about what is valued, not with what is valueless. Like the man who had little success in fishing. A bystander asked, "What bait are you using?"

"Blackberries," was the ready response.

"But fish aren't going to bite."

"Why not? I love blackberries!"

So much of our fishing in Japan, I discovered, was with blackberries.

To Strengthen Evangelism of the Sincere Seeker

The twenty-five-year veteran missionary looked despondent when she should have been exuberant a week before her fifth furlough. I asked what was so distressing, and she told a sad story. The centerpiece of this term's ministry had been a highly successful Bible study with a group of physicians. The night before, at her farewell party, the leader of the group had told her, "Now I understand what you are teaching about Christianity, and I want you to know I believe it." Elated, she responded, "Wonderful! You've become a Christian!" The physician was startled and blurted out, "A Christian? Oh, no! I said I believed it was true, but that doesn't have anything to do with me personally." My heart went out to the dejected veteran, but I wondered, *Why hasn't anyone told her that Japanese aren't interested in propositional truth when it comes to religion?* A very intelligent, right-brained logician, she had been fishing with blackberries—for twenty-five years—something very important to her in which they simply were not interested. They wanted to know, "What will this religion do for me—today? How will it make me feel—today? How will it help me cope—today?" Certainly the gospel offers much for today, but that is not necessarily what is uppermost in the missionary's mind.

I called out to the Christian bookstore manager in the next room, "There is a book on this desk. Do you believe that?" "Yes, of course, Sensei, if you say so," he responded. "Well, it's there because you believe it is, but if you didn't believe that, it wouldn't be there." I was preparing a sermon for Christians on evidences for the existence of God and wrestling with the issue that to many Eastern peoples, God exists for those who believe in him, but not for those who don't. Though I did not try to change unbelievers into my image in order to preach the gospel, I did still feel it important to deliver believers from the ancient East's version of contemporary Western postmodern thinking in which reality is concocted of what's "out there" and my perceptions of it. Hirota opened the door and said, "Huh? What did you say?"

I said, "If you believe this book is here, it is, but if you don't, it isn't." He exclaimed with astonishment, "Chimpunkampun!" This, by interpretation, is "fool stupidity." So I changed the sentence slightly, "If you believe God is there, he is, but if you don't, he's not."

"Oh," replied Hirota, "now I understand." Cultural studies can help communicate the gospel to people whose view of reality is radically different from our own.

Do I spend time seeking to bring the serious seeker under conviction of sin (which, in a shame culture, he may not even recognize as existing) by emphasizing what he is so constantly guilty of—lying? It's a big one for me. Why can't he see it? Because, as his proverb instructs him, "A lie also is a useful thing." My attempts to convict him of the heinousness of such a sin will no doubt prove futile. If I switch to sins he is acutely aware of, like relationships he has broken or his failure to meet his eternal obligations to his parents, however, I might make some progress in bringing conviction of sin—which my theology and good psychology teach me a person must have before he becomes interested in a Savior. I might even switch to shame instead of sin as an entering wedge, if shame is what his tightly knit culture recognizes. After all it is a shameful thing to fail in our obligations to God, and forgiveness of that shameful offense might prove desirable.

Cultural anthropology can alert the foreigner to the blocks to effective evangelism created by his own cultural entrapment. Many true values are held in every society, no doubt the result of general revelation, of the imprint of God's image that even centuries of error cannot fully erase. God loves beauty and so do the Japanese. American missionaries often do not. While the temples and their grounds are places of exquisite beauty, we erect Quonset huts with no garden at all and call them churches.

Another example of cultural handicaps in evangelism: we value individualism, rugged individualism. Otherwise we would never have become missionaries. The problem is we try to convert people into our image in order for them to qualify for receiving our message. The person who won't stand out against family and friends is not worthy. Yet, the African or Asian may not think such a trait desirable at all. He may value contrasting virtues to which we give slight attention, even though they may be major biblical themes. Community and loyalty, for example, honor of parents and human relationships, acceptance and affirmation are biblical attitudes which don't mix easily with individualism. Individual responsibility is a major strand of biblical teaching but it is not the only strand, and if not held in tension with balancing characteristics it can become demonic. Our own Western civilization may yet prove that.

In a society in which a person's all-important security is provided by those who guarantee his life, his family and employer, the offer of freedom and independence may not sound like Good News. This may be the Achilles heel of all Western efforts to democratize Islamic peoples. Cultural anthropology might help politicians too! We must include in our message values which we may have overlooked in our ethnocentric astigmatism if we are to be true to the whole revelation of God's will for us humans and if we are to convince people that we bring truly Good News. Thus, church growth anthropology—anthropological insights for more effective evangelism—will assist.

To Assist in Formulating an Indigenous Theology and Pastoral Approaches

My conviction is that only a spiritually mature indigenous church can make a full integration of biblical truth with the local culture, true to that culture and true to Scripture. The foreigner should always be modest about his insights. Of course, the indigenous church leadership may have been so acculturated to Western concepts that they, too, could benefit from the insights of anthropology, but the foreigner's basic stance should be one of learning.

For example, what is the objective of counseling? To enable a person to break free and assert his or her own rights with vigor and without a sense of guilt? I shall never forget the eerie feeling, in reading the first popular Japanese treatment of psychiatry, to discover the commonality with Western approaches to treatment until it came to the goal. There, for a person to be well, meant conformity. Until the counselor could help him relate to others in that way, his patient was destroying himself with antisocial behavior. The goal was the opposite of Western therapy. Or take marriage counseling. The chief obstacles to unity in marriage, it is said, are money, sex, and one's approach to child rearing. What could be more culturally specific? And yet we spend lavishly on getting our Western books about marriage translated into other languages without getting them translated into other cultures.

Consider suffering. In the triumphal aftermath of World War II and the euphoria of an expanding economy, what missionary would have written on the pain of God? Who among us worked at integrating this characteristic into his message, let alone into his life? Yet this is precisely what Japanese theologian Kazoh Kitamori did in his volume, *Theology of the Pain of God.*[9]

Stealing—taking by force what is not rightfully mine—is wrong by biblical standards in any culture, but culture defines "what is rightfully mine." Native Americans no doubt wished the Western invaders had studied anthropology. Maybe they wouldn't have staked out claims to private ownership of what had been public land!

My first term, before I completed my anthropological analysis of Japanese values, I trained the new believers in various leadership roles. We did TEE (theological education by extension) before it was invented and many became effective leaders. On the American model, that is. I was confident it was the New Testament model. But the first national pastor of that thriving church took as his first responsibility to squeeze out of the fellowship all "my" leaders. They didn't fit the cultural pattern; they were an intolerable threat to him. The second term, following my anthropological studies, we had similar evangelistic success, but I trained leadership on the Japanese model of leadership and the pastor who followed lost none of them.

This does not mean that the foreigner must abandon scriptural principles, of course. For example, we were applying for accreditation. As president of the Christian college, I was responsible for the final application papers for the government. I had frequent conflicts with the senior faculty member in charge of the preparation. I could not let falsehoods go in the report. After some months of unsuccessfully seeking to change my view of "true" and "false," the professor said, "Well, Sensei, it just may be that a lie is the cross God will ask you bear." We decided against taking up that "cross" because I could not abdicate my conscience. But most of the strong ethical, pastoral, and doctrinal stands I was tempted to take against my Japanese brothers were ill-advised. I tried to sit as a learner under their tutelage.

Another important area for integration is the creation of functional substitutes for culturally unacceptable rites and festivals. Is New Year's the chief celebration period of the year? The missionary must not merely forbid participation in a religion-intensive festival and expect seekers and new believers simply to abstain and sit at home while all the family and, indeed, the whole nation celebrates. Is there a solemn rite of passage into adulthood in the African tribe, a rite filled with anti-biblical behavior and attitudes? What substitute rite, of equal significance and excitement, can the missionary or church introduce? I cringe to think of the ordeal through which those early Christians in my ministry had to pass. Baptism scrunched up in a home

9. Kazoh Kitamori, *Theology of the Pain of God* (Richmond: John Knox, 1958).

ofuro (a small wooden tub), a public bathhouse, and a muddy, shallow river in the open countryside with no place to change clothes. Cultural insensitivity had added unnecessary barriers.

Even the agenda the preacher addresses needs to be related to felt needs, though often the prophet must raise to a place of "felt" biblical but unrecognized needs. My contention is that the person within the culture is best equipped for both of these endeavors. When I lived for a time in inner-city Atlanta, I visited sixteen black churches from the lowest to highest economic levels. In every case the agenda was social justice and the hope of heaven. In the midst of this immersion experience, I attended a white Christian business executive's breakfast and could hardly escape the fact that the theme of message, testimonies, and prayer requests were all economically oriented. That weekend I found myself in an adult Sunday school class in a large church in Bradenton, Florida, retirement capital of the nation. Everything in the lesson and in the many prayer requests had to do with ill health and the deceased. If I, a healthy, fifty-year-old, white and middle-class man, had been asked to speak to any of these groups I would never have addressed any of those topics. And I might not have connected with the audience at all. People on the inside are best able to identify biblically legitimate felt needs.

Generations of missionaries in Africa insisted that polygamists must divorce all wives but one in order to qualify for church membership. In other words, they forced the men to commit a sin roundly condemned by Scripture (divorce) in order to correct a practice which was more heinous in their view (polygamy), even if it was not directly condemned in Scripture. With a view to studying Scripture through the lens of their adoptive culture, they might have come to different conclusions and saved untold misery for the divorced wives who had no place to go.

When I returned to the States I had reverse culture shock. Sitting in chapel I was extremely uncomfortable with the clapping for some musical "performances," as I called them. Why, they even clapped for a good sermon. Once I was in a church where they applauded a rousing prayer! A colleague saw my dis-ease and leaned over to whisper in my ear, "Just imagine you're in a remote village in Africa and go with the flow." In an instant he opened my eyes to the value of anthropological principles for cross-cultural communication with what I had mistakenly assumed was "my" culture. My conversion in viewpoint in that chapel service helped prepare me for the "music wars" that convulsed the American church world in days to come.

Anthropology is a wonderful bridesmaid to help the Bride ask the Bible questions that have not been asked and find solutions that are at once biblically authentic and culturally attuned. But the tools can be hazardous.

Hazards in Using the Tools of Anthropology

The former general director of the Evangelical Missiology Society, David Hesselgrave, wrote in 1994, "Missiology itself has become more and more dependent upon the social sciences while its foundation in biblical revelation shows signs of gradual erosion. . . . Edward Rommen fears that missiology is being 'detheologized.'"[10] I'm not convinced this trend is so recent. In the July, 1979 issue of *MARK*, Ed Dayton traced the history of the emerging "new science of missiology" and described it as a combination of research, communications (derived, he said, from anthropology, sociology, and psychology) and management theory. The result of this "new science" so derived was reflected in a note I received in 1984 from a graduate student who was agonizing over his gradual loss of missionary passion as he studied anthropology and cross-cultural communication in one of our premier evangelical seminaries. He said the more he studied, the more he realized two things: because of the cultural encapsulation of Scripture and his own entrapment in ethnocentrism he was not sure of the truth of any message he might give. Secondly, he was quite convinced that even if he could salvage some "truth," he could never communicate it cross-culturally, so high and complex were the barriers. This was no minimal-exposure college student. This graduate student appended a list of eighteen leading evangelical anthropologists and theologians whose books and articles he had read. I encountered a similar experience in many graduate students from many schools throughout the seventies and eighties. Many hot-hearted young men and women lost the vision of missionary service in studying cultural anthropology unharnessed to Scripture.

Indeed there are hazards. And what are they? Often culture is used as a grid for determining what in Scripture is normative rather than using Scripture as the grid to determine what in culture is acceptable. In chapter 1 of this study we introduced such a grid. Here let's apply it to the issue of cross-cultural communication.

Hell and the Way of Salvation

Increasing numbers of Bible scholars and missiologists who consider themselves evangelical are calling into question the traditional ideas about hell and the way of salvation. The first question to ask, a question often skipped, is, "What are we talking about?" In other words, definition must come first. Are you advocating universalism, that all people will ultimately be saved? Or are you advocating that many may be saved without the knowl-

---

10. David Hesselgrave, *Scripture and Strategy: The Use of the Bible in Postmodern Church and Mission* (Pasadena: William Carey Library, 1994). Hesselgrave refers in this quotation to his *Today's Choice for Tomorrow's Mission: An Evangelical Perspective on Trends and Issue in Mission* (Grand Rapids: Zondervan, 1988) and Rommen's "The Detheologization of Missiology," in *Trinity World Forum* (Winter 1994). Later, Hesselgrave brought these themes to a climax in his classic *Paradigms in Conflict* (Grand Rapids: Kregel, 2005).

edge of Christ? Or do you merely mean that salvation by grace through faith alone is no longer a biblical non-negotiable? After determining what the issue actually is, that concept must be rigorously examined in the light of Scripture. Have we identified all passages which deal with the issue, and have we examined all teachings of Scripture which correlate with this teaching? Having identified all the passages, not a select few, have we done the rigorous work of applying all principles of interpretation to determine the meaning intended by the author of each passage and correlating all those passages and all those doctrines?

For example, have we given decisive weight to the clear teaching over the obscure text, to the abundant teaching over the occasional, to the New Testament over the Old? Only with such rigorous, honest work can we claim to be doing missions under the functional authority of Scripture.

Increasingly, the way of salvation is being redefined and the lostness of those out of Christ is being called into question. For example, when salvation is treated as a direction, not an event, so that Muslims are acceptable to God when headed in the right direction, godward, culture has imposed its authority over Scripture in the most critical of missionary affirmations.[11] Again, increasing numbers of those who consider themselves evangelical no longer believe in hell; it doesn't fit the postmodern mentality.[12] And that is in the process of cutting the nerve of the missionary enterprise. Scripture is not in functional control of missiological reasoning when such conclusions emerge.[13]

Ethical Issues

According to some interpreters, Christ's teaching against divorce, Paul's teaching against homosexuality, and biblical norms for the role of the woman in marriage are all culturally bound teachings and not normative. Therefore, they do not demand obedience in every culture of every age. I was once seated across the luncheon table from an anthropologist who was head of linguistics in a major mission. We were discussing the question of what teachings in Scripture are normative.

"What do you think," I asked, "should be required of all people in every tribe and culture?"

He responded immediately, "Those teachings which are culturally universal."

---

11. See, for example, Charles Kraft, *Christianity in Culture* (Maryknoll: Orbis, 1979), 231, 240–41, 250.

12. James Davison Hunter, *Evangelicalism: The Coming Generation* (Chicago: University of Chicago Press, 1987), 33–34. Note that Hunter lays a lion's share of the blame for loss of evangelical convictions in our evangelical colleges on the faculty in the social sciences and humanities (p. 176).

13. This issue is considered by the author in greater detail in two books: *Perspectives on the World Christian Movement*, Ralph D. Winter and Steven C. Hawthorne, editors (Pasadena: William Carey Library, 1999), chap. 26; and McQuilkin, *The Great Omission: A Biblical Basis for World Evangelism* (Waynesboro: Gabriel Publishing, 2002), chap. 3. Also, this text treats the theme in chap. 14.

"For example?"

"Well . . ." He hesitated. "I'm not altogether sure."

"Something like the forbidding of murder?" I suggested.

"Why, yes," he said, "That would be a cultural universal."

"I am surprised to hear that," I replied. "I would have thought that killing and perhaps even eating the victim, would be a virtue in some societies."

"Well, I guess you're right."

This is doing Scripture under the authority of anthropological principles, not doing anthropology under the authority of Scripture.

Or take liberation theology. Let us run it through the flow chart. The first question we must ask is, "Precisely what do you mean by 'liberation theology'? Do you mean that we should preach a holistic good news, that Christ liberates both from the results of sinful behavior but also from the behavior itself so that the true Christian will seek justice and mercy in society? Or do you mean that we must bring about justice and mercy by taking up arms to enforce it?" Is violence in the cause of the gospel demanded by Scripture in direct teaching or in principle? Since it obviously is not, the next question must be asked—Is it compatible with scriptural teaching? Since Christ taught expressly against such a concept, the Christian is conscience bound to reject it. Actually, classical "liberation theology" was based squarely on "culture" and "history" as the authority with Scripture as a sometime resource for selected examples of God at work in history.

To run certain issues through the flow chart, such as oppression, injustice, poverty, is to quickly establish a biblical authority for addressing the issue. For others, such as racism and sexism, is to find biblical principles on which to build. But if the agenda or the approach toward biblically valid issues is built from extrabiblical sources, one may quickly lose biblical authority.

Power Encounter

In a remote jungle base in Latin America, the translators were giving reports at the annual meeting. One translator reported how she had finally resolved the problem of translating "demons" for a people who didn't recognize their existence. She had translated demonic references as "illness." This is doing theology by translation under the authority of culture.

Some go the opposite direction, also guided by culture more than by Scripture. In the 1994 EMS annual meeting a paper was read by Robert Priest, "Missiological Syncretism: The Animistic Paradigm." The paper exploded across the missiological world because it challenges some of the newer concepts of spiritual warfare. Priest and his associates demonstrate that some of the newer missiological concepts such as the genealogical transmission of demons, territorial spirits, vulnerability to demons through curses, had not been derived from Scripture by their proponents, but from animistic cultures or from the testimony of demons themselves. Priest pitched the battle at the place it belongs: what does Scripture teach? Teaching and activity not based on Scripture cannot claim divine authority.

The Nations

One of the major battles waged in missiological circles today is whether the biblical ethne refers to an ethno-linguistic group or to a group defined sociologically as one in which the gospel can move without cultural barriers. The issue is critical for establishing other missiological matters. For example, this definition will determine whether there are 400, 4,000, or 12,000 ethne still unreached. That, in turn, impacts directly the practical matters of targeting the most needy groups, of deciding what the goals of evangelism are, of establishing the validity of a completion date, such as the year 2000 which at least eighteen major coalitions had targeted in the '90s. Much more rests on this definition, practical matters such as constituency, promotion, turf. Also, unintended results such as confusion among God's people and the promotion of unrealistic expectations.

What would result if everyone had stopped to do a rigorous word study to determine what the Bible did and did not mean? I am confident the result would be that the biblical term, *ta ethne,* was not defined by biblical authors by contemporary social science definitions at all, any more than it meant the modern political nation-state, what we call a "nation." If we did not try to claim biblical authority for our preferred definition of *ethne* and our resulting definition of the evangelistic mission of the church, we would be freed to use our preferred definition on the basis of what authority we do have: anthropological insight. This would have great utilitarian value in determining the best approach and what our first and long-range goals should be.

For example, those who preferred, would be free to concentrate on the "Bibleless" tribes, who need the Word. Others might concentrate on the initial penetration of all homogeneous groups that have no witnessing church movement. Again, others might concentrate on the full evangelization of large groups that are still out of reach of effective gospel witness. In other words, since Scripture does not describe what the evangelistic task will look like when it is finished, we can get on with the task of being sure that every person on earth has the opportunity to hear the gospel and that a congregation of God's people is established in every community. And until that goal is accomplished, the church cannot say, "It is finished. The task you gave us to do we have accomplished."

God may choose to say, "It is finished" before we do, but obedience to the command means that the church must pursue the goal of evangelization and church planting until then. To have more restricted, targeted goals is legitimate for tactical purposes as part of the overall task, but it is not biblical to make a limited goal and market it as the biblically required task of the church.

Self-image

The ultimate value of accepting and affirming oneself may not seem to accord with Christ's demand for self-denial, but the concept is not confined to evangelical psychologists. Anthropological missiologists urge this concept just as strongly for our missions enterprise.[14] Both for evangelism and for pastoral care nothing could be more important than to view self from a biblical perspective, yet the prevalent view of "self" as espoused by the social sciences, so destructive of personal redemption and human relationships, is urged on us by fellow missiologists because Scripture, if referenced at all, is done under the aegis of relativistic psychological and cultural understandings.

Teaching and Leadership

I have heard more than one evangelical anthropologist teach that nondirective, participatory interaction is the only legitimate mode for teaching, counseling, and leadership. The worst kind is directive and authoritative. No matter that Moses, Paul, and even Jesus seemed to operate at the lower levels of acceptability on this scale. Where does such a theory get its biblical authority?[15]

If one ministry approach is considered better than other options because of research data, let us state openly the basis of our recommendation and not paper it over with a few biblical texts and treat it as God's own truth. To follow this procedure of allowing anthropological theory to stand on its own merits would have the added benefit of allowing us to adapt to varying cultures and individual circumstances without fear of violating divine mandate.

When the formulation of mission thinking and the planning of mission strategy are accomplished under the functional control of Scripture and the study of human attitudes, relationships, and behavior is also done under the authority of Scripture, the missionary enterprise can be strengthened. But if Scripture does not control both endeavors, if naturalistically based scientific theory skews or displaces the teaching of Scripture on a given subject, to that extent the missionary enterprise suffers loss. Let us covenant together to use every new tool that holds promise of advancing the cause of Christ, while

---

14. See, for example, Marvin K. Mayers, *Christianity Confronts Culture: A Strategy for Cross-Cultural Evangelism* (Grand Rapids: Zondervan, 1974), chaps. 2 and 3.

15. For a procedure to ensure the functional authority of Scripture over any existing cultural form or proposed change, see *Understanding and Applying the Bible, op cit.* All the principles of the book are necessary, but the principles dealing with applying scriptural truth to contemporary contexts are found in chaps. 19 and 20. See also pp. 32–35.

doing so diligently under the functional authority of Scripture. Anthropology must remain no more than a bridesmaid, assisting the Bride to understand and apply her only authority for missionary faith and practice, the Word of God.

Thus I wrote for the missionary, but the principles apply to all cross-cultural ministry. And don't forget: "All communication of divine truth is cross-cultural"!